Frederic J. Leger

Beyond the Therapeutic Relationship
Behavioral, Biological, and Cognitive Foundations of Psychotherapy

Pre-publication
REVIEW

"**L**eger sets himself a most ambitious goal: to go beyond conventional loyalties to one psychotherapeutic approach; to attempt an integrative approach to psychotherapy; to focus on the variables that make for patient change; and to try to relate his observations and formulations to the behavioral, biological, and cognitive foundations of psychotherapy. The result is a very interesting and thought-provoking work."

Sol L. Garfield, PhD
Professor Emeritus
of Psychology,
Washington University,
St. Louis, MO

Beyond the Therapeutic Relationship

Behavioral, Biological, and Cognitive Foundations of Psychotherapy

THE HAWORTH PRESS
Advances in Psychology and Mental Health
Frank De Piano, PhD
Senior Editor

Beyond the Therapeutic Relationship: Behavioral, Biological, and Cognitive Foundations of Psychotherapy by Frederic J. Leger

How the Brain Talks to Itself: A Clinical Primer of Psychotherapeutic Neuroscience by Jay E. Harris

Cross-Cultural Counseling: The Arab-Palestinian Case by Marwan Dwairy

The Vulnerable Therapist: Practicing Psychotherapy in an Age of Anxiety by Helen W. Coale

Beyond the Therapeutic Relationship

Behavioral, Biological, and Cognitive Foundations of Psychotherapy

Frederic J. Leger

Foreword by
Arnold A. Lazarus

The Haworth Press
New York • London

The Haworth Press, Inc., 10 Alice Street, Binghamton, NY 13904-1580

Cover design by Monica Seifert.

Library of Congress Cataloging-in-Publication Data

Leger, Frederic J.
   Beyond the therapeutic relationship : behavioral, biological, and cognitive foundations of psychotherapy / Frederic J. Leger.
      p.   cm.
   Includes bibliographical references (p.) and index.
   ISBN 0-7890-0292-2 (alk. paper).
   1. Psychotherapy—Philosophy. I. Title.
RC437.5.L44 1997
616.89′1401—dc21   97-16975
                                                                                                          CIP

This book is dedicated to all whose work is cited in this volume, especially the founders of the three so-called main forces in psychotherapy: Carl Rogers, Frederick Skinner, and Sigmund Freud, upon whose pioneering foundation psychotherapy currently rests, and Arnold A. Lazarus, the father of eclecticism and integration.

ABOUT THE AUTHOR

Frederic J. Leger is a psychologist in private practice in Edmonton, Alberta. He has been a psychotherapist for over twenty-five years and is a member of the Canadian Psychological Association. Also a Chartered Psychologist with the Province of Alberta, he has practiced in mental health, social service, correctional, and private settings, both in institutional and community-based programs. He began his helping career with a two-year volunteer assignment to Ethiopia with the Canadian University Service Overseas (CUSO), and is the author of *A Behavioral and Biological Approach to Counseling and Psychotherapy* (1989).

CONTENTS

Foreword

Talk about scholarship! Fred Leger has devoted five years of his life to the inception and completion of this impressive tome. The vast majority of books on psychotherapy seem to deal with an author's pet school of thought, a writer's idiosyncratic notions of eclecticism, or some clinician's personal odyssey. Leger transcends these parochial trends and addresses the general or theoretical underpinnings of the field and their fundamental relation to contemporary practice.

One of Leger's main concerns is that most therapists and many well-known theorists are extremely insular, and as a consequence they function in isolation from one another. More important, however, is his view that *theoretical isolation as a field* characterizes the enterprise of psychotherapy, that without awareness of and inputs from neurology, information processing, nonverbal behavior, and the study of consciousness, knowledge will not be gained but instead, the same ideas will continue being recycled.

It is astonishing to read the range of crucial issues that are carefully documented throughout this entire book. In his search for universal characteristics, Leger has identified several significant heuristic factors that can point theorists and therapists toward the most fruitful avenues for meaningful research and creative clinical practice. As I have already mentioned, it took five years to amass the crucial materials that Leger has so ably distilled and integrated. Thanks to his labors and scholarship, we have a collection of the most erudite issues that any committed scientist or devoted practitioner needs to know. I can but hope that this book will be widely read and properly appreciated.

—Arnold A. Lazarus, PhD
Distinguished Professor
Graduate School of Applied and Professional Psychology
Rutgers—The State University of New Jersey

Preface

This book offers an empirically supported, integrated theory cutting across the multifarious therapies to unite psychotherapy's disparate forces. In so doing, it draws upon and relates existing research in the broader area of human behavior to the field of psychotherapy. Combining relevant physiological, social, and psychological research into a transtheoretical psychodynamic therapy, this *qualitative* (Horowitz, 1994) research endeavor thus identifies universal therapist behaviors and client change processes that supporting *quantitative* research suggests to be therapeutic. It was written ex post facto—presenting behavioral, biological, and cognitive evidence for, as it describes the process of, my twenty-five-year-old psychotherapeutic approach.

Making this volume more comprehensive and readable, this psychotherapeutic approach incorporates recent developments in psychotherapy eclecticism and integration inspired mainly by the positive reinforcement of Dr. Arnold Lazarus, whom I first met at the 1990 Evolution of Psychotherapy conference in Anaheim, California, and who graciously contributed the Foreword to this book. The theoretically consistent approach to psychotherapy described herein therefore shares elements of *technical* (Lazarus, 1992) and *integrative* (Messer, 1992) eclecticism within *common factors* (Norcross and Newman, 1992) and *transtheoretical* (Prochaska and Diclemente, 1992) integration. Hence this book offers, for the scrutiny of the therapeutic field, a scientifically grounded, integrated, or higher-order theory designed to guide applied psychotherapeutic research and integrative eclectic practice.

Acknowledgment

An expression of gratitude is extended to the distinguished faculty and staff of the 1990 and 1995 "Evolution of Psychotherapy" conferences in Anaheim, California and Las Vegas, Nevada. Their informative presentations were invaluable.

Introduction

The modern psychotherapies draw an aura of legitimacy and operating authority from their standing as forms of science applied to the human condition. Yet the science of which most of them were born is not that of today but of the *belle epoque*, a century past.

—David Orlinsky, 1994

Mechanism now lives next to fanaticism: Societies are in the hands either of the commercially powerful but spiritually empty or, to a lesser extent, in the hands of fanatical zealots under the sway of unscientific myths and emotion. Perhaps when we understand and accept a scientific view of how our mind emerges in the world, a richer view of our nature and more lenient myths will serve us.

—Gerald Edelman, 1992

Therapy in a pluralist age, is in constant danger of fragmentation. . . . It lacks the unifying glue provided by the concepts of a single theory. . . . A replacement still waits to be found for the protective and stabilizing shell that was once supplied by unitary theory and school.

—Haim Omer, 1994

Knowledge grows from that which precedes it. The heuristic contribution to psychotherapy of Carl Rogers's work on the therapeutic relationship is well established and evidenced by the fact, as others have pointed out, that virtually all schools of therapy acknowledge the need for some form of therapeutic bond with the client as a precursor

1

to change (Lambert, 1992; Beutler and Consoli, 1992; Prochaska and Diclemente, 1992). A half century after Roger's groundbreaking work, *Counseling and Psychotherapy* (1942) and *Client-Centered Therapy* (1951), however, just how therapeutic change is fostered within the relationship—or what behavioral, biological, and cognitive processes may be involved—largely remains unexplored. As Gelso and Carter (1985) conclude in their review of literature on this issue, sound theoretical and empirical work on relationship factors is virtually at a standstill—a situation prompting them to call for a paradigm shift.

Similarly, and more recently, Sexton and Whiston (1994) acknowledge, from their review of studies intended to identify the current understanding of the "real" or Rogerian aspect of the psychotherapy relationship, that there is little in the literature since Gelso and Carter's work to end this apparent impasse in the field. In their words:

> Investigations into the nature of the real relationship might also lack direction because there does not seem to be a theoretical foundation on which to base comprehensive research. In the era prior to this review, the real relationship was narrowly defined as the 'necessary and sufficient' conditions proposed by Rogers (1957). The lack of empirical support for the facilitative conditions model has left us without a unifying theoretical model to guide our understanding and lend theoretical validity to the results of empirical research (Strong, 1991). Further understanding of this area of the relationship might be enhanced by expanding the more traditional definition to include other perspectives. (p. 55)

Possibly because of the relative lack of scientific knowledge of change processes within the therapeutic relationship, the field has witnessed a profusion of therapies, most legitimately claiming some measure of therapeutic success. However, as others have noted (Lambert, 1992; Efran, Lukens, and Lukens, 1990), there is little evidence to suggest the superiority of any one therapy over another. Furthermore, as Phillips (1990) points out, "outcome predictions of psychotherapy (all variables, all participants) are unable to account for more than 10-20 percent of the variance"—a fact, he says, which "most therapists seem to disregard" (p. 116). Elliott and Anderson (1994) reinforce this point as follows:

> Psychology has more than its share of messy, chaotic phenomena to deal with, in the guise of 80-95% of the variance left unaccounted for in the typical study. Psychotherapy researchers in search of the challenge of chaotic or complex systems need look no further than the 'error variance' in their studies, including unexplained individual differences in clients' treatment outcomes, or unexpectedly strong client reactions to routine therapist interventions. (p. 67)

These unexplained effects, and the fact that psychotherapies largely yield similar results, Phillips (1990) contends, argue in favor of "commonalities" (p. 115) which reside in the conditions of the therapeutic relationship, not internally within the therapist. Phillips therefore advocates the development of an approach to psychotherapy based upon circumstances rather than the traditional characterological or intrapsychic attitudes of the therapist—an orientation to psychotherapy research which this book supports. As L.S. Greenberg (1994) concludes from his assessment of the therapeutic encounter in relation to current approaches to psychotherapeutic research:

> The alliance is thus not independent of technique; rather, a good alliance is characterized by the use of appropriate technical methods, and prediction will probably be enhanced by addition of specific processes to the alliance (Luborsky et al. 1988). If psychotherapy is to be understood in all its complexity, it will be necessary to understand the interaction of different aspects of the conditions facilitating therapeutic change and the specific 'work' that goes on in therapy. (p. 117)

However, from the current profusion of therapies on the market, it appears that the "work" of therapy may have been largely explored from a variety of narrow, within-school perspectives, and on an "experimental" or "hit-and-miss" basis—an approach to advancement of the field which seems to have contributed little toward paradigmatic direction. This state of affairs may further have been influenced by what Edelman (1992) (Nobel laureate in Physiology and

Medicine, 1972) claims to be insufficient biological grounding of psychological concepts. At one time, Edelman observes, psychological pursuits often had to be undertaken "in the absence of fundamental biological data" (p. 34). However, he says, given the recent progress achieved in the biological sciences, this is no longer the case.

The urgent need to integrate biological knowledge with psychology, Edelman (1992) maintains, is based on the inescapable fact that "the fundamental basis for all behavior and for the emergence of mind is animal and species morphology (anatomy) and how it functions" (p. 41). He further explains:

> Psychology itself has not fared very well in the absence of knowledge of the brain and nervous system. This is not to say that an enormous amount of useful and important information has not been accumulated since William James at Harvard in 1878 and Wilhelm Wundt in Leipzig in 1879 founded the first laboratories of experimental physiological psychology. Instead of a unified theory of mind, however, a series of schools subsequently sprang up, each with different views on behavior, consciousness, and on the relative significance of perception, memory, language, and thought. (p. 36)

Factionalization of psychology notwithstanding, Edelman nevertheless maintains that as modern methods of measuring brain function promote greater understanding of the brain, the opportunity exists for psychology to become better grounded in physiology to "guard against extreme errors" (p. 35). In the absence of neurological knowledge, Edelman contends, psychology can only be "provisionally pursued (as it always has been) while awaiting biological interpretation" (p. 40).

Factionalization of psychology into different competing schools may also have resulted in fractionalization of the person. Therefore, as Edelman (1992) explains, "Putting the mind back into nature has precipitated a series of scientific crises, for the data of the brain, mind, and behavior do not correspond to the pictures we have been using to explain them" (p. 65). He acknowledges, however, that "putting the mind back into nature" may seem to some as an "audacious conclusion—unwarranted, premature (more facts will clear things up!), or even downright unhealthy." On the contrary, Edelman explains, "the best time to be working in a science is when it is in a crisis state." For it is then, he says, that "one is prompted to look at a new way of looking at the data, or of a new theory, or of a new technique to resolve the apparent paradox" (p. 65).

This "paradox" in psychotherapy and some of the other social sciences may further have developed, Edelman (1992) contends, because studying mental matters in the absence of knowledge concerning the "structure, function, development, and evolution of the brain" is, in his estimation, "intellectually hazardous" (p. 68). With respect to psychotherapy, for example, this lack of biological grounding, coupled with theoretical division and isolation within competing schools, may have delayed paradigmatic realization. In this respect, therefore, and because of the importance of the concept of paradigm, the following description of this theoretical construct, proffered by Lynch (1985), will preface this book's discussion:

> In his seminal *Structure of Scientific Revolutions* (1970), Thomas Kuhn describes a phenomenon he calls the "scientific paradigm." Kuhn defines the term *paradigm*, in its most general meaning, as a construct embracing the entire constellation of beliefs, values, techniques, and attitudes that are shared by members of a given scientific community. As he outlines it, the paradigm determines how scientists approach the study of phenomena in their specific area of interest and how they understand and interpret the data they observe. The paradigm is a way of looking at the scientific data, and one remains in force until enough conflicting data accumulate to cause it to be seriously questioned. A shift in paradigms occurs when an alternative way of looking at data is developed and found to deal more effectively with the conflicting data. (pp. 56-57)

With respect to the lack of paradigmatic direction in this field, Gardner (1993) suggests in his commentary on Kuhn's work that disciplines such as psychotherapy and some of the social sciences are themselves often termed "preparadigmatic." Within this early developmental stage of the discipline, Gardner observes, studies are often carried out by researchers "in the absence of agreed-upon bodies of knowledge, methods of investigation, or signs of progress" (p. 95). Today, however, almost a century after Freud developed his theory and half a century after the "heyday" of behavior-ism, Gardner says, anything but a consensus exists about the "merit of either of these psychological revolutions." Such an underdeveloped science, he states, "features conflicting schools, rather than a normative paradigm that the field as a whole acknowledges and that all members situate themselves around" (p. 117).

Gardner goes on to explain that while the concept of paradigm has been prominent in the physical sciences, paradigms change with the evolution or growth of knowledge in particular disciplines. He elaborates:

> In each case, the earlier paradigm has been widely accepted by scientists for a period of time, with research and experiments being comfortably carried out under its aegis. Problems that begin to arise are at first ignored; then they become increasingly noticed, obtrusive, and troublesome. At such times, as Einstein himself put it . . . "it was as if the ground had been pulled out from under one, with no firm foundation to be seen anywhere, upon which one could have built."
>
> At such times of crisis, one or more scientists eventually put forth a scheme, a set of principles, a theory that holds the promise of reconciling discrepant findings and somehow incorporating them within a broader framework, which subsumes much, if not most, of the earlier synthesis. (p. 96)

Gardner's latter comments further appear consistent with the aim of the eclectic and integrative movement that arose primarily in response to the lack of paradigmatic direction in psychotherapy. Eclectics (Lazarus, 1967) and integrationists (Norcross and Goldfried, 1992) believe that an "alternative way" of looking at the data may be achieved through exploring common factors (Norcross and Newman, 1992), transtheoretical systems (Prochaska, 1979), and/or mechanisms of change (Leger, 1989) possibly operating across therapies.

This book joins in this eclectic and integrative paradigmatic search whose objectives are outlined by Wachtel (1990):

> It aims, first, for a theoretical model that is internally consistent and attuned to the full range of observations on which the various schools base their thinking and, second, for a melding and reworking of their concepts and methods so that what

results is not merely a mix of simple elements from different sources but rather a true synthesis of those elements that mark the evolution of new concepts and methods.

A key assumption is that most of the present schools have remained viable because they are each based on significant observations—observations that in turn are ignored or minimized by proponents of other schools. Therefore an integrative approach takes as its aim to attend seriously to what has been observed by proponents of all the major schools and to incorporate those observations and the methods they have spawned into a framework that is comprehensive, coherent . . . (p. 235)

The need for paradigmatic direction is urgent, eclectics and integrationists maintain, because the field is at a "crossroads" (about which more will be said in Chapter 1 which recommends moving beyond the therapeutic relationship). Goldfried, Castonguay, and Safran (1992) explain:

Until recently, it has been alternately described as being "in a mess" (Rogers, 1963), a "bewildering world" (Frank, 1972), a "therapeutic jungleplace" (Parloff, 1976), and a field best characterized by "sibling rivalry" (Beitman, Goldfried, and Norcross, 1989). Not only has there been growing proliferation and confusion among different schools of thought, but even within a given paradigm, clinicians have begun to acknowledge that their theoretical constructs and methods fall short of dealing with what they are likely to see clinically (Norcross and Newman, 1992). (p. 593)

These appraisals and criticisms of the state of psychotherapy, some say, characterize a field which appears in "disarray" (Zeig and Munion, 1990, p. 3) or in a state of "confusion" (Phillips 1990, p. 118) and whose "processes and mode of relief are almost entirely unknown at this time" (Langs, 1990, p. 62).

Kuhn (1970), on the other hand, views this state of affairs as normal preparadigmatic development, or "experimentation," for a relatively young discipline such as psychotherapy. Throughout this "experimental" stage, the eclectic work of Arnold Lazarus (1967, 1976, 1989, and 1992) has served as a reminder of the limitations of single-school adherence and of the need to promote the evolution of psychotherapy, or search for causal foundations, through empirical evidence rather than hypothetical constructs. As Norcross and Newman (1992, p. 27) observe, Lazarus's work in multimodal therapy has "paved the way" for some of the questions that the integrative psychotherapist is asking, such as, "Why not be prepared to give strong emphasis to the 'interaction' of cognitions, behavior, and affect?" Norcross and Newman cite, as well, the work of Steinfield (1980) and Staats (1981), who similarly support the adoption of a "unified-interactive framework" which includes cognition, behavior, and affect. They add, however, that there must be "an accompanying theoretical model" from which to support a "systematic program of research" (Norcross and Newman, 1992, p. 27).

Consistent with this objective of the eclectic and integration movement, therefore, this book attempts to formulate a "theoretical model," or *higher-order theory*, from the author's twenty-five year clinical practice supported by existing behavioral, biological, and cognitive research in psychotherapy and from disparate allied fields. Toward this end, eclectics and integrationists may espouse a broader view because, as Efran, Lukens, and Lukens (1990) observe, therapists can often become so engrossed in "listening with the third ear" that they may "neglect to make use of the first two" (p. 183). Or as L.S. Greenberg (1994) explains:

> Science proceeds by observation, measurement, explanation, and prediction (Hempel, 1966). In psychotherapy research to date, however, limited attention has been paid to the initial three steps, especially to observation and explanation. In fact, intensive and rigorous observation of how change takes place has probably been the most sorely neglected. We need to observe the process of change in order to identify patterns that will lead to the kind of explanation that involves understanding of what actually occurs, instead of automatic theoretical explanations from our favorite (often too strongly held) theory. (p. 118)

As a result of the field's apparent lack of attention to scientific precepts, Edelson (1994) points out that therapists have therefore learned "not to pin their hopes on prediction." When they are interested in causal explanation at all, he says, they are interested "not only in what causes what but in how any number of causes combine to bring about an effect by specific means or mechanisms." However, he observes, "Psychotherapy research rarely explicates causal mechanisms or even traces the steps leading from one state of affairs to another" (p. 69). Nevertheless, Edelson states, psychotherapists *are* "interested in explanation, which even after the fact can help them make sense out of what has happened" (p. 69).

It may further be because of this urgent need for meaning—to "make sense" of, or to understand psychotherapeutic processes—coupled with a lack of attention to scientific protocol—that therapists have had to resort to their "favorite theory" for explanation. However, Efran, Lukens, and Lukens (1990) point out that everyday emotional contradictions are not necessarily best understood in terms of "deviously operating unconscious mechanisms or internal mind entities" (p. 183). With respect to such hypothetical constructs, Strupp (1973) holds a similar view, stating that "new departures in psychotherapy derive from technical procedures, not from theoretical reformulations, however sophisticated the latter may appear" (p. 88). This view appears to be consistent with that of Davison and Lazarus (1995) as well when they state: ". . . Innovations by clinicians are the lifeblood of advances in the development of new therapeutic interventions" (p. 96). In their view, the major clinical discoveries are generally made by clinicians and then investigated by more experimentally minded researchers whose subsequent findings may persuade others "that the previously unbelievable technique is worth a closer look" (p. 96). Davison and Lazarus (1995) elaborate:

> There is nothing mysterious about the fact that repeated exposure to any given set of conditions makes the recipient aware of subtle cues and contingencies in that setting that elude the scrutiny of those less familiar with the situation. Clinical experience enables a therapist to recognize problems and identify trends that are usually beyond the perceptions of novices, regardless of their general expertise. It is at this level that new ideas can come to the practitioner and often constitute breakthroughs that could not be derived from animal analogues or tightly controlled investigations. It is when we try new things

that true innovators have the capacity to appreciate relationships that may go unnoticed by less resourceful and less obser-
vant workers. Different kinds of data and differing levels of
information are obtained in the laboratory and the clinic. Each
is necessary, useful, and desirable. (p. 96)

Consistent with these views, therefore, and seeking to provide a
theoretically consistent rationale, or scientific explanation, for the
therapeutic results accruing from my psychotherapeutic approach
(which provided the "blueprint" for this volume), Chapters 2, 3,
and 4 of this book draw upon behavioral, biological, and cognitive
research (from the behavioral sciences, in general, as well as the
psychotherapy literature) supporting the existence of universal variables operating across psychodynamic therapies and revealing a
possible transtheoretical "pattern" (L.S. Greenberg, 1994, p. 118)
or "higher-order theory" (Goldfried and Newman, 1992). The perspective from which this book approaches this objective is consistent with the view of Robertiello (1990) who observes that, given
the current confusion in the field, "to be anything but eclectic is
equivalent to being narrow-minded" (p. 54). In any other science,
he explains, "it is important to be familiar with all contributions
from various sources." "Why," he asks, "should this not also apply
to the field of psychotherapy?" (p. 254).

Robertiello (1990) further acknowledges that as the founder of
psychoanalysis, Freud's contributions were "major ones." But, he
adds, "Freud died forty years ago. To infer that science stopped
growing then is ridiculous" (p. 54). This view is also similar to that
of Peterfreund (1971) who maintains that although Freud never
thought of psychoanalysis as a "closed system," for many analysts,
he contends, it has nevertheless "indeed become" such a system.
This closed system is then used, Peterfreund states, as a body of "a
priori truths" into which the data are then "forced regardless of the
clinical empirical evidence" (a criticism which may apply to other
schools of psychodynamic therapy as well). This insular tendency,
Peterfreund further states, "can only markedly delay the necessary
revisions in Psychoanalytic theory"—revisions which he says are
"the hallmark of every progressive science" (p. 88).

This observation appears to be supported by L.S. Greenberg (1994) as well in the following description of the kind of the research task facing the field and his recommended course of action:

> We need to specify the active therapeutic ingredients or curative elements in different treatments. In doing this, however, we should not be in too much of a hurry to rush to our theories [psychotherapeutic] for answers to the question of what carries the therapeutic action, as our predecessors have been; rather, we should turn to the therapeutic process itself in order to discover what actually changes and how this occurs.
>
> Two major hypotheses about the change process have logically emerged from the findings of no difference among treatments. The first is that a set of common ingredients across all treatments accounts for change; the other is that different specific processes account for about the same amount of change in each treatment, and that we need to specify more closely the processes that mediate change in different therapies. (p. 115)

However, this task is hampered, according to Ferrara (1994), by the fact that psychotherapy is "a highly complicated activity." To penetrate its complexity, she therefore suggests, "studies from many differing perspectives are called for" (p. 4). Or, as researcher Orlinsky (1994) puts it, the "plausibility" of modern psychotherapies increase to the extent that they draw appropriately on "concepts currently accepted in other scientific disciplines." And in so doing, he contends, psychotherapeutic constructs "need periodic updating and reformulation" (pp. 101-102).

Accomplishing this task of updating and reformulation in psychotherapy, which is at the heart of the scientific enterprise, will thus likely require more than the gross outcome studies traditionally conducted from within schools of therapy (Davison and Lazarus, 1995, p. 104). As discussed in greater detail throughout this book, such outcome studies, while supporting the particular hypothetical constructs such schools espouse, appear to have accomplished little in the way of identifying therapeutic processes cutting across the multifarious therapies. This result therefore argues in favor of the need for greater process research to develop a stronger paradigmatic base—behaviorally, biologically, and cognitively—a view which

Rhodes and Greenberg (1994) appear to share when they state the following:

> As psychotherapy process researchers, we focus our sights on the palpable, describable level of therapeutic phenomena to build a bottom-up view of how people change in psychotherapy. We do not, however, propose a mindless, theoretically ungrounded empirical investigation of phenomena. . . . Theoretical views guide the selection and observation of change events. The goal is to look for the process patterns of change in the events. (pp. 229-230)

Thus, in an eclectic and integrative vein, and because "science looks for universals" (Davis, 1994, p. 13) to guide in the selection and observation of change events in psychotherapy, this book therefore presents an overview of research from diverse disciplines relevant to psychotherapy—empirical research which supports the existence of universal variables embedded in the interpersonal transactions and nonverbal behaviors of therapist and client. (These universal interactional factors may, in turn, activate cognitive and psychobiological therapeutic processes within the client as discussed in Chapters 6 and 7.) As Efran, Lukens, and Lukens (1990) note, "Therapists do not change clients, nor do clients change themselves. Clients and therapists interact, and their interaction yields outcomes that might not otherwise have occurred" (p. 62).

ATTENDING TO THERAPEUTIC CATALYSTS

Because interactional factors are still considered "nonspecific" (Garfield, 1992, p. 183) or "noise" (Norcross and Newman, 1992, p. 13), they currently exist, for the most part, outside the therapist's working awareness or external to the focus of therapeutic attention. As this book attempts to show, however, interactional factors nevertheless have behavioral, biological and cognitive bases. The process by which this "nonconscious" (Lazarus, 1992, p. 235) omission may occur could further be similar to the "figure-ground" phenomenon popularly described in Perceptual Psychology. As Combs, Richards, and Richards (1976, p. 28) explain using a diagram of a white candlestick on a dark background, depending upon the viewer's point of visual focus or attention, the picture can appear (or achieve forefront materialization) either as a candlestick or the profiles of two faces.

This phenomenon may further be a biological function of the selective property of human attention, itself, prompting Edelman (1992) to ask, "How is it that conscious attention is so narrow— usually able to focus on one or at most two targets at the same time?" In reply to his question, Edelman observes that motor plans and programs in the brain are "more or less exclusive (that is, they will not accommodate contradictory actions that are simultaneous)" (p. 143). Edelman also believes this selective characteristic of attention to be a product of our evolutionary history (a property which may have had survival value particularly at a time when vigilance and alertness were necessary to capture prey and/or protect against predators).

In this regard, Edelman maintains that attention is differentiated from wakefulness or consciousness because attention "lends a directional component to behavior, and it modulates an animal's responsiveness to the environment" (p. 141). Edelman (1992) expands upon this selective property as follows:

> Indeed, attention reveals the "fragility" of consciousness: it focuses our minds on its objects and obliterates or attenuates surrounding "irrelevancies." It does not seem possible to pay specific attention to more than a few objects or lines of thought; attention is highly selective, apparently obligatorily so.
>
> Many theories of selective attention are based on the notion of "filtering out" input signals, either early or late. But there is a variety of evidence suggesting that such filtering does not occur. (p. 141)

This selective attention phenomenon may also account for Einstein's observation, as quoted by Rossi (1993), that "it is the theory which decides what can be observed" (p. 235). In this sense, the profusion of therapies currently on the market may therefore be due to therapists focusing on variables (hypothesized by their favorite theory as being therapeutic) to the exclusion of other, possibly equally important, variables supported by other therapies. In other words, potential variables may be disregarded, and others remain unspecified, possibly due in part to the narrowness of vision imposed by the type of selective attention described above.

THE COMMON FACTORS HYPOTHESIS

In any event, such variables in psychotherapy are generally categorized as nonspecific, Garfield (1992) explains, because an understanding of their role is still unclear and because variables, other than those hypothesized by particular therapies, appear to play a role in therapeutic change. As one of the founders of the humanistic school, Abraham Maslow (1970) once put it, at this stage in the field, "we must accept the fact that therapeutic results may occur to some degree independently of theory, or for that matter, with no theory at all" (pp. 244-245). The significance of these *common factors* is further underlined by Norcross and Newman (1992), who observe that noise is being reconsidered by some as "the main signal element" in treatment, and Lambert (1992), who suggests that common factors "may account for most of the gains that result from psychological interventions" (p. 104). This view also appears to be indirectly supported by the findings of Fred Fiedler, as cited in Goldberg (1992), which found that as therapists become more experienced, their work tends to resemble the work of other senior therapists of different theoretical orientations than that "of less experienced therapists of their own persuasion" (p. 28).

L.S. Greenberg (1994) explains why this common factors view has developed into a major hypothesis in the field. The common-elements approach, he says, "arises from the view that since the search for differential effects has proven rather unproductive, there is a strong possibility that the preponderant weight of psychotherapeutic change is borne by psychological forces that are shared by the various therapeutic approaches, despite the fact that different languages are used to explain the approaches" (p. 116) (or despite the fact that different therapies stress different catalysts or variables in the therapeutic process). And, as the empirical evidence cited in this book and the author's clinical practice suggest, these factors may function universally as processes of change, or as the more immediate stimuli or catalysts intervening between the Rogerian therapist attitudes—empathy, congruence, and unconditional positive regard—and client change. As Wexler (1974) observes, it is doubtful whether the communication of attitudes, alone, "is a particularly potent therapeutic tool to be relied upon." Therapists, he says, "do indeed do specific things on a moment-to-moment basis that have observable effects. The client-centered therapist is no exception" (pp. 95-96).

While this suggestion might initially seem "heretical" to practitioners of Rogerian therapy, i.e., proposing the integration of therapist attitudes with behavioral and biological phenomena, this book nevertheless remains consistent with progressive humanistic thought. However, it goes beyond Rogers's global or molar theorizing by proposing specific therapist behaviors which may flow from these therapeutic attitudes and thus function as interactional processes of change. The advantage of such a behavioral approach to psychotherapy, as Hayes (1990) explains, is that "it can lead readily to the development of data, both basic and applied," at a time when much of clinical psychology is "desperately in need of a strong empirical base, especially for the theoretical concepts used." Behaviorists, Hayes contends, may therefore be of "real assistance in this area to clinicians of a variety of persuasions" (p. 143).

THE NEED FOR GREATER SCIENTIFIC GROUNDING

The need for greater empirical exploration of the common therapeutic processes playing a crucial role in psychotherapy is emphasized by Beutler (1990), who believes that to emerge from the ranks of an "interesting pseudoscience" and to assume its place as a legitimate professional practice, a treatment must pass the tests of "theory, empiricism, and practicality" (p. 228). Rachlin (1994) echoes a similar view. The claim of cognitive psychology to be scientific, he says, "to be useful for predicting, controlling, and explaining behavior—rests on standard, well-understood scientific practice: observe behavior; form a theory, based on those observations, of an underlying mechanism; use the theory to predict future behavior; test the theory by further observation; revise the theory based on differences between observed and predicted behavior" (p. 20). These scientific preconditions, particularly the need for closer observation of behavior and for the revision or evolution of psychotherapeutic theory, are further emphasized in relation to client-centered therapy, for example, by Lietaer (1992):

> In client-centered therapy (Gendlin, 1970; Rogers, 1961), the basic attitudes of the therapist—acceptance, empathy, and genuineness—together with intense experiential exploration on the part of the client, are seen as the essential factors in constructive personality change. The question remains, however, as to what extent the client-centered theory of change coincides with what actually happens in practice. As has been shown by many psychotherapy process studies (Lambert, Shapiro, and Bergin, 1986; Orlinsky and Howard, 1986), there is still a gap between the theory and what goes on during therapy. In other words, the "common ingredients" may prove to be more impactful than the specific factors advocated by the theory. (p. 134)

Others, such as Rice (1992), also report being "disturbed" by the fact that client-centered theory mainly concerns itself with the qualities of the therapist participation, with the only conditions stated for the client being that he or she perceive the qualities of the therapist and that the client be vulnerable, anxious, or in a state of "incongruence." As Rice (1992) explains, "We felt strongly that the style of the client's participation needed to be examined in more depth." This was further motivated, she says, "by our awareness of current developments in theoretical psychology as well as the potential importance of developments in cognitive information processing in understanding human functioning" (pp. 12-13). Martin (1992) echoes these sentiments by explaining, "Therapy is clearly a two-way street." Therapists can assist clients to change, he says, but they "cannot change them in the absence of complementary change-directed activity on the part of clients themselves." Moreover, any attempt at change that does not directly "engage the conscious agency of clients", he maintains, "is unlikely to succeed in the long term" (pp. 124-125).

Consistent with these views, Chapter 5 therefore examines the topic of the *client's* participation in therapeutic change (through discourse and self-disclosure) as central to the *intensive experiential exploration* mentioned above. Chapters 6 and 7 of this book then incorporate research from linguistics, neurology, psychobiology, information processing, cognitive science, and philosophy in exploring possible *psychobiological* change processes occurring within the client (hypothesized to result from *dialogical* and *interactional* change processes occurring between the therapist and client). The relevance to psychotherapy of such an integrative approach to the study of intra- and interpersonal cognitive processes appears to be supported by Gutsch (1990) when he observes that cognitive science is "reality-based." In other words, he says, the therapist "does not have to ponder empathy or personal warmth (which are difficult to define), but can deal primarily with the application of psychological principles to the problem at hand" (p. 154).

To disregard scientific knowledge, from whatever source, and operate strictly from within theoretical schools of psychotherapy (which appears to have occurred for most of this discipline's history), seems inconsistent with the general protocol of science itself. As DeBerry (1990) cautions: "The danger of theoretical models is that we sometimes follow them literally and forget that they are metaphors." Theoretical models, "like good maps," he says, "are necessary and useful; however, it is extremely important not to confuse the map with the territory." Existence and the human mind, he further contends, "will always be greater than any map is able to indicate" (p. 196). With respect to psychotherapy, in other words, this suggests a need for theory revision through transtheoretical communication and the integration of empirically relevant knowledge from diverse allied fields of human behavior.

THE NEED FOR INTEGRATION

With respect to revising hypothetical constructs, Carl Rogers (1959), himself, appeared to recognize this need, through integrating knowledge, when he made the following prediction:

I visualize the same type of rapprochement with learning theory, where in my judgement we have much to offer in the way of new directions in that field, as well as being able to use much of the material available there. It also seems likely that a number of hypotheses we are formulating may be tested in the laboratory, some on human and some on animal subjects, thus linking the field of personality and therapy with so-called experimental psychology. (pp. 249-250)

Others from the humanistic school, as well, appear to favor the kind of *holistic* integrative approach advocated herein. In the words of Combs, Richards, and Richards (1976):

> Some psychologists have been and will remain content with only the study of behavior. Other psychologists have been and will remain content with only the study of personal perceptions and meanings. Both groups, undoubtedly, will continue to extend our understanding of persons and their functioning. . . . We would like to propose a third alternative—an approach which attempts to integrate the study of an individual's behavior and his perceptions or meanings. (p. 2)

Despite these early appeals for integration, and Lazarus's warnings of the limitations of single-school adherence, however, it has taken decades for integration and eclecticism to become established as the *preferred treatment orientation* of therapists (seemingly by default, however). Or as Mahoney (1991) states, it has taken psychology a long time to "put the person back together" as we begin to realize the complexity and individuality of human experience. Behaviorists, he says, "have emphasized action, cognitivists have been partial to insight and reflection, and humanists have encouraged emotional experience and expression." Only in the last decade, he adds, have there been genuine dialogues among the rival groups and "a growing appreciation for the complex interdependence of their respective realms of preference" (p. 21).

This integrative trend is also supported, as previously noted, by the transtheoretical work of Prochaska and Diclemente (1992) who believe that integration across systems of therapy will likely occur at an "intermediate level of analysis between theory and technique," or at the "level of the processes of change" (p. 302). In this regard, Goldfried, Castonguay, and Safran (1992) note that a number of researchers now agree that efforts should be directed at investigating change processes, rather than therapeutic orientations, mainly due to the "failure to find uniform differences in the efficacy of various treatments" (p. 600). The rationale for doing so, they say, also derives from the fact that "treatment orientation is too large a unit of analysis to help us refine our understanding of what works" (p. 601). Prochaska and Diclemente (1992) expand upon these therapeutic processes of change:

> The processes of change, then, may be best understood as a middle level of abstraction between the basic theoretical assumptions of a system of psychotherapy and the techniques proposed by the theory. A process of change represents types of activity initiated or experienced by an individual in modifying thinking, behavior, or affect related to a particular problem. Although there are a large number of coping activities, there appear to be a finite set of processes that represent the basic change principles underlying coping activities. (p. 302)

With respect to the possible "nonconscious" characteristic of these interactional behaviors or proposed "change principles," Ekman and Friesen (1975), and others who work in the area of nonverbal communication, maintain, for example, that interpersonal nonverbal behavior is mostly learned out of habit or "automatically" (Beck, 1984). For this reason, due to its current "nonspecific" status in psychotherapy, it generally remains outside the therapist's main focus of attention when attending to, or concentrating upon, other variables (i.e., those which the therapist's working model or theory proposes to be therapeutic). And, as Zeig and Munion (1990) note, these "other" hypothesized therapeutic variables are numerous:

> What does the therapist consider to be the "quark" or essential unit in psychotherapy? Depending on one's background, a therapist may choose one of a number of things as the essential unit-of-analysis, for example emotion, behavior, thought, or relationship. Also, some therapists emphasize the past, others the present, and still others, the future. Some therapists emphasize what goes on within the client; others emphasize the process between the therapist and the client. Others emphasize the process among clients. Some emphasize method, others theory. Some emphasize research; others eschew research. Some elevate the importance of growth. Others orient toward the symp-

tom. Some emphasize conscious processes; others focus on unconscious processes. Some derive models of therapy from art, others from science. (p. 9)

This issue of theoretical perspective is important, Zeig and Munion explain, because the "units-of-analysis," or the hypothesized therapeutic catalysts to which therapists attend, become "theoretically determined, implanted lenses" which are not only intellectually but perceptually based ways of "seeing a problem" (p. 13). Or, as previously noted, the theory then "decides" what can be observed. Garfield (1990) concurs and contends that a therapist bound by one specific theoretical orientation tends to view events from that perspective and to credit, as therapeutic variables, "those designated by the theory." However, Garfield cautions, "this process could distort what actually occurred, and other explanations could be of equal or greater validity." For example, he says, in some instances, "the opportunity to unburden oneself to a noncritical and empathic healer might be the variable of significance and not the transference relationship per se or a particular interpretation" (p. 242).

Zeig and Munion (1990) further contend that therapists acquire these theoretical lenses early in their training, in addition to the lenses that develop during their own personal history or upbringing. Moreover, problems often arise, they say, when these lenses rigidify over time and hinder flexibility in therapy, thus leading to "counterproductive results" (p. 13). They go on to explain that this selective attention within particular schools occurs not only by therapists in relation to processes of change but also by clients with respect to differing perspectives regarding the concept of *disorder.* For example, depression, they say, can be defined as "a behavior, a feeling, a relational pattern, or a biological event"(p. 11). This definition, they further state, "can be offered by the patient *or* the therapist, and sometimes the two have to fight it out to see whose definition will prevail because both patient and therapist alike tend to emphasize one element to the exclusion of others" (p. 11).

In view of these differing hypothetical opinions which, as previously noted, may be less an issue of right or wrong than one of *selective perspective* (similar to the figure-ground phenomenon described earlier), this book therefore aims to broaden the perspective on the psychotherapeutic relationship. It attempts to do so by bringing therapist nonverbal behavioral processes, and knowledge of client psychobiological processes, to the therapist's working focus. This need in psychotherapy is further underlined by the nonverbal behavioral work of Ekman and Friesen (1975) who conclude, for example, that interpersonal nonverbal behavior is mainly based on unwritten rules of convention, "politeness, and intimacy" (p. 16) rather than on *efficacy of communication*. In other words, if such nonconscious, conventional, interpersonal interaction occurs in the broader area of human behavior, then given the current "nonspecific" status of nonverbal behavior in psychotherapy, this must also be the case with respect to the therapeutic encounter. For this reason, the particular relevance to psychotherapy of research in nonverbal behavior is addressed in Chapters 3, 4, and 7.

The need to bring nonverbal variables to the therapist's working awareness or focus, in a process which itself relies heavily upon facilitating effective communication, both interpersonally and intrapersonally, would appear to be fundamental to this field. Furthermore, until the fundamental or foundational bases of psychotherapy are established, the structure of the field will be weak and, as Efran, Lukens, and Lukens (1990) explain, our knowledge of human behavior will remain stunted "within a limited range of conceptual possibilities" (p. xiii). In the absence of consensus in this area, however, Efran et al. observe that trends in the mental health field, throughout psychotherapy's preparadigmatic phase, have mainly involved a shuffling of emphases among the same few areas of focus:

> . . . We have shifted around among biochemical, intrapsychic, and interpersonal foci. Emotions, behaviors, and cognitions have each been placed temporarily in the limelight. Also, we have alternately focused our attention on the individual, the family, and the sociology of the community. In our estimation, the murkiness that currently characterizes work in the field cannot be cleared up simply by inventing more techniques or introducing additional theoretical refinements to existing models. To break out of the current conceptual morass will require a review of the core epistemological assumptions on which our thinking has been based. (p. xiii)

This view is also shared by Sexton and Whiston (1994), who conclude that for a true paradigm shift to occur, it may be necessary to "critically investigate the very ontological and epistemological assumptions on which we base our theoretical models" (p. 59). Or as Gardner (1993) puts it, the more challenging work of science "transcends the solution of problems already posed by others." What occurred in Einstein's formulation of "relativity theory," Gardner says, was in effect "system building." Having considered the concepts and phenomena in a domain, and having found prevailing views to be inadequate, Gardner says, "scientists in a sense go back to the drawing board" (p. 132).

The first two chapters of this book therefore address this issue of "core assumptions" involving the topics *therapeutic relationship* and *universal variables* in an attempt to retrace foundational roots and establish a clearer perspective. Without sufficient scientific consensus in this area, crucial issues will continue to plague the field— issues such as "efficacy," for example, which Strupp (1978) believes to be "the single most important problem overshadowing all others and placing them in perspective" (p. 7) in psychotherapy today. This lack of efficacy may further be a function of the tenuous scientific foundation upon which psychotherapy currently rests— hence the proliferation of therapies fueling a well-meaning, but thus far unproductive, attempt to address this indefinite situation. In this regard, as Efran, Lukens, and Lukens (1990) point out, the same history: "initial enthusiasm followed by a more realistic appraisal, increasing skepticism, and at least partial disillusionment" (p. 16), has characterized the birth of virtually all techniques and models in this field.

To break out of this redundant developmental stage of *experimentation* and to benefit from the ideas and experiences of others, Norcross and Newman (1992) maintain that consensus or knowledge has to be achieved. As they observe in quoting S.A. Appelbaum, "Only knowledge can unite the disparate schools, techniques, and views of man and change. Only knowledge is boundaryless and infinite" (p. 29). Therefore, in their acknowledged pessimistic view, Efran, Lukens, and Lukens (1990) see an urgent need to stop the psychotherapeutic community from operating like "a giant rumor mill," where conceptions are more likely to be "self-fulfilling than self-correcting"—instead of being "a repository of carefully sifted information" (p. 17). Lazarus (1992) voices a similar concern stating that the field is still "replete with cult members" (p. 258) or devout members of specific schools of thought. In his estimation, the proliferation of different, rival, and competing therapies has "produced more contention than convergence and no shortage of divarication." Preconceived agendas are heavily promoted, he says, and "we have to contend with cults and similar in-group mentalities that are the antithesis of science" (Lazarus, 1993a, p. 674). In other words, Goldfried, Castonguay, and Safran (1992) point out, we seem to be "writing for ourselves" with little communication with others. The discoveries or developments in each particular school, Goldfried, Castonguay, and Safran maintain (and, one might add, within other allied areas of human behavior), have therefore traditionally failed to contribute to the growth of other approaches, as if they were themselves emerging from "incommensurable paradigms" (p. 603).

Herein, then, lies the promise of the eclectic and integration movement in which Mahoney (1991) and others have observed a growing trend in the field toward *convergence of knowledge* in psychotherapy. Or as Bergin and Lambert (1979) advocated at an earlier stage of the integration movement: "We particularly value the kind of integrative review that resynthesizes data or reintegrates data in such a way as to come out with some new insight." Many fields of inquiry, they note, "have been significantly advanced by . . . the analysis of existing data as opposed to simply churning out additional reports on familiar topics" (p. 54). This view is also supported by Efran, Lukens, and Lukens (1990) who maintain that it is useful to have the freedom to "change lenses" from time to time, first using one level of analysis and then shifting to a "larger, smaller, or different unit of study." Some of the great discoveries of science, they note, "were simply a matter of widening or changing the boundary definitions of a phenomenon" (p. 95).

This movement toward integration and convergence has been slow, however. Despite the growth of therapies since 1889 when the term *psychotherapy* was first coined, Efran, Lukens, and Lukens (1990) point out that paradigmatic realization has remained elusive and that "nothing remotely resembling a consensus has been achieved" (p. 18). Given this relatively long-standing state of affairs, the move toward eclecticism by Arnold Lazarus in the 1960s should probably have been more popular than it reportedly was at that time (Lazarus, 1992). Today, however, as Jensen, Bergin, and Greaves (1990) report, and as Lazarus (1992) himself observes, 59 to 72 percent of therapists espouse an eclectic approach. In addition, this is apparently so despite the fact that, as Efran, Lukens, and Lukens (1990) point out, the selection of therapeutic strategies is still a "seat of the pants operation" guided mainly "by personal predilections, intuitions, and financial considerations than by hard facts" (p. 12). Or as Lazarus (1992) similarly acknowledges, eclecticism offers no modus operandi for selecting treatments of choice, matching therapeutic "styles" to particular client variables, or choosing the "type of relationship stance" most likely to facilitate "growth and change" (p. 235). Nevertheless, as Spengler et al. (1995) point out, "Paul's (1967, p. 111) question for psychotherapy research, '*What* treatment, by *whom*, is most effective for *this* individual with *that* specific problem, under *which* set of circumstances?'" presents a seemingly impossible agenda for researchers. Yet, they say, "counseling psychologists face this reality on a daily basis" (p. 516). And therapists may face this daily predicament, as the thesis of this book suggests, due to the lack of paradigmatic direction.

While this book recognizes the need for such direction, or for a universal modus operandi in the field, it nevertheless questions the apparent widespread assumption, noted by Beutler and Consoli (1992), that efforts should be directed at what may be an "endless and unattainable task" (p. 270), i.e., the matching of countless "style" and "relationship stance" therapist variables with similar client variables. On the contrary, the proposal of such a seemingly complicated and subjective research task, as with the current profusion of psychodynamic therapies, may have arisen as a result of the lack of paradigmatic realization rather than as a possible means of achieving it. Therefore, instead of providing a way out of our increasingly complicated "quagmire of psychodynamic theorizing" (Lazarus, 1992, p. 233), such an approach might further divert research efforts away from the paradigmatic quest given the current weakness, or lack of specification of the foundational bases of psychotherapy, upon which this proposed solution to the psychodynamic dilemma would be constructed.

This book therefore suggests the alternative approach of delineating the processes of change, first, as a means of addressing the secondary issue of therapeutic efficacy—both objectives being consistent with what Beutler and Consoli (1992) define as "the most pressing needs" (p. 292) in systematic eclectic psychotherapy today. Toward this realization, and in addition to *technical eclecticism* —which Lazarus (1992) describes as the systematic or practical application of psychological science within theoretically consistent guidelines—this book also incorporates elements of *common factors* and *transtheoretical* integration. Further rationale for *integrating the integrationists* is provided by Norcross and Newman (1992) who state: "No technical eclectic can totally disregard theory, and no theoretical integrationist can ignore technique." Without some "commonalities" among different schools of therapy, they say, "theoretical integration would be impossible." And even the most ardent proponent of common factors, they point out, "cannot practice 'nonspecifically' or 'commonly'; specific techniques must be applied" (p. 14).

Additionally, as Goldfried, Castonguay, and Safran (1992) observe, the days have long since past when it was possible for a lone scientist to arrive at important discoveries in almost complete isolation from colleagues. In their words, "We all have our reference groups, and it is hard to imagine how we could function professionally without them" (p. 601). In fact, as Rossi (1993) observes in his quote from Carl Jung, "There is not a single important idea or view that does not possess historical antecedents." Ultimately, he says, "they are all founded on primordial archetypical forms whose concreteness dates from a time when consciousness did not think, but only perceived." In this sense, Jung observes, thoughts were "objects of inner perception, not thought at all, but sensed as external phenomena—seen or heard, so to speak" (p. 276).

In building upon or integrating previous knowledge, Norcross and Newman (1992) therefore describe the common factors approach as one which seeks to determine the "core ingredients" which psychodynamic therapies have in common in order to improve therapeutic efficiency. They believe that what these therapies share may be more significant in effecting therapeutic change than their apparent differences. However, without openness and informed cooperation in the integration process, they warn, as does Lazarus (1992), that potential differences among integrationists could repeat the problem of the competing schools of rigid adherence, i.e., designating "integrative psychotherapy" as "another therapeutic school" at a time when there is no consensus as to "what specifically should be integrated" (Goldfried, Castonguay, and Safran, 1992, p. 610). This possibility notwithstanding, Norcross and Newman (1992) nevertheless express hope that the integration movement will instead create an "open system of informed pluralism, deepening rapprochement, and empirically grounded practice"—one that leads to "improved efficacy of psychosocial treatments" (p. 32). Or as Messer (1992) explains, ". . . we want to be able to draw upon any theoretical ideas or techniques that are backed by evidence, are potentially useful, and can be assimilated in a contextually meaningful way. We want to be rational and reasonable, not dogmatic" (p. 156).

Moreover, the current lack of efficacy or "superiority" (Lambert, 1992) of any one therapy over another, across broad categories of behavioral and psychological disorders, lends support to the assertion of Lazarus (1992) that his eclectic approach, multimodal therapy, probably has greater efficacy than "less comprehensive approaches" (p. 225). However, as previously mentioned, more fundamental than the issue of efficacy, the specification of the behavioral, biological and cognitive bases of psychotherapy, when established, would simultaneously resolve the secondary issue of efficacy by fostering paradigmatic direction. Lacking such direction, therapists presently attend to a variety of variables (which may or may not be among the actual therapeutic catalysts facilitating change) thereby resulting in inconsistent effectiveness across therapists and an absence of quality control in the field. This issue further has import, as Meltzoff and Kornreich (1970) observed over a quarter of a century ago, because the onus is on the profession to provide services that have been tested and actually consistently perform that which they purport to accomplish. Failure to do this, they contend, results in far greater injustices to the client population, in general, who are then forced to utilize services with very little consumer protection.

With the help of the eclectic and integration movement, this book therefore describes, for heuristic purposes, a transtheoretical psychodynamic therapy which derives support from existing empirical research in psychotherapy, and from the behavioral sciences in general, and is grounded in the author's clinical practice. With respect to applying research from the behavioral sciences to the clinical domain, Norcross and Newman (1992) view this as a legitimate means of enhancing knowledge of change processes in psychotherapy by integrating "basic knowledge on cognition, affect, development neuroscience, biological substrates, interpersonal influences, and community interventions" (p. 14). Goldfried, Castonguay, and Safran (1992) agree and add that drawing on such knowledge from basic research disciplines, with their standardized terminology, may, in their opinion, "provide a partial solution to the problem of different therapeutic language systems" (pp. 606-607) (about which more will be said in Chapter 2). In this respect, therefore, the integrated eclectic approach described herein is proffered as a transtheoretical proposal for future scientific foundational research in psychotherapy, as well as for guidance in integrative eclectic practice.

Until the foundational bases of psychotherapy are established, confusion in the field will likely continue. As Efran, Lukens, and Lukens (1990) observe:

> In the absence of a theory that provides a firm basis for predictions, even positive outcomes may not be entirely satisfying to therapists. Since ours is a field in which success is not more easily understood than failure, favorable outcomes do not automatically serve as a grounding for details of clinical practice. Therapists continue to crave—but for the most part have not been able to find—a solid footing in the amorphous theoretical and methodological landscape of the field. (p. xii)

Compounding this "amorphous" state of affairs for therapists, Efran, Lukens, and Lukens (1990) note, is the fact that the situation for clients is understandably not much better. In their words:

> The illusion that there are objective treatments that can be described in psychotherapy "shop manuals" has dissuaded some clients from shopping for a therapist who might truly suit their purposes. They think of therapies and therapists as basically interchangeable, except for relatively minor differences in experience, competence, or "bedside manner." Thus they go about

picking a therapist the way they might choose a physician, lawyer, or real estate agent. They fail to appreciate that the essence of therapy is the match between client and therapist, not the therapist's technical competence in applying set procedures. (p. 194)

This artistic-like situation, or *personality matching*, is likely further currently necessitated by the lack of scientific foundation in the field which, in turn, results in inconsistent efficacy across therapists. For this reason, the words of Strupp (1973) seem applicable today, when he asked: "How does it come about that one person, by virtue of what he is or what he does, can exert such a lasting influence on another person that the changes that result from this encounter may be termed therapeutic?" In reply to this question, Strupp recommends the following *dyadic* course of action:

> . . . As psychologists and researchers we have set ourselves the task of arriving at a better scientific understanding of the forces operating within the dyadic framework of the therapeutic relationship. Our aim is (or should be) not merely the achievement of therapeutic results—important as this goal unquestionably is—but a conceptualization of "how" these results are achieved as well as the parameters of our efforts. . . . Furthermore, if our goal is to develop a psychotherapy as a "scientific discipline," together with an improved technology for effecting therapeutic change, I believe this course of action represents our best hope. (p. 19)

The problem remains, however, how to create a "scientific discipline" from the study of the psyche. Despite the fact that mental events may not be among the data of science, Dennett (1991) nevertheless maintains that this does not mean we cannot study them scientifically. Black holes and genes are not among the data of science, he says, but we have developed good scientific theories about them. The challenge, Dennett says, is to construct a theory of mental events "using the data that scientific method permits" (p. 71). Combs, Richards, and Richards (1976) further describe such an approach to theory building in relation to the field concept utilized by other sciences:

When something occurs at one point in space apparently because something else happened at another point with no visible means by which the "cause" can be related to the "effect," the scientist often says the two events are connected in a field. The field serves as a kind of bridge between cause and effect. Using this concept the scientist can deal with a problem even though he may not be clearly aware of all intervening aspects. No one has ever seen electricity, for example, nor are we entirely certain just what it is or exactly how it works. In spite of this lack of exact knowledge, however, we are able to deal with the phenomenon by assuming the existence of an electric field. . . . It makes it possible to deal with events that behave lawfully even though we may be ignorant of why or how. That an event can be utilized in a lawful way is sufficient to make it useful for the scientist's purpose. (p. 21)

Dennett (1991) also points out that neuroscientists are right to insist that you do not really have a good model of consciousness "until you solve the problem of where it fits in the brain" (p. 256). The same might also apply to a scientific theory of psychotherapy— its neurological or biological basis within the client, and its interactional basis between therapist and client, have to be more firmly established. As Rossi (1993) observes:

No theory of mind-body communication and healing can be considered complete until therapists are able to specify, at least in general outline, the major pathways of communication from what they do on the mental-behavioral level to the cellular-genetic responses that are an inherent part of the mind-body communication loop. (p. 284)

In this regard, toward advancing the scientific objective of proposing a transtheoretical paradigm of the psychodynamic process, Carl Rogers's work on the therapeutic relationship, as discussed in Chapter 1, may have helped narrow the quest by marshalling consensus concerning the *designated area* in which to search for universal variables composing a higher-order theory. Chapter 2 then explores these common or universal factors which are amplified in subsequent chapters and integrated, in the final chapter, into a trans-theoretical psychodynamic therapy, or modus operandi (Lazarus, 1992), deriving its support from the empirical literature as well as the author's clinical practice.

In summary, the field of psychotherapy may have reached a "crossroads"—some might say, a "crisis point"—with little apparent scientific foundation from which to sustain paradigmatic direction. As a result, not only clients and therapists appear to have suffered but, presumably, therapist training programs, as well as research of the therapeutic alliance currently reported to be at a standstill. Reasons offered for this indefinite state of affairs mainly relate to the lack of behavioral, biological, and cognitive grounding of psychotherapeutic concepts as well as the need for transtheoretical communication and construct revision, which are at the heart of the scientific enterprise, but which have been lacking in this field.

Single-school adherence, possibly due to the human *selective attention* phenomenon, may further have prevented knowledge from becoming "comparative and cumulative," thus contributing to the current crisis state. The limitations of these schools now seem more widely acknowledged, as well as the need for an integrated theory generating sufficient scientific consensus to unify the field. Since science deals in universals and observables, doing so will therefore likely involve moving beyond the current intrapsychic preoccupation whose paradigmatic value largely appears to have become defunct. In other words, there may be a need to move beyond the therapeutic relationship—toward greater behavioral, biological, and cognitive grounding of the interactional change processes occurring between therapist and client, resulting in psychobiological change processes occurring within the client. Once established, this scientific field theory could provide the paradigmatic direction required to sustain future research resulting in greater efficacy of treatment and more effective therapist training programs.

In conclusion, supporting this kind of higher-order theory building, Goldfried, Castonguay, and Safran (1992) observe that the future of psychotherapy in general, and psychotherapy integration in particular, could be enhanced "if our knowledge of the change process is informed by both empirical and theoretical knowledge acquisition strategies" (p. 610). Theory, they say, "typically guides our research, and empirical findings are especially valuable if they can help us in revising our theoretical constructs" (p. 608)—both processes being vital to the growth of knowledge itself and the advancement of any science.

Chapter 1

The Therapeutic Relationship: Beyond This Point of Convergence

Early on, Freud (1910/1957) himself insisted that the truth of an interpretation, while necessary, was not a sufficient guarantee of therapeutic efficacy. The correct interpretation will be ineffective or even pathologic unless the patient has formed a "sufficient attachment" to the analyst.

—Jay Greenberg, 1994

The attempt to think about psychotherapy, to investigate it empirically, and to demand a certain amout of accountability, does not have to blind one to the mystery that lies at the heart of the process. On the other hand, the insistence that psychotherapy cannot or should not be empirically investigated is often associated with a type of arrogance and unwillingness to engage in self-examination that in the long run can only be harmful to the field and to our clients.

—Jeremy Safran and Christopher Muran, 1994

Whichever viewpoint one embraces—technical eclecticism, common factors, or theoretical integration—there is one theme that has captured the imagination of many psychotherapists in recent years, namely, that existing theoretical frameworks and their associated techniques are insufficient to account for complex clinical phenomena and to enable the clinician to formulate the most efficient, effective, and humane interventions.

—Gerald Davison and Arnold Lazarus, 1995

As the integrationists Beutler and Consoli (1992) point out, most theorists and therapists including Rogers (1957), Guidano (1987), Bowlby (1979), Larson (1987), Mahoney (1991), Lambert (1992), and Prochaska and Diclemente (1992) acknowledge the need for developing a relationship or alliance with the client as a vehicle for therapeutic change. While therapists may differ on the degree of importance ascribed to the relationship, the general consensus surrounding its necessity nevertheless tends to lend credence to the view of humanists at the extreme end of the psychotherapeutic spectrum who believe, as Derlega et al. (1991) put it, that "the relationship *is* the therapy" (p. 6).

The main reason for this convergence or coalescence around the therapeutic relationship is outlined by Beutler and Consoli (1992):

> From empirical research has come an appreciation of the power of the therapeutic bond. Numerous investigators have asserted that the relative inability to distinguish outcomes of different psychotherapies suggest that they all work through the same basic mechanisms—the therapeutic bond, or alliance (Luborsky, Singer, and Luborsky, 1975; Sloane, Staples, Cristol, Yorkston, and Whipple, 1975; Smith, Glass, and Miller, 1980). (p. 265)

Goldfried and Newman (1992) agree and add that the convergence of schools of thought on the centrality of the therapeutic relationship is even supported, in the treatment of personality disorders, by some cognitive behaviorists who view "interactions in the therapeutic relationship as being central to assessment and treatment, not merely a prerequisite to treatment" (p. 76). Lambert (1992) echoes this view pointing out that reviewers are "virtually unanimous" in their support of the therapeutic relationship as a critical factor in the process of therapeutic change—but a factor which they claim "is more ambiguous than was once thought" (p. 104).

This ambiguity may further derive from the fact that, aside from the Rogerian therapist attitudes previously mentioned, just what behavioral, biological, and cognitive factors may be involved in such an alliance has remained unexplained—thus probably fueling much of the preparadigmatic propagation of therapeutic approaches within the last fifty years. Prochaska and Diclemente (1992) point out the inherent limitations of developing a field primarily through inventing new therapies. In their view, "each therapy system focused more on theories of psychopathology and single mechanisms of change than on exploration of the process of change." In this respect, they state, "unconditional positive regard, authenticity, living in the here and now, confrontation of beliefs, social interest, conditioning and contingencies are valuable rules for human functioning, but are not sufficient to explain therapy change" (p. 300).

Furthermore, there is reason to believe that Carl Rogers and Abraham Maslow, the founders of the humanistic school and themselves the chief proponents of the therapeutic relationship, rather than purporting to profess "gospel," recognized the function of humanistic theory—as a heuristic guide to the search for processes of change. For example, Rogers (1965) prefaced the formulation of his "Client-Centered Theory of Therapy, Personality, and Interpersonal Relationships" by stating:

> I believe that there is only one statement which can accurately apply to all theories . . . from the one I will present to the one I hope will replace it in a decade—and that is that at the time of its formulation, every theory contains an unknown. . . . To me this attitude is important, for I am distressed at the manner in which small-caliber minds immediately accept a theory—almost any theory—as a dogma of truth. If theory could be seen for what it is—a fallible, changing attempt to construct a network of gossamer threads which will contain the solid facts—then a theory would serve as it should, as a stimulus to further creative thinking. (p. 472)

And the similar view of Maslow (1970):

> In the past, as we have said, the character structure of the therapist was far more important than any theories he held, or even more important than the conscious techniques that he used. But this must become less and less so as technical therapy becomes more and more sophisticated. In the total picture of the good psychotherapist, his character structure for the last decade or two has slowly receded in importance and will almost certainly continue to do so in the future, while his training, his intelligence, his techniques, his theories have steadily become more important until, we may rest assured, some time in the future they will become all-important. (p. 260)

Like Rogers and Maslow, Freud, too, as a neurologist and neuro-anatomist by training, believed until his death, according to Gardner (1993), that "all psychic mechanisms must have a material basis" (p. 68) as he searched for physiological grounding of his psychoanalytic constructs. In fact, Gardner maintains that in his "Project for a Scientific Psychology," Freud attempted to formulate a comprehensive framework or theory of human behavior which would include normal, abnormal, conscious, and unconscious phenomena. Gardner further quotes Freud, who defined the purpose of his "Project" as being: "To furnish a psychology that shall be a natural science; that is, to represent psychical processes as quantitatively determinate states of specifiable material particles, thus making those processes perspicuous and free from contradiction" (p. 66).

However, as Gardner explains, Freud's efforts in this regard may have been premature, and would have had to await greater scientific exploration in neurology (and, one might also add, in areas of human functioning closely allied to psychotherapy such as linguistics, information processing, interpersonal communication, and nonverbal behavior). Nearly a century later, however, the processes of change within the therapeutic relationship remain unspecified. Commenting upon this state of affairs, Wexler (1974) observes that the curative effect of the therapeutic relationship is still believed to accrue from the therapist's establishing an "understanding" atmosphere which "permits growth and change" (p. 95). However, Wexler says, this general truth does not provide much insight into the "specific properties of understanding" or the nature of "its direct effects" upon the client.

Toward greater specificity, Smith (1966) appeared to recognize fairly early on that the interpersonal communication between client and therapist differs from that of everyday relationships in that therapists develop "specialized techniques" (p. 196) to play their role effectively—a process which he acknowledges requires a great deal of supervised practice and experience. Smith concludes, therefore, that the role and techniques of the clinician, rather than his personality or his sensitivity, might be what fosters therapeutic change. Moreover, this ambiguity may derive from the fact that, as Kolden, Howard, and Maling (1994) point out, the therapist "is both the provider and the instrument" of therapy. That is, they note, the therapeutic relationship "serves major functions as a component of the context of change (along with other therapy processes) as well as a primary mechanism for change" (p. 82).

Given this dual function of the relationship, as Wexler and Rice (1974) further explain, extending humanistic theory to incorporate therapist behavioral expressions of intrapsychic states need not necessarily contradict it. It merely recognizes the *synergistic* existence of mind and behavior, they say, which may further ultimately address the problem of operationalism in client-centered therapy. In their words:

> The practice of client-centered therapy . . . seems to be moving further and further away from a strictly "school" approach, and toward the use of a variety of different techniques . . . . This move away from orientational orthodoxy does not seem to be leading in the direction of becoming atheoretical. The theoretical formulations are simply taking a different form. The trend is not toward dealing in whole orientations, but toward the *specification* of different kinds of therapist operations . . . . (p. 205)

This evolution of client or person-centered theory further seems necessary because, as Cochrane and Holloway (1974) note, Rogers was not explicit as to how his therapist attitudes were conveyed to the client. In this regard, however, they go on to explain that "Nonverbal communication, as in voice quality, posture, and the like, may be particularly important" (p. 273). Similarly, others who espouse an eclectic and integrative view suggest that the facilitative attitudes would likely not have the stylistic impact hypothesized by Rogers unless they were accompanied by the corresponding behavioral signals. Empathy, for example, has been described by such integrationists as "a combination of understanding the other's feelings and providing feedback to the other via attentive behavioral cues which signal that the process of empathy is taking place" (Norton and Pettegrew, 1979, p. 15). This view further appears to be supported by that of humanists Truax and Mitchell (1971), who state:

> When empathy is defined in terms of operational scales measuring the therapist's responses to the client, it becomes clear that what is being measured is an interpersonal skill rather than simply an attitude or personality attribute, since a person can have an

understanding or empathic attitude, and even actually be sensitive and accurately understand, without making an accurately empathic response. In short, you have to understand to make an accurately empathic response, but the absence of an accurately empathic response tells us nothing about the depth, extent or accuracy of the understanding. (p. 319)

To clarify how theoretical formulations can "take a different form" or, more specifically, how attitudes relate to, or translate into, "interpersonal skills," the description of the relationship between attitude and behavior supplied by Gordon Allport (1967) may help. He describes an attitude as "a mental and neural state of readiness, organized through experience, exerting a directive or dynamic influence upon the individual's response to all objects and situations with which it is related." Or conversely, as Combs, Richards, and Richards (1976) put it, behavior "represents the externally observable manifestation of what is going on inside a person" (p. x). Allport (1967) goes on to explain that an attitude characteristically "provokes behavior that is acquisitive or avertive, favourable or unfavourable, affirmative or negative toward the object or class of objects with which it is related" (p. 8). Further expanding this view, Harre and Gillett (1994) note that because of the synergistic relationship between attitude and behavior, attitudes are in turn dependent upon *context*, or come into existence, "in displays expressive of decisions and judgments and in the performance of actions" rather than being "semipermanent mental activity" (p. 22).

Despite these apparent heuristic contributions to the growth of knowledge, however, rigid adherence to a specific school may have delayed what would seem to have been the next logical step in the evolution of humanistic and/or psychotherapeutic theory, i.e., the specification of behavioral and physiological *expressions*, or manifestations, of therapeutic attitudes. This delay in the evolution of psychotherapeutic theory may further have occurred as a result of the field becoming obfuscated by the plethora of therapies on the market and by a redirection of a large portion of the treatment focus away from individual therapy and toward group and family therapy—a factor which continues to impact psychotherapy research today. That is, including more human beings in the therapeutic process naturally increases the complexity of the research task thereby likely resulting in even greater obscuration of the change processes (those operating within the basic interpersonal or dyadic components of such treatments). As Elliott and Marmarosh (1995) point out, "Despite the rich history of research and practice of group psychotherapy in the counseling psychology literature, little work has examined structural and interpersonal factors in change-producing groups from social-cognitive perspectives" (p. 676).

The significance of this move toward systems and group emphases in the field, without understanding the change processes occurring within the basic dyad, lies in the fact that, just as atoms and molecules have different characteristics than the elements or compounds they form, the group or systems contexts of such therapies may influence therapeutic change through processes additional to, or possibly different from, those occurring in dyadic therapy. In our haste to adapt the current "ineffective" psychotherapy to the masses, therefore (or to capitalize upon ideological investment), research efforts may have been diverted away from exploring the behavioral, biological, and cognitive bases of what would appear to be a foundational building block of psychotherapy—*the interpersonal dyad*—an omission which likely perpetuates much of the current confusion in the field. For, while group and family therapy may be as efficient as the current "ineffective" individual therapy (as their adherents may legitimately point out), these systemic therapies may nevertheless *not* be as efficacious as "effective" individual therapy (once the behavioral, biological, and cognitive foundations have been established), given the greater number of clients in these systemic therapies and the logistics of meeting their diverse idiosyncratic needs.

In any event, without a more comprehensive understanding of the basic dyadic components of such therapies, limitations to group and systems processes will likely result as well. Expanding upon this point, Efran, Lukens, and Lukens (1990) state:

A teacher can lecture to an entire classroom, and a family therapist may elect to meet with many members of the same family at once. However, each individual in the classroom is learning something different, and each client at a family meeting is pursu-

ing an individual agenda. The analysis is complicated because
everyone is together—each interaction can therefore trigger multiple responses—but the basic principle is unchanged. Each person is on his or her own therapeutic journey. (p. 190)

Furthermore, as Feldman and Powell (1992) explain, behavioral
changes in families or groups may become blocked by the dysfunctional cognitions and emotions of individual members. When these
intrapsychic factors are neglected, they maintain, therapy often
"becomes bogged down in frustratingly repetitious efforts to promote
change by means of interactional change processes alone." Reduction
or elimination of intrapsychic blocks in such situations, they say,
"allows behavioral change to proceed" (p. 519). Along similar lines,
Feldman and Powell (1992) point out that individual and family
concerns are maintained by a combination of intrapsychic and interpersonal factors, together with the interactions between them. In
order to interrupt the problem maintenance process, they say, often both "intrapsychic" and "interpersonal changes are needed"
(p. 521)—each type of change process "facilitating and strengthening
the other" (p. 519).

In other words, a comprehensive understanding of *all* forms of
psychotherapy, derived from and constructed upon the dyadic
foundational building block, would seem necessary for the scientific
maturation of this field. For this reason, as suggested earlier, a
review of the basic epistemological assumptions or core principles,
i.e., "going back to the drawing board," may be required to break
out of this conceptual "quagmire." This review therefore begins
with an outline of the general environmental or interpersonal conditions under which psychotherapy normally occurs. Expanding upon
their universal nature, discussions of each of these common interpersonal factors, or universal variables, follow in subsequent chapters exploring how they may interact to form a higher-order theory.

This approach to theory building further appears consistent with
the early views of Haley (1963) who observed that a scientific
approach to determining the causes of therapeutic change would
involve "examining and describing the various contexts which
bring about change to determine what they have in common" (p. 2).
This would further seem necessary, as previously mentioned,

because common factors may hold the key to establishing greater paradigmatic direction. In other words, as stated earlier, if theory provides the map for the "therapeutic journey," the need for an empirically grounded or standardized "blueprint" to replace the current multiplicity of "road maps" is underlined by Beutler (1990). In the trenches, he maintains, "there are no theoretical purists—all theoretical views are modulated and tempered by personal experiences and beliefs." These are what the patient learns in effective treatment, he says, and these are "what guide the goals and subgoals of treatment" (p. 229).

TOWARD A STANDARDIZED TERMINOLOGY

Developing a more solid foundation in psychotherapy than that provided by "personal experience and belief" would seem to require, among other things, a standardized terminology to ensure that the same phenomena are being discussed. As Russell (1994) explains, "the quest for an observational language free from any and all theoretical influence—one whose terms point unambiguously at their material referents, and provide the final adjudicatory bedrock in relation to which frameworks must be comparatively assessed and their competing claims justified—has in fact failed" (p. 173). Despite this apparent failure, however, this task may not be as difficult as might first appear. In standardized, universal terms, for example, it is generally assumed that psychotherapy occurs face-to-face, that it involves self-disclosure or dialogue on the part of the client about a particular concern or concerns, and that through this disclosure, the therapist facilitates change in, or by, the client to ameliorate these concern(s).

This process was first described by Freud as "the talking cure" (Gardner, 1993, p. 58). However, to date, little attempt has been made to explain how talking, in the presence of another receptive human being, actually "cures." Nor is it known what therapist behaviors, interpersonal transactions between therapist and client, or physiological processes within the client (occurring as a result of these discursive transactions) likely facilitate that "cure." As Ferrara (1994) notes:

> Despite a general awareness on the part of the public about the availability of mental health resources, the practice of psychotherapy is still opaque. . . . Few people know what really goes on in therapy sessions [including the therapists, for that matter] or have any idea about how talking to a stranger can be beneficial to mental health. What is it about therapeutic discourse that is so therapeutic? Why is the therapy hour so powerful in the lives of troubled people if all they do is talk? (p. 3)

In his therapeutic work with hypertensive clients, Lynch (1985) offers a possible reason for the delay in exploration of such *therapeutic talk* by observing that Freud lacked the present-day technical capacity to monitor the human body and, thus, could not have appreciated, for example, "the dynamic connection between the human cardiovascular system and talking" (p. 294). One might also add that this would apply as well to today's sophisticated medical equipment for scanning the brain through magnetic resonance imaging (MRI) and positron emission tomography (PET). Despite such technical assistance, however, the dearth of knowledge concerning psychotherapeutic change processes still persists, as noted by Strupp (1978):

> The therapist attempts to be helpful to the patient or client. However, since there are considerable disagreements about the purpose of psychotherapy, the goals of treatment, and how therapeutic change is brought about, there is no consensus concerning the role and function of the therapist. . . . Most professionals agree that the therapist must acquire special skills, but for the reasons mentioned above, there is less agreement on the nature of these skills or how to perfect them. (p. 6)

Not surprisingly, therefore, this indefinite state of affairs likely extracts a considerable toll. As Efran, Lukens, and Lukens (1990) observe with respect to psychotherapy trainees, for example, who, despite extensive classroom training, often still feel at a loss when faced with a live client:

> . . . Practicum and internship supervisors often fail to provide them with the basic "how to" information they feel they need. Supervisors often act as if these *basics* are simply too obvious to

discuss. However, the central tenets of practice are never obvious to trainees, and their befuddlement about how they are supposed to "cure" anyone by just talking to them may last for years. They, too, feel as if there is a conspiracy of silence about the fundamental underpinnings of psychotherapeutic practice. (p. 4)

As a result of this uncertainty in the field, therefore, Haley's (1963) criticism still appears valid today—that knowledge in the field is inappropriate to describe the behavior of the psychotherapist and client in the therapeutic dyad. More important, he states, the transactions between therapist and client cannot be conceptualized through "the theoretical models which are the basis for these terms." Nevertheless, he points out, as yet, "there is no adequate substitute for the usual psychiatric concepts" (p. 4).

A decade later, however, Bordin (1974) offered this heuristic contribution to the debate:

Students of psychotherapy, whether clinical psychologists, psychiatrists, or representatives of other related disciplines, are subject to conflicting orientations and motivations as they confront the problem of understanding psychotherapy and of verifying this understanding. By its very nature, psychotherapy concerns itself with some of the most complex and, therefore, most baffling aspects of human phenomena, encountered, moreover, under conditions of human suffering. A psychological treatment process places the helper-healer in a personal encounter unaccompanied by the impersonalizing and objectifying effects of biochemical treatments or of surgical interventions. His interventions are of a personal nature; the specific therapeutic agent is his reaction to the patient. (p. 1)

Others in the field have put forth similar views. Over three decades ago, Haley (1963), for example, noted a gradual shift occurring in psychotherapy from an emphasis on intrapsychic phenomena to exploring relationships "between" people. It is only when the focus is upon "behavior within a relationship," he states, that psychotherapy becomes "describable." This is so, he explains, because "by definition, psychotherapy is a procedure which occurs in a relationship" (p. 3). Danziger (1976) offers a similar view. To understand the processes which foster change in psychotherapy, he notes, one must start with the fact that it involves at least two people. Its intraindividual effects, Danziger states, are generated by patterns of social interchange—the "motor" of therapeutic change being the "interpersonal processes" (p. 108). If this were not so, he observes, the same effects could just as well be produced by "individual meditation or by the perusal of enlightening literature" (p. 108).

Consequently, as Haley (1963) points out, when the focus in psychotherapy shifts to the two-person context, it enters the field of interpersonal communication which describes individuals in terms that apply to the exchange of "communicative behavior" (p. 5) between two people. It therefore follows, Danziger (1976) maintains, that if therapeutic effectiveness depends upon particular interpersonal transactions between therapist and client, it should be possible, in his estimation, "to establish empirical relationships between these interpersonal variables and appropriate measures of therapeutic outcome" (p. 108). In this respect, therefore, the general orientation of this book is consistent with the view that entering psychotherapy involves participating in a "special kind of interpersonal communication" (Danziger, 1976, p. 111).

Providing biological support for this interpersonal communication view in his psychotherapeutic work with hypertensive clients, Lynch (1985) states:

Human communication clearly involves two intertwined components—talking *and* listening—each of which has a powerful influence on the regulation of human blood pressure. Human dialogue is a seesaw, whose rhythm is sensitively registered by the vascular system. Dysfunctional speaking patterns appear to be accompanied by equally dysfunctional listening skills.

As the computer systems traced the blood pressure responses during therapeutic dialogue, it became apparent that there are two aspects of the vascular response to human communication: That is, in addition to the elevation in blood pressure when a person speaks, there is a *decrease* in blood pressure when one listens. (p. 160)

Lynch further contends that the hypertensive problem is extended to include not only the person whose blood pressure is elevated, but also those with whom he or she comes into contact. From his physiological research, he therefore concludes that significant others frequently contribute inadvertently to the general problem of hypertension. In other words, blood pressure not only transiently responds when a client talks to a mate or therapist, but his or her overall resting blood pressure is also influenced by the "quality" (p. 318) of such interpersonal communication.

INTERPERSONAL COMMUNICATION
AND THE THERAPEUTIC RELATIONSHIP

That the integration of interpersonal communication and psychotherapy is not exactly a new proposal in the field is noted by Vaughn and Burgoon (1976):

> Parsons (1951) maintains that therapy becomes necessary when the control mechanisms inherent in the reciprocities of ordinary human relationships break down. These control mechanisms are intimately bound up with human communication, for it is primarily through communication that individuals influence and are influenced by one another (King, 1975). Only by observing the constraints of a particular set of socially agreed upon behaviors can the individual hope to communicate (Harre and Secord, 1973). Thus, communication as a mode of social influence is central to the well-being of both the individual and the larger social unit; both depend upon it for their existence. (p. 256)

The apparent relevance of interpersonal communication to the therapeutic process then begs another question: How does interpersonal communication relate to humanistic or client-centered theory? The following explanation by Rogers (1972) may illuminate this connection:

> What relationship is there between providing therapeutic help to individuals with emotional maladjustments and the concern

of people today with obstacles to communication? Actually, the relationship is very close indeed. The whole task of psychotherapy is the task of dealing with a failure in communication. The emotionally maladjusted person, the "neurotic," is in difficulty first because communication within himself has broken down, and second because as a result of this, his communication with others has been damaged. (p. 71)

Similarly, Harry Stack Sullivan's (1970) book, *The Psychiatric Interview,* describes phenomena which "interfere with the freedom of communication, as they are revealed in the special instance of two people sitting down together for a supposedly common purpose." Sullivan further states that a major goal of the psychiatric interview is to understand such "blocks to communication" which reflect "underlying anxiety and anticipation of hurt from another human being" (p. xvi). Furthermore, the important ingredient of successful therapy, he states, is more adequately conveyed "by gesture and tone of voice than by words" and is executed "by the interviewer's being keenly responsive to the needs of the interviewee, and doing nothing to lower that one's self-esteem" (p. xxi).

The question remains, however, as explored in greater detail in Chapters 3, 4, and 7: Which therapist nonverbal behaviors facilitate interpersonal communication and which ones conceivably hinder it? As Dittman (1972) points out, communication habits are deeply ingrained and are usually removed from awareness so that "misunderstandings, or at best partial misunderstandings, may well be the rule rather than the exception." He further explains that a person "may 'blurt out' a response—if this term may be applied to channels other than language—in a way that he does not know about, at any stage of acquaintance" (p. 140). And since these communication habits and nonverbal behaviors are still categorized as nonspecific in psychotherapy, further exploration of these variables would therefore seem warranted.

With respect to the significance of the lack of integration of interpersonal communication research with psychotherapy, Vaughn and Burgoon (1976) maintain that in the final analysis, the emphasis on disrupted social functioning "highlights" the role of interpersonal communication in the "origin, diagnosis, prognosis, and treatment" of a wide range of organic and behavioral disorders. Because of the centrality of communication to social functioning, they say, it is therefore possible to view disrupted social functioning as "disturbed communication" (p. 256). Or as Derlega et al. (1991) put it: "If a client's inability to form or maintain close relationships is, as Sullivan (1953, 1954) suggests, a cause as well as a sign of psychological distress and if, as other work we have noted suggests, the ability to disclose and communicate responsively is crucial to the formation and maintenance of close relationships, then one of the chief tasks in therapy will be to teach clients more responsive communication patterns" (p. 141).

NONVERBAL BEHAVIOR
AND THE THERAPEUTIC RELATIONSHIP

Given the apparent significance of interpersonal communication to psychotherapeutic theory, how then might nonverbal behavior relate to these two areas of human inquiry? As Ekman and Friesen (1968) explain, "Nonverbal behavior can be considered a relationship language, sensitive to, and the primary means of, signaling changes in the quality of an ongoing interpersonal relationship." While the verbal discourse may conceivably duplicate this information, they say, "usually such matters are too direct or too embarrassing to be easily stated" (p. 180). The relevance of nonverbal communication to psychotherapy, Brooks and Emmert (1976) further maintain, is particularly evident in the work of Albert Mehrabian (Mehrabian and Ferris, 1967) which found, for example, that the amount of liking we have for another person is primarily communicated through nonverbal channels. Brooks and Emmert elaborate:

Mehrabian's formula indicates that of the total affection or liking which we communicate to another person, only seven percent is communicated by words. Thirty-eight percent is communicated by how we use our voice (rate, pitch, and volume of speech). Fifty-five percent is the result of facial expressions (smiles, eye contact, and frowns). Thus, nonverbal communication is very important. (p. 118)

Considering this, what would appear to be fundamental knowledge relevant to psychotherapy in its search for greater paradigmatic direction, this book therefore draws upon and integrates research, not only from the attitudinal sphere, but also from the nonverbal behavior, interpersonal communication, information processing, linguistic, and physiological areas of human functioning. The need for a better integrated scientific grounding of psychotherapeutic processes is expressed by Rossi (1990):

> Most forms of psychotherapy today . . . are still locked in the phenomenological realm, just as were the founders of depth psychotherapy such as Janet, Freud, and Jung. The founders all recognized that psychological processes could not be divorced from the physiology of the body but acknowledged that the physiology of their day was not yet advanced enough to be related to the psychological. This is no longer the case. In fact, I would say that today the true innovators in psychology are coming from the ranks of molecular biologists, who are discovering profound relationships between mind and molecule. (pp. 359-360)

In this regard, Rossi (1993) later asserts that the basic idea behind what he terms "the psychobiology of mind-body healing" is that information (or knowledge) is the "central concept and connecting link between all sciences, humanities, and clinical arts." Psychology, biology, and physics, he states, "now have information as their new common denominator" (p. 23) (an integrative and eclectic thrust upon which this book capitalizes in its exploration of psychotherapeutic change processes).

LIMITATIONS OF THE INTRAPSYCHIC APPROACH TO PSYCHOTHERAPY RESEARCH

The apparent stasis of the more orthodox humanistic researchers who tend to remain "locked in the phenomenological realm," disregard therapist behavior, and primarily attempt to measure therapeutic attitudes through self-report measures and analyses of verbal discourse, may, in the process, sacrifice integrative knowledge. As Messer (1992) observes:

> It is probably true to say that humanistic therapy has had more impact on behavior therapy (e.g., Curtis, 1976), on cognitive therapy (e.g., Safran and Segal, 1990), and on psychoanalytic therapy (e.g., Appelbaum, 1979; Kahn, 1985; and Stolorow, 1976) than it has been influenced in any fundamental way by them. It appears that humanistic therapists have been willing to forego the potential advantages of an integrative vision. (p. 147)

Various explanations have been offered for this seemingly insular tendency. Garfield (1992) observes that it is understandable that therapists who have been trained in a given form of therapy, and have been identified with it, are "reluctant to acknowledge the importance of common factors—factors they essentially share with other forms of psychotherapy" (p. 173). Norcross and Goldfried (1992) similarly suggest that since the prestige and financial security of psychotherapists hinge on their ability to present their particular approach as more successful than that of their rivals, "little glory has been traditionally accorded the identification of shared or common components" (p. 10). And Prochaska (1979) suggests that perhaps some therapies hold on to their general theoretical concepts in order to place responsibility for change on the client, possibly because, he asserts, the field "has been unable to generate techniques powerful enough to produce adequate change in the behaviors of clients" (p. 195).

These possible motives notwithstanding, the neglect of behavior by the humanistic school may also have been influenced by the view, as expressed by Combs, Richards, and Richards (1976), that behavior "is only a symptom." To try to understand people exclusively in behavioral terms, they say, can provide only "partial answers to questions about what people are like and why they behave as they do" (p. x). While this statement may generally apply to therapists attempting to understand *clients* solely from their behaviors, it has little relevance with respect to discerning the possible effects that *therapist* behavior may have upon the client or upon processes of therapeutic change. On the contrary, as the thesis of this book suggests, exploration of therapist behavior would appear to be the next logical step in the evolution of humanistic *and* psychotherapeutic theory.

Orlinsky and Russell (1994) provide further rationale for the integration of behavior with client-centered theory in their following critique of the Rogerian model:

> . . . It is probably fair to say that process research during the 1960s was largely dominated by the intensive efforts of client-centered researchers to provide objective evidence of the validity of Rogers' (1957) elegant theoretical formulation concerning the necessary and sufficient conditions of therapeutic personality change. Paradoxically, although Rogers' theory emphasized the client's experience of the "facilitative conditions" (therapist empathy, warmth, and self-congruence), positivist methodological biases led most researchers to use objectified, nonparticipant-observational measures of therapist behavior (Truax and Mitchell, 1971; but see also Mitchell, Bozarth, and Krauft, 1977). Nevertheless, the net result of this peculiarly flawed research was to document the singular importance of relationship factors, especially in client-centered therapy, although this line of work on the Rogerian conditions virtually ceased in the mid-1970s. (p. 194)

In addition to avoiding this apparent self-serving kind of within-therapeutic-school research, the particular merit or rationale of approaching psychotherapy research from the perspective of therapist nonverbal behavior and client self-disclosure, as opposed to therapist intrapsychic states, was noted decades ago by Jay Haley (1963). As he points out, "interior processes must be inferred" (p. 4) and are therefore difficult to test empirically. Furthermore, as Derlega et al. (1991) explain, while empathy, for example, involves the ability to feel with others and to take their perspective, indicating that one is doing this, they maintain, will, by definition, involve "responsive action." In their opinion, therefore, future studies need to describe the "verbal and nonverbal behaviors of more empathic therapists in greater detail, rather than merely relating therapist empathy scores to client disclosure or therapeutic outcome." When such future research is undertaken, Derlega et al. further predict that therapists higher in empathy "will maintain more eye contact and display by their nonverbal behavior more interest in and attention to their clients" (pp.139-140).

Contrary to the traditional humanistic stance, therefore, this book does not approach the exploration of therapist interventions solely from the narrow intrapsychic perspective but recognizes the reality of the simultaneous and synergistic existence of both internal and external frames of reference or spheres of therapist and client functioning. Furthermore, these spheres may not be as diametrically opposed as might initially appear. As Rachlin (1994) explains:

> Behavioral analysis and the study of mental life seem like contrary if not contradictory activities not only in popular understanding but also in contemporary psychology and philosophy. This attitude, though understandable, is wrong. Not only is behavioral analysis not really contrary to the study of mind, behavioral analysis is potentially the best way to study mental *life* (as opposed to mental *mechanisms*) both of humans and other animals. (p. v)

Nor is there reason to believe that even the most orthodox behaviorists deny the existence of mental processes. In this respect—possibly partially influenced by the previously mentioned selective attention phenomenon—mental states may just not happen to be within their particular realm of study or academic interest. As Skinner (1953) states, for example, "The objection to inner states is not that they do not exist, but that they are not relevant in a functional analysis." We cannot account for the behavior of any system, he says, "while staying wholly inside it; eventually, we must turn to forces operating upon the organism from without" (p. 35). Nevertheless, disregarding intrapsychic human states, no matter how behavioristically self-serving, does not help resolve the human dilemma, and reality, of behavior being a product of a psychological mind existing within a biological brain.

On the other hand, the apparent antibehavioral stance of the humanists appears equally untenable since, as Selltiz, Wrightsman, and Cook (1976) point out, although humanistic investigators usually report their research findings in terms of abstract concepts (attitudes); they and other readers must keep in mind that what they have actually found is "a relationship between two sets of data or of operations that are intended to *represent* their concepts" (p. 73). Or as Hill (1994) observes in her critique of the review of literature on the therapeutic relationship by Sexton and Whiston (1994), for example: "One could question whether working alliance measures actually assess the unique construct of working alliance or whether they measure a more global 'good guy' factor such as has been found for empathy measures" (p. 94).

This indefinite situation may further prevail because, as Rennie and Toukmanian (1992) note, despite the existence of only one *scientific method*, the study of "personhood" (or human behavior and intentionality) has, in the past, required two approaches to psychotherapy process research: The first being the paradigmatic, deductive, or "demonstrative and quantitative approach," and the second, the narrative/phenomenological, or "inductive, hermeneutical and qualitative" (p. 235) approach. Since the former studies the "process" of therapeutic change and the latter deals with the participants' "experience of therapy" (p. 236), in order to obtain a more complete picture of the therapeutic process, Rennie and Toukmanian (1992) therefore advocate integration in this sphere of psychotherapy as well. In their words:

> There appears to be a need for methodological pluralism and/or epistemological synthesis. By methodological pluralism, we mean the combination, in the same study, of procedures expressive of both the narrative and the paradigmatic approaches to explanation. Epistemological synthesis refers to the incorporation, into theorizing done within the one approach to explanation, of information derived from the alternative approach to explanation. (p. 246)

Again, another seemingly complicated and subjective research proposal, the prospect of integrating the narrative/phenomenological research approach with objective scientific methodology may be being advocated as a result of the lack of paradigmatic direction in psychotherapy rather than as a viable means of achieving it. This integrative proposal may also have been advocated because while the intrapsychic approach to psychotherapy research may have contributed toward generating correlational knowledge and formulating global hypotheses, it has nevertheless lacked in ability to establish specific probable cause. This may further have influenced Skinner's (1979) remark that there must be some reason why psychology has "failed to make the same kinds of technological advances in the management of human behavior that are so obvious in other fields." The reason, he says, may involve "our lingering commitment to the individual as initiating agent" (p. 15). (Implied in Skinner's statement may also be a criticism of the phenomenological model and its inherent subjectivity—thus the call by Rennie and Toukmanian [1992] for an integrated research model which better reflects the totality and reality of human experience.)

Similarly, Beutler, and Sandowicz (1994) offer additional criticism of the intrapsychic model, the literature on which, as previously noted, was reviewed by Gelso and Carter (1985) and Sexton and Whiston (1994). As Beutler and Sandowicz (1994) explain:

> The most obvious example of limitations in the original model was revealed as the authors attempted to operationalize the distinctions made by Gelso and Carter among "real," "unreal," and "working alliance" components of the relationship. This distinction is difficult to maintain from either an empirical or a rational stance, a point that is only partially acknowledged when Sexton and Whiston pointed out the limitations of this model—specifically, its failure to indicate either how these three relationship components interact or the means by which they account for client change. (p. 98)

Possibly contributing to this failure in establishing probable cause, Fisher (1978) notes inherent difficulties and limitations in the use of the specific instruments or inventories, themselves, for measuring intrapsychic states. In his words:

> Validation of such inferential measures is probably inevitably inconclusive. . . . The problem is an age-old philosophical one of providing correspondence rules for theoretical terms: that is, the problem is one of operationalizing (making observable) theoretical concepts so that differing operations are equivalent. Do Likert scales, Guttman scales, or Thurston scales, for example, measure the same thing, which we have called an "attitude"? We assume that each of these techniques measures "attitude" even though operational definitions in any two studies may be quite different. (p. 155)

Fisher (1978) further explains that when observation of any phenomenon is indirect or inferred (such as an intrapsychic state), proving the superior validity of any measuring instrument is "highly problematic" (p. 155). In other words, he observes, if you do not know what an attitude "looks like," how do you know when you are measuring one? Add to this difficulty the "conceptual multidimensionality" and complexity of cognitive, affective, and behavioral components, he says, and the difficulties in the measurement of attitude "increase dramatically." In his estimation, therefore, the problem of assuring the validity (i.e., whether the instrument actually measures what it purports to be measuring) of any technique for measuring a covert concept, is "virtually insurmountable." According to Fisher, the real question therefore becomes what "degree of invalidity you are willing to tolerate" (p. 155).

SUMMARY AND CONCLUSION

In summary, while scientific consensus appears to have coalesced behind the therapeutic relationship as central to psychotherapeutic progress, the behavioral, biological, and cognitive processes underlying such change nevertheless still remain unspecified. Lacking scientific grounding and theoretical integration, not only from within the psychotherapeutic field but also in relation to the major *allied* areas of human inquiry (from which psychotherapeutic theory itself should have evolved), the various psychotherapeutic schools have therefore seemingly operated within theoretical "vacuums," or in *theoretical isolation*, thus influencing the burgeoning growth of therapies and contributing to the current lack of treatment efficacy and quality control. The intrapsychic or characterological preoccupation (i.e., the apparent humanistic reluctance to recognize the synergistic existence of both phenomenological *and* behavioral realities), together with what may have been a "premature" shift to family and group emphases in the field, may further have diverted attention away from observables within the foundational therapeutic dyad (thus thwarting research efforts and maintaining psychotherapy's artistic state).

While research technology and knowledge of human physiology may have been limited in Freud's day, this is no longer the case.

Relevant psychobiological knowledge exists but has not been integrated with psychotherapeutic theory. Thus, while Freud may have given birth to the field, and pointed the way to explicating its change processes by labelling psychotherapy "the talking cure," little progress has seemingly been achieved in determining *how* talking "cures" or what behavioral, biological, and cognitive change processes may be involved in this "cure."

Other forefathers, Harry Stack Sullivan and Frederick Skinner, for example, contributed additional pieces to the therapeutic puzzle by highlighting interpersonal factors and behavioral and environmental contingencies. Carl Rogers then appeared to provide the most recent heuristic advance by marshalling consensus around the therapeutic relationship as the *designated area* in which to search for therapeutic change processes. Finally, Arnold Lazarus, as the father of eclecticism and integration, broadened the perspective of the field by proposing the integration of knowledge, not only from within psychotherapy, but from disparate allied areas of human inquiry such as nonverbal behavior, interpersonal communication, information processing, and the biological sciences.

In conclusion, given the apparent scientific limitations to the study of internal states, a redirection of the intrapsychic focus of the field— toward the behavioral, biological, and cognitive *expressions* of these facilitative attitudes—may be necessary. Toward this end, the next chapter addresses the need for what has been termed, a higher-order theory, begging the following question posed by Lazarus (1992): "What concepts and observations (not theories) [hypothetical constructs] from any source are necessary to provide a basis for understanding human psychology and creating a comprehensive and scientific approach to psychotherapy?" (p. 235).

Chapter 2

Universal Variables:
Toward a Higher-Order Theory

Psychotherapy for the experienced practitioner, as for the beginner, continues to have its uncertainties and failures. Psychotherapy is not a science that can be decisively mastered. It continues to be difficult because there is never a final perfect therapy form that can be endlessly manufactured for all diverse clinical situations and individuals.

—Carl Goldberg, 1992

. . . There has grown up, over time, a gradual decoupling of theory from data. Deprived of a common set of facts that might represent the gist of our collective wisdom, theory is free to tell whatever story it chooses.

—Donald Spence, 1994

The enemy is ideological fanaticism, whether it comes in the form of an antiempirical attitude that fails to recognize the potential contributions of empirical research of any kind or a scientific approach that involves a rigid and superficial understanding of the way in which science really operates. . . . When we are required to articulate in operational terms the clues on which our intuitions are based, we are compelled to observe the relevant clinical phenomena in a more rigorous fashion *and* to examine our own implicit theories more carefully. Operationalizing terms thus reduces the gap between theory and phenomenon.

—Jeremy Safran and Christopher Muran, 1994

57

> The problem that confronts us is the need to construct a meta-perspective of personality and intervention that encompasses all that we have learned thus far and that fosters growth and development in the field without uncritically approving any method simply because it is new and holds promise.
>
> —*Jeffery Zeig and Michael Munion, 1990*

The quest for paradigmatic direction in the form of a higher-order theory has been one of the main objectives of the eclectic and integration movement since its inception. The need for such a guiding theory is contained in Leslie Greenberg's advice to the field, "Discover the important phenomena before proceeding to tests of causal relationships" (Orlinsky and Russell, 1994, p. 204). In this regard, advocates for the integration of theories of psychotherapy, Goldfried and Newman (1992), note that others, not primarily identified with the integration movement, also believe the time is right to aim at developing greater paradigmatic direction. In their words:

> A number of authors began to suggest that the field of psychotherapy needed to develop a new, higher-order theory that would help us to better understand the connections between cognitive, affective, and behavioral systems (Beck 1984; Greenberg and Safron, 1984; Mahoney 1984b; Ryle, 1984; Safron, 1984). These writers maintained that attempts to answer the question of how affective, behavioral, and cognitive systems interact would move the field toward the development of a more adequate, unified paradigm. (p. 64)

Similarly, achieving such paradigmatic direction would also presumably explicate the nature of higher-order consciousness as well, which, according to Sacks (1995), would involve "the explicit concept of self, or so-called theory of mind, and of history" (p. 33).

While some theorists believe such an integrated higher-order theory awaits greater maturity of the field, others such as Garfield (1992) appear confident that it will be formulated and will include "a proper emphasis on common factors" (p. 197). Toward this end, Norcross and Goldfried (1992) note that as a result of progress thus far, integration has already emerged as the orientation preferred by therapists. They further observe that the last fifteen years have witnessed a general decline in ideological struggle, as well as the stirrings of "rapprochement." The debates across theoretical systems, they say, appear to be less polemical and more issue-specific. Consequently, the theoretical substrate of each system is undergoing intensive reappraisal, they state, as psychotherapists "acknowledge the inadequacies of any one system and the potential value of others" (p. 3).

To support their claims, Norcross and Goldfried (1992) cite the conclusions of a recent National Institute of Mental Health conference on research in psychotherapy integration which maintains that treatments of greater "efficacy, efficiency, and safety" could result from integrating the best elements from different schools of psychotherapy. Additionally, Norcross and Goldfried note that the general consensus from that conference was that research on integrated treatment models could lead to the development of a "comprehensive model of psychotherapy process that will have solid empirical backing" (p. 4). Consistent, as well, with this aim of promoting the scientific development of psychotherapy, the three "Evolution of Psychotherapy" conferences, organized by the Milton H. Erickson Foundation, brought together representatives from the major schools of psychotherapy in an attempt to foster greater understanding across theoretical lines.

While Lazarus (1992) agrees that psychotherapists need to "broaden" their "theoretical bases," he nevertheless questions how the "worthy ends" of psychotherapy integration will be achieved, particularly at the hypothetical construct level. Herein lies the problem, he says, "people cannot agree on an acceptable *modus operandi*" (p. 259). Garfield (1992) adds that it is difficult to provide systematic research data on an integrative eclectic approach since there is considerable uniqueness and variation among eclectic practitioners. Perhaps even more than is true of other approaches such as psychoanalysis, behavior therapy, or person-centered therapy, Garfield observes, "there is more individuality among eclectic practitioners in how they conduct their psychotherapy" (p. 195). This apparent problem notwithstanding, however, Garfield (1992) nevertheless notes that eclecticism currently remains "the most popular approach to psychotherapy" (p. 194).

Offering a possible explanation for this popularity, Goldfried and Newman (1992) cite Beck (1984) who maintains that the various theoretical perspectives have "varying degrees of explanatory power." By relating them to each other, Beck maintains, we may be able to construct "an integrated model that will have greater explanatory power than the individual perspectives" (p. 72). Goldfried and Newman (1992) agree and add that even though the myriad theoretical orientations may focus on different aspects of human functioning, they can all be effective because of the "synergistic effects that one area of functioning may have on another" (p. 48). In this regard, they refer to Marmor (1971) who maintains that the psychodynamic therapies and behavior therapies "simply represent different teaching techniques"—their differences based partly on "differences in their goals" and partly on "the assumptions of the nature of psychopathology" (Goldfried and Newman, 1992, p. 54).

Similar support for this view comes from Norcross and Newman (1992) who, citing the work of W.M. Pinsof, suggest that theoretical schools may not be contradictory, but "complementary"—each modality and orientation having "its particular 'domain of expertise,'" domains which they believe can be "interrelated to minimize their deficits" (p. 26). This complementary relationship of the behavioral and psychodynamic schools, and their different emphases, is more clearly enunciated by Goldfried and Newman (1992):

> Whereas behavior therapy may be characterized as emphasizing *realism* (the world existing independently of its observers), *objectivity* (the existence of a common frame of reference for all), and *extraspection* (seeking the external motivators of behavior), psychoanalytic (or psychodynamic) therapy reflects *idealism* (the world is of one's own making), *subjectivity* (each person's frame of reference is unique), and *introspection* (searching for the internal motivators of behavior). (p. 71)

The reality recognized by this book, however, is that both perspectives are legitimate and, in a manner similar to the "figure-ground" phenomenon previously described, can be shown to exist simultaneously and synergistically depending upon the therapist's working focus. In other words, there is a behavioral reality (environmental contingencies) for both therapists and clients, as well as an intrapsychic one, whose forefront materialization depends upon which perspective therapists attend to or direct their therapeutic attention. Developing greater paradigmatic direction in the field will therefore require a working theory which incorporates both perspectives, in addition to having sufficient explanatory power to account for and clarify the basic emphases or "observations" (Davison and Lazarus, 1995, p. 108) of the major therapeutic schools.

While at first glance, this might not seem an easy task, Norcross and Newman (1992) and L.S. Greenberg (1994) nevertheless offer encouragement. For example, Norcross and Newman observe that the so-called pure form psychotherapies are themselves "second generation integrations." They further contend that in factor analytic terms, nearly all neo-Freudian approaches would be labeled "second order" constructs—"a superordinate result of analyzing and combining the original components (therapies)" (p. 22). As they explain, "Just as Freud necessarily incorporated methods and concepts of his time into psychoanalysis (Francis, 1988), so, too, do newer therapies." All psychotherapies, they state, may therefore be viewed as "products of an inevitable historical integration—an oscillating process of assimilation and accommodation" (Sollod, 1988, p. 22) (i.e., Knowledge grows from that which precedes it).

A DISCOVERY INVESTIGATION—UNRAVELING "WHAT HAS ALREADY OCCURRED"

L. S. Greenberg (1994), as well, voices optimism for research in a field which he believes to be "ripe for a discovery-oriented investigation" (an ex post facto approach which this book emulates). Greenberg describes this form of basic or theoretical research as follows:

A critical feature of psychotherapy research is that it involves the investigation of a domain in which a vast amount of practice already occurs, guided by theoretical [hypothetical constructs] knowledge and beliefs but not by scientifically based understanding. The researcher's task is both complicated and enhanced by this state of affairs. There is no need to start from scratch and begin to build a knowledge domain based on research or controlled experiments alone: a rich and complex domain of practice already exists, and the researcher's task is to make sense of it. This aspect of psychotherapy research is more like the task of the detective attempting to unravel what has already occurred, rather than that of an experimenter setting up a controlled experiment to study the effect of specific variables. A discovery orientation thus has special relevance to the study of psychotherapy. (p. 114)

This view appears to complement that Davison and Lazarus (1995) and Kiesler (1994) in their description of the symbiotic relationship existing between psychotherapeutic practice and research. In Kiesler's words:

Psychotherapeutic practice always will take the lead, with theory and research following. The hallmark of research is *not* to innovate, *not* to discover exciting new techniques or interventions, *not* to dramatize new learnings via enthralling clinical anecdotes. The researcher systematizes, standardizes, and operationalizes available techniques; validates promising interventions that have emerged from clinical theory and practice; and attempts to isolate and validate the essential ingredients of the change process. Seldom, if ever, can studies offer new clinical discoveries or settle theoretical controversies. In short, psychotherapy research always "plays catch-up" to psychotherapy practice. (p. 143)

As for the existing research attempts at "unraveling what has already occurred," or isolating and validating "the essential ingredients of the change process," Beitman (1992) contends that, unfortunately, many approaches to psychotherapy integration thus far bear strong resemblance to those created by "rigid psychoanalysts, rigid behavior therapists, and manual-driven psychotherapists" (p. 202). He therefore advocates an alternative approach to psychotherapy integration, creating a model with sufficient flexibility to: assimilate new ideas generated from other psychotherapies and research; to accommodate the "psychotherapy schemas" of each individual therapist; and to be adaptable "to the schemas of each patient." In other words, rather than being a solid form, he says, the elements of this approach would be "like the molecules of a liquid in that they would fit the cognitive containers of their users" (p. 202).

Messer (1992) similarly observes that this approach to integrating the differentiated parts of psychotherapy, at a higher level, would be consistent with the philosophical concept, "organicism." According to Messer, the organicist believes that there exist, in any individual's world, "fragments of experience" (such as the observations of a particular school of therapy). Although these may appear connected, the narrower model, Messer contends, inevitably encounters contradictions, gaps, or opposition from other fragments of experience (such as observations or therapeutic variables espoused by other schools of therapy). Within an organicistic model, Messer says, the various fragments tend to be resolved by incorporation into an "organic whole" which was implicit in the fragments, all the while, and which transcends the previous contradictions by means of a "coherent totality" or "an integrative eclecticism" (pp. 133-134). Messer elaborates:

> By organizing the data at a higher level, the appearance of conflict is dissolved into the reality of the organic whole. Progress is achieved by including more and more of the fragments into a better integrated whole.
>
> In terms of integrating parts of one therapy with parts of another, the integrative eclectic, like the organicist, would argue that the apparent contradictions were never really contradictions at all because they vanish when the integrated system is constructed (see Beitman; Garfield; Prochaska and Diclemente; Wachtel and McKinney; all 1992). Nothing is lost in such a system because it takes in the pieces of one therapy and joins them to another. Individual pieces get aggregated into wholes that are greater than the sum of their parts. . . . In joining parts of different theories or therapies, we are contributing to that unity which is, in fact, the natural order of the psychological (and physical) universe. (p. 134)

This "natural order of the universe" may further eventually materialize through what Rossi (1993) terms, "a more comprehensive future philosophy of information and communication," comprised of "all the arts and sciences," which he believes may some day illuminate "the essence of everything of comprehension and special interest to the human mind" (pp. 146-147). It is in this respect, therefore, that the problem of grasping the essence of human nature may be less an issue of scientific methodology which, according to Friedman (1992, p. 10), the more orthodox humanists have criticized as being too narrow or reductionistic. Rather, it may more specifically involve one of integrating, or organizing into a coherent whole, the existing knowledge already accumulated with the help of this very scientific method. In other words, why shoot the "messenger" if the problem is one of integrating the various "messages" already received?—a responsibility seemingly residing more with the recipient of the message than with the medium itself. As Edelman (1992) explains:

> We are now in a position to use what we know about biology, psychology, and philosophy to postulate a theory of consciousness that will be an essential part of a theory of how the brain works.
>
> Most scientists consider such efforts premature, if not downright crazy. But the history of science suggests that we progress not by simply collecting facts but by synthesizing ideas and then testing them. It also teaches us that nothing is so effective in promoting new thoughts and experiments as a theory that one can amend or even knock down.
>
> The theory must be a scientific one: Its parts must be testable, and it must help to organize most, if not all, of the known facts about brains and minds. (p. 71)

In other words, formulating such a higher-order theory would involve maintaining the scientific character of psychotherapeutic theory or scientific objectivity. Furthermore, Elliott and Anderson (1994) point out that the important intricacies of therapy process and outcome can be addressed "without giving up the search for general heuristic principles." This is necessary, they say, to "allow psychotherapy research to join the other 'emerging sciences of complexity' at the boundary between 'order and chaos'" (p. 105). That boundary is further maintained by what Stanley Strong terms, "the notion of intersubjective agreement" (Strong, Yoder, and Corcoran, 1995), as central in scientific work. As Strong explains: "The job of the scientist is to array evidence that will enable others to grasp and observe what the scientist declares to be so." This, in itself, does not set science off from other social enterprises, he says, for "the entire social world is fundamentally negotiated social agreements." What differentiates scientific work, Strong adds, "is the scientist's insistence that empirical evidence is the essential backing for assertions" (p. 382)

While this scientific precept may not always have been adhered to in psychotherapy (thus contributing to the current indefinite state of the field), the scientific objective of psychological field, in general, nonetheless appears to have been advanced by the "cognitive revolution" of the last two decades as well as the "second" cognitive revolution which Harre and Gillett (1994) suggest is imminent. This second cognitive revolution, which they term "discursive psychology" and which is discussed in greater detail in Chapter 6, may further help resolve one of humanistic psychology's main dilemmas and criticisms, i.e., that natural science currently studies the client (as well as the therapist) without reference to his or her "meaning system" or "intentional relations to the world" (Friedman, 1992, p. 10). In this respect, however, as this book attempts to show, the problem of illuminating the human essence may be more one of perspective, and of "putting the human being back together," than of abandoning a necessary scientific tool for establishing cause and effect. Or, stated in metaphorical terms by Rossi (1993), this task may be more one of rising "above the timberline to gain the perspective we need to see the entire forest" (p. 298).

In addition to (or possibly as a result of) this lack of *holistic* perspective in psychotherapy, Russell (1994) maintains that few researchers have formulated links between the meaning of the "categories in their systems" and the "larger theories" of, for example, language and discourse from which, he states, they should have been "explicitly derived and critically articulated" (p. 174). In this regard, for example, such help may eventually arrive from the allied field of linguistics—some of their leading proponents currently maintaining that understanding language "offers the prospect of integrating biological and humanistic views of 'the way we are'" (Jackendoff, 1994, p. 4). For without such an integrative holistic grounding of how the myriad psychodynamic therapies fit into the larger human behavioral and biological picture, research efforts could prove meaningless—lacking appropriate empirical grounding—thus further delaying paradigmatic realization. When assessing research on therapeutic discourse, therefore, Russell (1994) maintains that we should be asking broader theoretical questions such as: "What (larger) theories help us to understand the meaning of the therapist's or patient's linguistic 'objects?' Or, better still, what theories need we refer to in order to comprehend the meaning of a given class label, such as 'interpretations' or 'disclosures?'" Currently, he says, "we seem to have pitifully few" (p. 174).

NARROWING THE RESEARCH FOCUS

While Freud may have attempted to achieve a holistic perspective or integration with psychoanalysis, Gardner (1993) points out that compared to the achievements of Einstein, for example, Freud's creations were relatively loosely formulated and presented. This occurred, Gardner believes, not only because psychology was a young science at that time, but also because Freud "dealt with a whole ensemble of issues, rather than with a focused problem or set of problems" (p. 75). In addition, further complicating and possibly limiting Freud's efforts was the fact that his work was mainly supported by case studies and observation (Gardner, 1993, p. 133) rather than the wealth of rigorous scientific research employing the sophisticated statistical and computerized technology of today.

To narrow the focus to a workable degree, therefore, this book does not directly address the concept of disorder. As Prochaska and Diclemente (1992) explain, while disorder is important for taxonomy and classification purposes which aids in understanding a problem, in their view, knowledge of a disorder by itself has "limited value" (p. 314) in prescribing *psychodynamic* therapy interventions. Because, as Goldfried, Castonguay, and Safran (1992) observe, psychotherapy and psychopathology are two distinct areas of inquiry. Advancement in psychotherapy process research, they say, can shed light on *how* change occurs, while knowledge of psychopathology can address "*what* needs to be changed" (p. 606). Furthermore, they assert, "although therapists have not struggled with all the particular problems faced by different clients, all therapists have had some experience with the processes of change" (pp. 314-315). This view (and that of this book) therefore appears consistent with that of Reamy-Stephenson (1990), who maintains that "Psychotherapy focuses on accessing personal resources, not defining pathology" (p. 288).

Excluding the concept of disorder also facilitates generalization. As Kolden, Howard, and Maling (1994) explain, there is indirect empirical support for generalizing across clients at the process level. In their words:

> Thus there is some faith that generalization is possible—that clients have enough in common to permit generalization from one to the other. So we search for general principles and causal structures that could provide a basis for such generalization. It is in this context that the phenomenology of the participants becomes salient. Because our goal is to facilitate changes in the client, the client's perspective on the process of therapy tends to be the most causally relevant. In fact, the positive relationship between the client's perception of the therapeutic relationship and outcome is perhaps the most consistent finding in the entire empirical literature on effective psychotherapeutic processes (Orlinsky and Howard, 1986). (p. 85)

Thus, consistent with the systematic eclectic psychotherapy of Beutler and Consoli (1992), the approach described herein, while excluding the concept of disorder, focuses instead upon the "nature of the interpersonal forces and mechanisms that instigate or inhibit change" (p. 267). That is, it explores the *interactional* dynamics between client and therapist which may activate processes or *resources within the client*—in turn possibly serving to ameliorate the presenting symptom(s) or concern(s). The objective of such an undertaking therefore appears consistent with the view of de Shazer (1990) when he states: "The goal of therapy is to meet the client's goal; that is, if the client says he wants to stop being depressed, then the success of therapy can only be measured by the client no longer saying to the therapist that he is depressed." For this change to be possible, he says, "one does not even need to know what the problem is; perhaps it cannot be known, and therefore client and therapist together need only to begin a solution" (p. 278).

The search for "solutions," processes of change, or active ingredients in psychotherapy has also prompted an approach to psychotherapy research which Stiles, Shapiro, and Harper (1994) term, "the drug metaphor." Due to its parallels with pharmacology research and its respect for scientific objectivity, this model precludes the intrapsychic or intentional participation of the client, however, of which, as mentioned earlier, humanists have been critical. Stiles, Shapiro, and Harper (1994) outline other limitations of this research model as well:

> Increasingly, authors have been re-examining the philosophical basis of the drug metaphor and the underlying medical model of psychological disorders and treatment. For example, Butler and Strupp (1986) have argued that, unlike drugs, psychotherapeutic interventions concern meaning; hence they depend upon the active, conscious participation of both patient and therapist, with their idiosyncratic meaning [self] systems. From another angle, Russell (1986) has argued that positivistic attempts to define psychotherapeutic techniques independently of specific theoretical contexts are ultimately empty. Any adequate description of an intervention must be given in terms compatible with the theory from which it derives. Such theories are not universally accepted, but are the objects of dispute and incomprehension by adherents of other systems. (p. 38)

In other words, any proposed higher-order theory would presumably have to close this so-called "gap" in psychotherapeutic theory by including not only behavior, but the client's "meaning" or "self-system," as well (discussed in greater detail in Chapters 5 and 6).

Further narrowing the research focus, this book does not directly address the phenomenon of transference/countertransference. As Derlega et al. (1991) note, "For humanistic therapists, it is the real relationship that counts; relatively little attention is given to either the working alliance or transference/countertransference" (p. 12). This delimitation can further be made, as Sexton and Whiston (1994) explain, because transference and countertransference are not "direct aspects of the interaction between client and counselor" (p. 29)—a factor which R.D. Laing (1990) appears to recognize when he states metaphorically: "It seems to me that the mutative zone in the relationship, the domain whence positive change occurs, is in that territory not heavily mined by transference or countertransference; or, to change the metaphors around, where both the client and I can sense the sun through our rain and clouds . . ." (p. 207).

Further extending this line of reasoning, Sexton and Whiston (1994) note in their commentary on Gelso and Carter's (1985) work that transference/countertransference is a "perceptual mistake, a distortion, misperception, or misinterpretation of events in the counseling relationship by either the client or counselor" (p. 29). Consequently, Kolden, Howard, and Maling (1994) explain:

> Transference, countertransference, and relationship patterns are not part of the therapeutic process; they are personal behavioral characteristics that patients and therapists bring to therapy. They become important when they emerge as obstacles to change and become targets for therapeutic interventions (e.g., transference interpretations). Moreover, increased understanding of transference, countertransference, and relationship patterns can facilitate therapeutic progress; however, in and of themselves, they are not therapeutic. (p. 83)

DEVELOPING A COMMON FRAMEWORK

Beyond narrowing the working focus, the next question relevant to higher-order theory building is posed by Messer (1992): "If a truly integrative therapy is to be proposed and developed, how are the different languages to be joined? . . . How are we to understand ourselves and develop a common framework?" (p. 137). Norcross and Newman (1992) agree that "each psychotherapeutic tradition has its own jargon, a clinical shorthand among its adherents, which widens the precipice across differing orientations" (p. 25). They further maintain that this "seemingly intractable obstacle" to the establishment of a clinically sophisticated and "consensually validated integrative psychotherapy" will have to be overcome. As they explain:

> Isolated language systems encourage clinicians to wrap themselves in semantic cocoons from which they cannot escape and which others cannot penetrate. . . . The purpose of a common language is to facilitate communication, comprehension, and research. It is not intended to establish consensus. Before an agreement or a disagreement can be reached on a given matter, it is necessary to ensure that the same phenomenon is in fact being discussed. (p. 25)

Consequently, the main interactional therapeutic terms used in this book refer to behavioral and biological phenomena which can be observed, and therefore standardized, as a precondition to achieving scientific agreement. This is necessary, Dennett (1991) maintains, because we must have a neutral way of describing the data—a way that does not prejudge this issue—before we can "see what the theory actually says" (p. 71).

Once the focus has been narrowed and the terminology standardized, the resulting psychotherapeutic approach outlined in subsequent chapters of this book should correspond to an *integrative eclecticism* which Messer (1992) defines as proposing a "single, comprehensive, and unified therapy for all clients," as opposed to selective eclecticism, which entails the "use of different approaches with different clients" (p. 132). According to Messer (1992), underlying eclecticism itself is the belief that we can share a "common neutral language in psychology, replacing the diversity of theoretical and ideological terms we currently employ" (p. 132). And this can be done, as Garfield (1992) observes, because the various forms of psychotherapy may "appear more different" than is actually "the case" (p. 173). Consequently, he contends, some common variables or processes may be viewed as different even when they are "essentially similar" (or serve a similar function). Even potentially more significant, he says, is the fact that some "basic and important processes" are ignored because "they are not stressed in the formal descriptions of the individual forms of therapy" (p. 173).

Therefore, Garfield (1992) points out, investigators tend to investigate the processes and procedures "hypothesized to be of significance in their particular theories or orientations." Meanwhile, he says, "others tend to be disregarded, or are considered to be 'nonspecific' and of lesser importance" (p. 173). The consequence of this insular tendency (or selective attention), as Lambert (1992) explains, has been *molarity* of definition. That is, from existing research explicating the state of psychotherapy thus far, he says, only general conclusions can be formulated such as: "Psychotherapy, in general, has been shown to be effective. Positive outcomes have been reported for a wide variety of theoretical positions and technical interventions" (p. 99) (which does not say much for the degree of consensus achieved in explicating change processes during the past hundred years).

Given the apparent paucity of knowledge concerning change processes, and consistent with the basic principles of psychological change, Mahoney (1991) believes the most important task now facing the field is to devise a "conceptual base camp" from which to operate while exploring future scientific development. As he explains, such a base camp must be "pliable, portable, and itself capable of development, so that one's deep-felt commitments can be anchored in its abstractions while, simultaneously, one's unfinished lessons can be pursued within its moving expanse" (p. 266). This "base camp" or higher-order theory is necessary, says Mahoney, because knowing that change is possible is not the same as knowing how to facilitate it. As he states, "We yearn to learn technique because we desire the power of enacted knowledge" which he calls, the heart of *praxis*, or doing,—the "existential basis of being" (pp. 286-287).

Goldfried and Newman (1992) echo a similar view, but add that in the final analysis, any attempt at psychotherapy integration must be based "on what clinicians do, rather than what they say they do" (p. 61). In this respect, what clinicians do, at a higher level, is relatively clear. As outlined in the previous chapter with respect to Freud's "talking cure," the therapist establishes a face-to-face relationship with a client wherein the client engages in self-disclosure about a particular concern or concerns. During the course of their encounter, the therapist's physical presence, or behavioral and psychological interaction with the client, facilitates change in, or by, the client. This, of course, has been known since Freud's time and the inception of psychotherapy. However, what was not available, at that time, is the wealth of research in psychotherapy, and fields allied to it (such as nonverbal behavior, interpersonal communication, information processing, and physiology) which could enhance knowledge of change processes in psychotherapy.

This factor, coupled with the growing momentum of the eclectic and integration movement, which some believe has created a "renewed respect for research evidence and an openness to procedures found to be clinically effective" (Goldfried and Newman, 1992), may have brought the field closer to paradigmatic realization. These salient factors further seem to be coalescing at a time when the stress of attempting to maintain caring relationships with *all* clients appears to be taking its professional toll. As Arkowitz (1992) explains in relation to the intrapsychic model of psychotherapy, "Although Rogers emphasized these attitudes as the foundation of his therapeutic approach, it is unlikely that every therapist can fully hold these attitudes with every client to the degree that Rogers would recommend" (p. 420). Or, as one advocate of the client-centered approach, Sanford (1990), puts it:

> It is true that the therapist who chooses to work in this way accepts a demanding discipline: to be congruently aware of self and the feelings flowing within from moment to moment; to be genuine and open enough to reveal them to the client at an appropriate moment; to be deeply empathic and secure enough to enter the world of the client, move comfortably within it, and then return to his or her own world; and to do all of this without judgment and with respect for another human being. . . . There is no expectation that any therapist can assume all of these attitudes all of the time, with all clients—or with any particular client. (p. 84)

As a result, there appears to be a developing realization among practitioners of the need for "tools" above and beyond "empathy" and "positive regard"—however admirable these attitudes may be. Of his pioneering work, Rogers (1977) believed that if he "could discover even one significant truth about the relationships between two people, it might turn out to be much more widely applicable." He then adds, "I don't mean truth with a capital T, but just an approximation of one truth about what goes on between a person with problems and a person who is trying to help." If we could discover that truth, he observed, "that orderliness, that lawfulness, it might have many implications" (p. 148). Furthermore, failure to more fully discover that "truth" may continue to extract a considerable toll from therapists and clients alike. In their work on therapist burnout, for example, Grosch and Olsen (1994) maintain that in the absence of reliable empirical support for many forms of therapy, "therapists may wonder if what they are doing is even helping, rendering them skeptical of the whole profession." In their estimation, while some of the systemic factors that lead to burnout may be inherent in the specific mental health setting, "others," they report, "are related to the practice of psychotherapy itself" (p. 24).

Goldberg (1992) agrees and points out that although each vocational career has its limitations and perils, there are some careers, he says, which are at times "downright dangerous." The practice of psychotherapy, he contends, "is one of these," having "profound effects upon our health and well-being" (p. 4). Supporting this view, Mahoney (1991) reports:

> The effects of serving as a mental health professional are particularly apparent, and although some of these effects are positive, others are decidedly negative. . . . In two surveys of psychiatrists, for example, over 90 percent felt they had suffered special emotional problems resulting from their role as psychotherapist, 73 percent reported having experienced moderate to incapacitating anxiety in their first years of practice, and 58 percent reported having experienced severe depression (Guy 1987; Guy and Liaboe, 1986). . . . It seems increasingly clear that the practice of psychotherapy is a significant factor in the development and exacerbation of many psychotherapists' personal distress and dysfunction. (pp. 356-357)

Consistent with the view that most of this therapist "distress" and personal "dysfunction" may be related to the lack of scientific development of the field, Efran, Lukens, and Lukens (1990) observe that since psychotherapy's inception, practitioners have "struggled to get this nebulous class of procedures to work at least reasonably well in everyday practice." And in the process, they state, therapists "have suffered through more than their share of angst." Efran, Lukens, and Lukens further describe the resulting feelings of inadequacy and panic with which novice, and sometimes experienced therapists, can relate:

> It has dawned on some of these therapists—sometimes right in the middle of a session—that they had little idea what they were doing or why they were doing it. They may have understood that "just listening" helps. However, the question troubling them was: Did they, as professionals, have anything more specific to offer clients than general support, attention, and empathy? (p. xi)

Further expanding upon this point, Efran, Lukens, and Lukens (1990) observe that although clients often report being helped by therapy, "neither therapists nor their clients seem entirely clear about what has been offered or what has been received." What's more, they maintain, surveys indicate that "no single set of premises about therapy is widely accepted by practitioners as an adequate grounding for what they do" (p.1). At this time, Efran, Lukens, and Lukens (1990) further assert, there is even little evidence to support the claim that high-level training in psychotherapy "enables therapists to provide services that are either unique or uniquely effective (American Psychological Association, 1982; Berman and Norton, 1985, p. 1)." In this regard, as Beutler and Consoli (1992) point out, scientists who have reviewed large bodies of research in the field have repeatedly concluded that "training in specific therapies and their associated procedures does not enhance the likelihood or magnitude of outcomes (cf. Luborsky et al., 1975)" (pp. 265-266).

Given these apparent consequences of the seemingly tenuous foundation upon which psychotherapy and the intrapsychic model of the therapeutic relationship currently rest, the remainder of this book therefore describes a behaviorally, biologically, and cognitively based therapeutic approach which is consistent with progressive humanistic thought—and scientific protocol. It should also be noted that in no way is the intention here to reduce the therapeutic process to a "cold, arid, cognitive process" (Goldfried and Newman, 1992) or to interfere with therapist empathy for clients. On the contrary, as Friedman (1992) points out, we need to keep building on the knowledge and experience of humanism. In his words:

... The old humanistic psychology has been criticized rightly by Viktor Frankl, Brewster Smith, and me for insufficient tough-mindedness about such central shibboleths as self-realization and self-actualization. In going "beyond humanistic psychology," I do not mean to leave behind what has been of value in that movement. On the contrary, it is my desire to help the movement itself and others who are interested in it to offer a more coherent live option to contemporary psychologists and psychotherapists. (p. ix)

While Friedman's seemingly progressive humanistic view seems generally consistent with the theory presented herein, rather than moving "beyond humanistic psychology," this book more specifically advocates moving beyond the therapeutic relationship in order to achieve what Wexler and Rice (1974) term, the "demystification" of psychotherapy. Observing, describing, and understanding the events of the therapeutic relationship, they maintain, would "improve training and enrich both practice and the development of new theory." Not only would this "*not* dehumanize the all-important therapy relationship," they contend, but in their view, it would "allow the participants a fuller use of their potentials" (p. viii). As they explain:

> It is about the process that hypotheses are formed and generalizations made, not about the personality dynamics of the client or the things he ought to explore. Each client must be free to move in whatever idiosyncratic direction he needs to go. Thus, there can be a technology of process together with a fluidity and spontaneity about what is explored and what is changed. (p. 207)

THE NEED FOR A SCIENTIFIC THEORY

The need for a higher-order theory to guide empirical research of these change "processes" in psychotherapy is advocated by Strupp (1978). He points out that the pressures for the development of treatments that are "effective, efficient, humane, and widely applicable" are mounting as society seeks "solutions to its multifarious human problems" (p. 17). Consistent with this view, this book therefore recommends moving beyond the therapeutic relationship toward exploring the kinds of facilitative therapist behaviors which the molar therapeutic attitudes may be engendering as they guide these interactive change processes—interactive processes which may further be promoting cognitive and physiological change processes within the client.

Explicating this more specific *guidance* function of the Rogerian attitudes, neurologist Damasio (1994) states, "Feelings, along with the emotions they come from. . . . serve as internal guides, and they help us communicate to others signals that can also guide them" (p. xv). Damasio further concludes from his neurological work that feelings therefore orient us in the right direction; they "take us to the appropriate place in a decision-making space, where we may put the instruments of logic to good use" (p. xiii). In other words, he says, "Emotion and feeling, along with the covert physiological machinery underlying them, assist us with the daunting task of predicting an uncertain future and planning our actions accordingly" (p. xiii).

Toward illuminating the possible "actions" or change processes involved in the therapeutic relationship, therefore, the integrative and eclectic approach described in subsequent chapters, and its underlying theory, attempts to build upon the following views of Garfield (1992) and Rossi (1993) concerning psychotherapy's current scientific status. As Garfield (1992) states in the following:

> It is difficult to spell out precisely the relative contributions of the various hypothesized therapeutic variables. What exist at present are, for the most part, opinions and formulations and not clearly demonstrated empirical facts. Thus, many statements should be viewed as hypotheses, although some postulated variables have received empirical support (Orlinsky and Howard, 1986). Within this context, I believe some aspects, such as a "good" therapeutic relationship, are a prerequisite for potential progress in psychotherapy. However, a good relationship alone does not ensure positive change; it is only a prerequisite. (p. 183)

And the views of Rossi (1993) on this issue as well:

> By now there are thousands of correlational studies that report statistically significant relationships between attitudes of mind, mood, and "sociocultural" factors with the ills of the body. These studies tend to leave many of us vaguely unsatisfied, however: We know that correlation is not causation. We really do not understand how something as insubstantial as "mind" can effect something as solid as our own flesh and blood. Where is the connection between mind and body? (p. xv)

In other words, as L.S. Greenberg (1994) points out, "correlating process to outcome, or even experimentally manipulating variables to produce effects reliably, does not explain the causal processes involved in change" (p. 136).

SUMMARY AND CONCLUSION

In summary, inspired by the need for a higher-order theory, proponents of the eclectic and integrative movement note that the birth of psychotherapy itself resulted from the kind of integration of knowledge to whose scientific precepts this movement has adhered. In this regard, however, they point out that (possibly due to the selective attention phenomenon described in Chapter 1) therapist working focus has nevertheless seemingly centered upon either internal *or* external foci rather than upon their synergistic existence within human and psychotherapeutic reality. The problem ostensibly has been how to study human behavior, and human intentionality or meaning, within the confines of scientific methodology leading to extreme suggestions ranging from the abolition of the scientific method, itself, to its integration with subjective phenomena. However, these suggestions may have been offered as a result of the lack of paradigmatic "direction" rather than as a viable means of achieving it since the issue seems more integration-related than medium-related. For, in the absence of communication with other major areas of human inquiry (from which psychotherapeutic theory itself should have been "derived and articulated"), research efforts will likely continue to prove groundless.

To facilitate the task of theoretical integration in this volume, the working focus has been narrowed by excluding the concept of disorder (what needs to be changed) and transference/countertransference (attitudinal biases which clients and therapists bring into psychotherapy). This book concentrates instead on integrating observable behavioral factors which instigate or inhibit change. A prerequisite to this unifying task, developing a common language, may further be simultaneously achieved through an integrative perspective which utilizes the standardized terminology of other established areas of human inquiry (as opposed to the hypothetical constructs and jargon of traditional psychotherapeutic theory). In other words, building an integrated scientific theory must be based on what therapists do rather than what they "say they do." And the consensus on "what they do," which has seemingly accrued since the time of Freud and the inception of the field, is that the therapist establishes a face-to-face relationship with the client wherein the client engages in self-disclosure about his or her concern(s). The therapist's behavioral and psychological interaction with the client, within the context of a therapeutic relationship, in turn facilitates psychotherapeutic change within the client.

In conclusion, how this change comes about, or what behavioral, biological, and cognitive processes may be involved, remains the central issue. Consequently, given the apparent designation of the therapeutic relationship as the general area in which to search for this "scientific explanation," the following chapters, supported by research in psychotherapy and related fields, explore therapist behaviors and interpersonal transactions—as well as physiological and cognitive processes occurring within the client—possibly contributing to therapeutic change. In so doing, this book offers a "realist" explanatory perspective described by L.S. Greenberg (1994) as an approach to theory building which involves "laying bare the underlying processes that connect observable inputs and outputs"— its objective being to help demystify such events by showing how they "fit into a causal nexus" (p. 136). And, as previously stated, this "causal nexus," or higher-order theory, may materialize with the help of the standardized terminology of the disciplines of nonverbal behavior, information processing, and interpersonal communication—the next topics of exploration.

Chapter 3

Nonverbal Behavior, Information Processing, and Interpersonal Communication in Psychotherapy

Anthropologist Don Brown has described in great detail the common characteristics of individuals in societies throughout the world. He calls these characteristics the traits of the "Universal People" (UP).

The UP have their cultural knowledge embedded in a language, which has a grammar and a set of phonemes. They speak in abstractions. Their phonemes are produced and channeled through the oral and nasal cavities. Their language allows them to think and speak in abstractions. They also lie and have symbolic speech. And they manage to express much more than their words indicate through nonverbal gestures, all of which are similar around the world.

—Robert Ornstein, 1993

. . . We create by being. We are not passive recipients of experience. Nor are we simple behavior respondents. Information processing studies teach us that we produce throughout our lives—less systematically at first, more systematically later—a constant stream of perceptual, imaginal, memorial, and behavioral objects.

—Wayne Anderson, 1974

. . . Human beings are actually unfinished animals, constantly in the process of change and development. At any moment, the maps of our brains may change as we learn new things and as the world changes.

—Robert Ornstein, 1993

Psychotherapy's search for its scientific roots and its quest for greater efficacy, as suggested earlier, may be enhanced by research in fields relevant to it such as nonverbal behavior, information processing, and interpersonal communication. This would appear especially so in a therapeutic field which lacks a strong empirical base and quality control. Given this state of affairs, for example, it is not surprising, as Mahoney (1991) notes, that "some therapists are significantly more helpful than others across diversities of clients and psychological problems" (p. 271). In fact, in his study of therapy outcome, Luborsky (1987) reports that therapist differences accounted for eight times as much variance as treatment differences. He therefore concludes that the study of the types of treatments is "drastically less enlightening" than the study of therapists. Yet, he observes, there are "phenomenally more studies of the former" (p. 58).

In addition, the argument that variability within samples of therapists has influenced the results obtained in psychotherapy research, according to Garfield (1992), is strengthened by the comparative outcome studies which report few differences among therapies (Lambert, Shapiro, and Bergin, 1986; Stiles, Shapiro, and Elliott, 1986). As a result, therefore, Kiesler (1979) states, the research literature "clearly shows that organismic factors interact with treatment variables." To assume that they do not by letting them vary "unsystematically," he says, "can only produce maximum 'noise' in subject variability and obscure important relationships" (p. 45). In other words, according to Garfield (1992), these data tend to support the existence of common factors, related to therapist behavior, cutting across therapies.

Furthermore, the failure of past gross outcome studies to identify processes of change, Garfield (1992) notes, is due to the fact that there were "no detailed observations or recordings of what individual therapists actually did" (p. 195). He further maintains that these limitations also apply to most of the research conducted in psychotherapy "until very recent times." In other words, he says, psychotherapy researchers have focused almost exclusively on type of psychotherapy, as if it "consisted solely of a set of standard technical skills, and the individual application of the therapist was of little consequence" (p. 195). It is not surprising, therefore, that such research appears to have contributed more toward confirming the existence of the therapeutic change within the client (however limited) than in explaining how it occurs or how it is facilitated or unwittingly inhibited by the therapist.

This may further account for the general belief in the field, as expressed by Stricker (1990), that "the limits of treatment may be set by the limitations of the therapist, for the patient cannot be taken any further than the therapist has travelled" (p. 278). This general view (that the amount of growth possible in the client is dependent upon the degree of personal growth achieved by the therapist) appears to be held by both humanists and psychoanalysts alike (Goldberg, 1992, p. 45)—a view which probably serves as a commentary on the current artistic state of the field as well as the need for greater scientific grounding. Given this current characterological or intrapsychic preoccupation, it is also understandable, for example, why high-level training programs for psychotherapists may have lacked success. For how is character building taught, or therapist growth for that matter, of the type required to produce effective therapists? Given the apparent ineffectiveness of such training programs, a shift from the intrapsychic model to one with a potentially stronger empirical base—one emphasizing therapist nonverbal behavior and client information processing—may therefore be warranted.

While the scientific value of viewing therapeutic change from a behavioral perspective has been previously noted, that for information processing is outlined in the following passage by Rice (1974) (about which more will be said in subsequent chapters):

> . . . For the therapist, the prescription of congruence, empathic understanding, and unconditional positive regard gives only general guidance toward the kinds of operations he should seek to maximize in his own behavior.
>
> It seems increasingly clear that the appropriate theoretical base for understanding the operations of client-centered therapy and the mechanism of change involved is some kind of information processing model. . . . This will be more than a semantic exercise. It is designed to lead to rather specific prescriptions for the kinds of operations on the part of both client and therapist that are likely to lead to maximal positive change. (pp. 292-293)

And that of Wexler and Rice (1974) who elaborate upon this view:

> What information processing fundamentally provides for the therapy theorist is a language, a language of events and processes that is free from many of the problematic assumptions of traditional personality theorizing, and unlike the phenomenological language of past client-centered theorizing, a language that is clearly rooted in empirical findings. Moreover, it is a language that is molecular, that gives a rich and detailed view of the complex internal events occurring within the individual. (p. 17)

The implications of an information processing perspective for psychotherapy notwithstanding, Strong (1995) nevertheless points out that in this social psychology model, the focus has been more on the "intrapersonal, not the interpersonal—on what goes on within rather than between people" (p. 688). Furthermore, if therapists wish to gain insight in psychotherapy, he says, they will have to "refocus on the interpersonal, on the space between in which they work" (p. 689). Thus, he concludes, "other information—another theory—is needed to inform counselors about what they should do in their interface with the client to stimulate 'correct' information processing in the client" (p. 687). In other words, he says, "this emerging theory needs concepts of how a more skilled person lends powers to a seeker who appropriates them for autonomous use, and of the timing and pacing of the equipping process" (pp. 688-689).

Toward this objective, this chapter therefore explores the integration of an information processing perspective, with that of interpersonal communication and nonverbal behavior, in the light of the previously cited finding that the factors which vary indiscriminately in psychotherapy are therapist-based rather than therapy-related. However, since therapist nonverbal behavior is still relegated to the category of "nonspecific," the next few sections explore the possible role such behaviors play in the therapeutic process.

AN OVERVIEW OF NONVERBAL BEHAVIOR IN INTERPERSONAL COMMUNICATION THEORY

Although the study of nonverbal behavior has been growing as an important area of exploration in psychology, most of its research to date has been carried out and applied to naturalistic environments as opposed to therapeutic settings. Despite the fact that considerable attention has also been given to nonverbal behavior in interpersonal communication theory, as yet little emphasis appears to have been placed on applying these findings to psychotherapeutic theory and practice in any systematic way. Further, in a field such as psychotherapy, where the interpersonal or therapeutic relationship appears basic, and in view of the fact that evidence appears to be accumulating (Argyle et al., 1970; Mehrabian, 1970; Mehrabian and Ferris, 1967) suggesting the nonverbal act to be "more important in interpersonal relationships than language itself" (Key, 1975, p. 20), research in the nonverbal area of interpersonal communication in psychotherapy appears warranted.

While interpersonal communication has long been considered by some in the field as a "central issue" (Perez, 1968, p. 14) in the psychotherapeutic process (Patterson, 1959; Williamson, 1959; Rogers, 1961; Haley, 1963; Perez, 1965; Watzlawick and Beavin, 1977), most communication research in individual therapy, as previously noted, has been approached from the perspective of analyzing the *verbal* or language component of the therapeutic relationship. These analyses of verbal *content* have further been done to assess levels of therapist functioning in relation to the facilitative conditions or therapeutic attitudes (Truax and Carkhuff, 1968; Rice, 1965; Watzlawick, 1978). However, research in nonverbal behavior suggests that language is only part of the communication process (Birdwhistell, 1970; Mehrabian, 1972; Siegman and Feldstein, 1978) and that the nonverbal component in therapy may be a more "important" (Parloff, Waskow, and Wolfe, 1978, p. 241) perspective from which to approach research in this area. Moreover, some in the therapeutic field, Bandler and Grinder (1979) for example, maintain that the "proper domain" of therapists, or "professional communicators," may not only lie in verbally transmitted content, but in "process" (p. 47). In other words, instead of concentrating primarily on analyzing the content of client disclosure, the therapist, they say, should also attend to the process of *how the client organizes his experience* which, they believe, is "much easier" (p. 47).

While some therapies may be process-oriented to some degree, as previously noted, the intrapsychic approach to psychotherapy research may nevertheless have been too global, or molar, to delineate change processes. In addition, research in nonverbal behavior, indicating its importance in interpersonal relationships, suggests the verbal approach to studying the therapeutic relationship may have been too exclusionist of other, possibly more important, channels of communication (Wexler and Rice, 1974, pp. 15-16). As a result, according to Wexler and Rice, in Rogerian theorizing, there has been somewhat of a "gap" between "therapist technique and client change" (p. 18). What the client-centered therapist does to be instrumental in helping the client, they say, has therefore "remained something of a mystery" (p. 18). Prochaska (1979) echoes a similar view stating: "While Rogers has written extensively about the conditions of the client-therapist relationship that allow for therapeutic change, he has had much less to say about the actual processes that occur in the interactions between the client and the therapist to produce such change" (p. 118).

Thus, because of their conceptual and often dispositional nature, researchers have begun to realize that attitudes (like other hypothetical constructs), while having thus far served as the global "road map" to therapeutic change, may nevertheless have contributed little toward understanding the properties of the "road" itself (processes of change), or of the "destination" (growth or therapeutic change). As Strupp (1973) observes: "We cannot rest content with the assertion that certain undefined charismatic qualities of the therapist exert a psychological influence on the patient that augment his powers to cope with life's problems and in turn lead to diminution or disappearance of particular symptoms." Unlike religious conversion or faith healing, he says, "it is precisely the task of psychotherapy as a scientific discipline to make explicit the psychological mechanisms that are instrumental in producing change" (p. 108).

As a result of this uncertainty in the field, Bordin (1974) recognizes the need to examine the questions and relevant hypothetical constructs in psychotherapy with a view to "converting them to observables" (p. 31). Likewise, Strupp and Bergin (1973) suggest that research in the field must seek to isolate psychological principles embedded in, and often obscured by, "divergent theoretical formulations" (p. 797). Paralleling this view, interpersonal communication researchers, as well, maintain that while it may be useful to know that therapists differ in relation to facilitative attitudes, to understand the therapeutic process, they believe it is also important to discover "just 'how' these qualities are communicated to the patient, and how the patient in his turn influences their expression" (Danziger, 1976, p. 109).

These views further appear to be supported by existing psychotherapy process research which suggests these therapist "qualities" to be communicated not only by verbal interaction but more so through nonverbal behavior (Fretz, 1966; Shapiro, 1968; Graves and Robinson, 1976; Smith-Hanen, 1977; Tepper and Haase, 1978). Therefore, in view of the relative lack of *outcome* research of nonverbal behavior in psychotherapy, which some social psychologists nonetheless consider to be the "relationship language" (Ekman and Friesen, 1968), research in this seemingly neglected or "nonspecific" area of psychotherapy might help provide a more complete view of the therapeutic encounter to augment research of the verbal component.

NONVERBAL THERAPIST BEHAVIOR AS NONSPECIFIC

While some Gestalt therapists—Perls, Hefferline, and Goodman (1977, p. 17), for example—along with the work of the some of the behaviorists (Mehrabian, 1970, p. 65), the neurolinguistic work with eye-movements of Bandler and Grinder (1979), and the EMDR technique of Shapiro (1995), do refer to observing and utilizing nonverbal *client* behavior as a means of improving intrapersonal communication, *therapist* nonverbal behaviors, as previously noted, are nevertheless still categorized by most theorists as "nonspecific factors" (Strupp, 1978, p. 12) associated with "attention" or "interest" in the client or treatment. That attention itself may be therapeutic is suggested by researcher Orlinsky (1994), who reports: "A substantial number of findings indicate that good outcomes are often associated with attention to the feelings and problems presented by patients" (p. 113). Applied to specific therapies, the relationship between therapist interest in the client and successful outcome has further been described by Shapiro and Morris (1978) as "the cornerstone of Rogerian client-centered therapy" (p. 381). This relationship has also been explored, in relation to other therapies, by Ginsburg and Arrington (1948), Goldstein and Shipman (1961), and Frank (1965).

That there may be a complex interaction among the variables of therapist interest in the client, the treatment, and the ultimate results is suggested by Shapiro and Morris (1978). They conclude, however, that how these factors influence results "is not clear" (p. 384). Nevertheless, the possibility that "attention" or attending to clients has therapeutic effects appears to have considerable support. As Prochaska (1979) states, "anyone who has been in therapy can appreciate the gratification that comes from having a competent professional give undivided attention for an hour" (p. 5). Just what it is about attention that contributes to therapeutic change, however, has not yet been specified. Nonetheless, Prochaska (1979) states, "researchers have frequently found that attention does indeed lead to improvement regardless of whether the attention is followed by any other therapeutic processes" (p. 5).

The conclusions of Bergin and Lambert (1978) also appear to parallel this perspective. In their view, psychotherapy is "laden with nonspecific or placebo factors (Frank, 1973; Strupp, 1973a); but these influences, when specified, may prove to be the essence of what provides therapeutic benefit." Instead of controlling for them in research designs by adopting "a spurious parallel with medical placebos," they state, we may be "dismissing the active ingredients we are looking for" (p. 180). In this regard, as Schwartz (1978) contends, the behavioral sciences may now have the potential of being able to delineate and specify "processes that contribute to the combination of uncontrolled psychosocial factors, brought together under the global concept of a nonspecific placebo response" (p. 83). The need for such delineation is suggested by Shapiro and Morris (1978), as well, who contend that nonspecific factors may underlie most of the observed effects in therapy.

This book therefore explores these relevant nonverbal therapist behaviors, associated with interest or attention, which may be therapeutically active in psychotherapy but which as yet, because they have not been clinically verified, are still relegated to the category of "nonspecific." Being nonspecific, such variables are supposedly not considered to be particular to any one system of therapy and are frequently not specified by theories, according to Prochaska (1979), as being of central importance. Still, he says, such variables are assumed to be part of any approach to therapy (or exist universally).

Nevertheless, he adds, nonspecific factors have been seriously overlooked by the major theories in psychotherapy. In his words:

> If therapists are to increase their impact, they can no longer afford to leave such factors unspecified. Well-controlled studies that have included placebo treatments to control for nonspecific factors frequently find that such factors account for as much as 50 percent or more of variance in therapy (Paul, 1966; Sloan et al., 1975). Therapists who have taken a close look at nonspecific factors suggest that such factors are indeed the essence of a transtheoretical process of therapy. (p. 366)

This view is supported by others in the field who similarly believe that the task of psychotherapy research in the future may well be, according to Strupp (1973), "to refine the application of relatively specific techniques in such a way as to markedly enhance the so-called nonspecific effects of psychotherapy" (p. 109). Similar observations have been made by Haley (1963, p. 13), Scheflen (1973), and from researchers in interpersonal communication as well. Danziger (1976), for example, believes that the practical effectiveness of psychotherapy is at best "minimally related to the theoretical content of psychotherapeutic systems" (p. 110). This is so, he maintains, because it has been shown that even therapists with the most diverse theoretical orientations are able to effect at least some therapeutic change. Therefore, it seems likely, according to Danziger, that such successes may be due to factors that are "common to psychotherapies practiced under the aegis of quite diverse theoretical orientations" (p. 111). These common features, he contends, may be found in the interpersonal interaction since he believes all approaches to psychotherapy involve the creation of what he calls "a special system of interpersonal transactions" (p. 111). Paralleling this view, Watzlawick (1978) suggests that there may exist in psychotherapy, a nonconscious language. He further states: "I would go so far as to claim that, when using this particular language, the question as to what particular school of thought a therapist subscribes to becomes quite unimportant, and probably most of those surprising and unexpected improvements— for which a particular theory does not provide a satisfactory explanation and which, therefore, are not 'supposed' to take place—

can be traced back to the unintentional and fortuitous use of these patterns of communication referred to above" (pp. 4-5).

Finally, at a time when the need for greater naturalistic observation in psychotherapy is being advocated (Hill, 1994; Rogers, 1975, p. 54; Goble, 1970, p. viii; Gross, 1972, p. 53), research in nonverbal behavior, with its naturalistic and standardized behavioral perspective, may be more amenable to promoting scientific consensus in psychotherapy than intrapsychic phenomena. Such agreement or consensus may further accrue, according to Horowitz (1994), not only through quantitative research but also through the kind of *qualitative* research endeavor proffered herein. As he explains:

> Seeking consensus in research does not always involve quantitative methodology (other than some checks on reliability). Qualitative research can consist of a repeated review of material. The aim is a sober and objective pursuit of pattern recognition leading to descriptive and then explanatory models. This type of approach in research is not unlike the clinician's tasks of objective case formulation and planning how change processes may occur, but it is often more time-consuming. (p. 197)

NONVERBAL BEHAVIORAL RESEARCH IN PSYCHOTHERAPY

The need for research of nonverbal behavior in psychotherapy becomes more apparent by the relative lack of controlled outcome studies attempting to identify specific interpersonal behaviors or interactions that might possibly influence therapeutic change. As Bergin and Lambert (1978) report, "although there is a growing body of knowledge that confirms the value of psychotherapy, differences in outcome between various forms of intervention are rare" (p. 180). This situation appears to further exist despite the fact that, as Gottman and Markman (1978) point out, the question: "What therapeutic processes lead to the most change?" (p. 26) still dominates psychotherapy. A review of research by Meltzoff and Kornreich (1970) and empirical analyses of psychotherapy by Garfield and Bergin (1978; 1986) indicate, for example, that the majority of studies employing appropriate controls are of the behavioristic type, emphasizing no therapeutic relationship. And, until recently, most of the existing psychodynamic research consisted mainly of studies comparing the effectiveness of two or more therapies, or studies attempting to determine the efficacy of therapies within particular schools.

Despite a relatively recent increase in the growth of process-outcome research, the existing efforts of the past two decades nevertheless appear to have yielded little in the way of consensus concerning behavioral, biological and cognitive processes involved in therapeutic change. Stiles, Shapiro, and Harper (1994) summarize this existing state of affairs:

> Psychotherapy is widely practiced as a treatment for psychological disorders, and reviews of research indicate that it is effective in this capacity (Lambert, Shapiro, and Bergin, 1986; Smith, Glass, and Miller, 1980). However, its mechanisms of action are poorly understood and disputed among competing schools. This issue is usually cast as the relationship between process and outcome—between what happens during a psychotherapy session and the overcoming of psychological problems. The poor understanding of this issue is not a result of lack of effort; there is a sizable literature reporting attempts to identify process-outcome relationships (Orlinsky and Howard, 1986). However, the results of this research have been disappointing. Although some individual studies have claimed significant advances, there is little indication of convergence on principles or methods that reliably point to what processes are effective (Shapiro, Startup, Bird, Harper, Reynolds, and Suokas, 1994; Stiles and Shapiro, 1989). (p. 36)

L. S. Greenberg (1994) further reiterates why the existing process research appears to have yielded little in terms of agreement or "convergence of knowledge" on the processes of therapeutic change:

> Unfortunately, the predominant manner in which process research has been done has stripped the behavior of its context. Observational coding systems abstract the information about certain features of behavior, independently of the context in which they occur; although this highlights certain aspects, it reduces our potential understanding of the situation by eliminating others. Failure to take context into account affects the

meaningfulness of our results. Context is critical in understanding human behavior, yet in observational coding and scientific study it is not treated as the resource it is for understanding in our everyday lives (Heatherington, 1989). (p. 122)

Whether attributable to methodological limitations or not, the end result is that existing research in the diversity of psychodynamic theory appears to have achieved little agreement in the field. It is for this reason, therefore, that knowledge derived from other related fields, through the eclectic and integration movement, may help "point to the effective processes"—an objective toward which the remainder of this book is directed. The need for greater paradigmatic direction is underlined by the results of Orlinsky and Howard (1978) who, in their review of psychotherapeutic research, conclude: "Among them all, there is no standard definition of what occurs in, or is distinctive of, therapeutic 'process'; no consensus about the intended effects of therapy, or no criteria of therapeutic 'outcome'; hence, no agreement concerning the selection and measurement of meaningful process and outcome 'variables'" (p. 284). Consequently, as previously noted, while research thus far may have supported the existence of psychotherapy, in general, as therapeutic (contrary to the early opinion of Eysenck (1952, 1966), little yet seems to have been achieved in terms of identifying the specific processes or mechanisms underlying change. Or as stated by Garfield and Bergin (1978), "a clearer understanding of what variables help certain types of clients with certain types of problems is still to be ascertained" (p. ix).

As a result of this nebulous state of affairs, Bordin (1974) observes that more than additional gross evaluative studies, we need "new ideas and investigations directed toward the criterion in change-oriented investigations" (p. 220). Further expanding upon this view, he states:

> I see a special need for two kinds of more restricted methodologically oriented investigations. One of these *is* a more thorough examination of the relations among different channels of observation of the process of psychotherapy, with particular emphasis on the cost/benefit of making available the full range

of sensory channels (visual, auditory, etc.) versus different degrees of restriction. The other need is for fuller investigation of the generalizability of various analogues through bridging research. (p. 220)

Support for this view also comes from the work of Orlinsky and Howard (1978) who state that "surprisingly few studies" exist which "relate therapists' instrumental techniques to therapeutic outcome" (p. 291).

Thus, consistent with the extreme humanistic view mentioned earlier—that the relationship *is* the therapy—therapeutic change, for the most part, still appears to be attributed to the client-therapist relationship, or to psychotherapy in general. Therefore, while research supporting the existence of therapeutic effects from psychotherapy may have contributed toward establishing it as a discipline, as stated earlier, such research nonetheless appears to have contributed little toward understanding how it occurs. It may be here, therefore, that nonclinical research in the nonverbal mechanisms of interpersonal interaction may prove helpful, when applied to a psychotherapeutic context, in delineating processes of change.

This kind of behavioral approach to the study of psychotherapy was recommended twenty-five years ago by Meltzoff and Kornreich (1970) when they observed that little had been done "to study gestural and expressive behavior in psychotherapy in an era that offers many sophisticated techniques with which to investigate these phenomena" (p. 480). Thus, as Paul (1969) notes, most research in nonverbal behavior has been carried out through laboratory-based designs in the form of experimental analogs as opposed to research performed in a clinical context. For this reason, he says, such research has been considered to be in the broader area of *behavior influence* rather than in the more specific psychotherapeutic context of therapeutic growth and behavior change. Despite this fact, he nevertheless maintains that such laboratory research can contribute knowledge of therapeutic processes of change without reference to clinical behavioral change. As he explains:

Laboratory studies have implications for the selection of specific variables for investigation in the behavior modification context to the extent that they have been isolated as prominent factors in other contexts of behavior influence. The findings of nonclinical laboratory studies may provide the basis for predicting relationships in the clinical context including the prediction that laboratory derived techniques or principles may be effective in altering clinical behavior in specified ways. As such, the experimental analog may form a solid basis for development of hypotheses to be tested in the context of treatment regarding the influence of new therapeutic techniques. . . . (p. 53)

Similarly, the opinion of Strupp and Bergin (1973) in this area suggests that advances in psychodynamic therapy may not necessarily only come from within the traditional clinical framework, but also from "basic research in disparate areas" or "through a combination of clinical and experimental methods within the clinical context" (p. 799) (an opinion also seemingly shared by Davison and Lazarus [1995]). Such observations would therefore appear to lend support to the approach of this book which integrates nonclinical research in nonverbal behavior, and other related fields of human inquiry, toward the formulation of a behaviorally, biologically, and cognitively grounded theory of therapeutic process. This proposed higher-order theory is further being offered, as previously stated, to stimulate applied research based on observable, and thus replicable, psychotherapeutic procedure and practice.

DELINEATING PSYCHOTHERAPEUTIC VARIABLES

In the past, as Paul (1969) observes, there is reason to believe that some psychotherapeutic procedures were based upon hypothetical constructs most of which, in his estimation, did not rest upon a firmly verified foundation but rather on what he terms, "personal conviction, investment, and observation" (p. 34) rather than scientific evidence. In this respect, psychotherapy research based on the relatively more solid empirical base in nonverbal behavior, interpersonal communication, information processing, and psychobiology (relevant to psychotherapy) may help contribute more toward delineating therapeutic therapist behaviors and client change processes than had previously been possible through the various narrower, esoteric psychotherapeutic therapies.

However, given the greater number and complexity of variables in psychotherapy than, for example, in most physical science research, the need for proper identification, description, and control of therapist variables, where possible, is necessarily of concern. While research in psychotherapy poses its own set of problems, according to Meltzoff and Kornreich (1970) such special requirements should nevertheless not deter it. In their view, psychotherapy is amenable to research and can occur without sacrificing "experimental rigor" (p. 9). They admit, however, that approaching research from the point of view of intrapsychic states may have produced an antiresearch stance in the field possibly implying, as Meltzoff and Kornreich observe, that "therapeutic relationships are so unique as to make experiments nonreproducible" (p. 11). This, on the other hand, might be where research based on therapist behaviors, rather than attitudes, could provide a more concrete basis for replication as a prerequisite to generating consensus.

Another factor supporting the need for clearer specification of therapist variables or therapist "style" (Parloff, Waskow, and Wolfe, 1978, p. 241) was identified by Watzlawick and Beavin (1977). They state, for example, that the therapist's own behavior may often be "overlooked" or "difficult to see" because, in their view, it is "like breathing, largely out of awareness, until drawn to our attention" (pp. 56-57). These seemingly basic ideas concerning therapist behavior may be obvious, Watzlawick and Beavin contend, but they are still "neither systematized into an adequate theory of communication nor consistently utilized in research" (p. 57). Thus, as Strupp (1973) concludes (expressing a view similar to Maslow's [1970] quoted earlier), "one can practice the art of psychotherapy without being aware of the principles one is employing" (p. 781).

In this regard, Key (1975) points out that nonverbal communication researchers have been aware of this lack of specificity for some time. She observes, for example, that Sapir (1927) was among the first in the behavioral sciences to note that "we respond to gestures with an extreme alertness and one might almost say, in accord with an elaborate and secret code that is written nowhere, known by none, and understood by all" (Key, 1975, p. 12). Part of the reason for this apparent nonconscious state of understanding in nonverbal behavior, Key suggests, may be because, as previously noted, most of the system of nonverbal communication is learned "out of awareness" (p. 15). Moreover, Galin (1979, p. 19) further suggests that due to hemispheric specialization, the right hemisphere may play the dominant or major role in such nonconscious nonverbal learning. This knowledge from allied fields would therefore appear to support the need for identifying or bringing therapist behavior into greater *working focus,* or attention. Or as Watzlawick (1978) observes, there may be a need to translate the learnings of the right or nonverbal hemisphere into a language that the left or "verbal" (p. 21) hemisphere can understand.

Watzlawick (1978) further believes that psychotherapy may now "hold the key to an objective understanding of those functional mental mechanisms and disturbances (for example, repression, depersonalization, delusion, and others), for whose explanation we have for so long had to rely on nebulous, speculative hypotheses" (pp. 17-18). Reasoning from the hemispheric brain theory, for example, Watzlawick (1978) suggests that the possibility may now exist "that the conceptual distinction of conscious and unconscious processes (and with it all the manifold consequences for our understanding of psychopathology and psychotherapy that necessarily flow from this distinction) may have to be modified" (p. 38). And this would seem to follow since, as Whitely and Fretz (1980) observe, "the biological bases of behavior, particularly in learning, memory, and emotion, are being increasingly understood." However, they state, "this new knowledge is only peripherally incorporated within the psychology literature." Psychobiology as a content area, they nevertheless contend, "should become part of our traditional curriculum, not a haphazard source of ideas for practice and research" (p. 101).

Such observations from within the psychotherapeutic profession would therefore appear to lend support to the objective of this book—toward identifying, and thus operationalizing, psychotherapeutic processes, i.e., therapist interactional behaviors and client psychobiological responses, possibly contributing to therapeutic change.

THE NEED FOR OPERATIONALISM
IN PSYCHOTHERAPY

If, as some therapists contend, psychotherapy is still an art (Gottman and Markman 1978, p. 30) concerned primarily with affective ideas, concepts, and emotions and less with methods and specific human behaviors, justification for advocating greater operationalism in psychotherapy, through studying therapist nonverbal behavior, may seem warranted. Part of the rationale for such an approach was proposed by Parloff, Waskow, and Wolfe (1978), Strupp (1973), and Thoresen (1974). For example, Parloff, Waskow, and Wolfe (1978) maintain that "the category of studies dealing with experimental research on therapist and patient interactions within the treatment setting remains essentially null" (p. 234). Strupp (1973) echoes a similar view, noting that the psychodynamic "psychotherapist-technician has no techniques per se" (p. 113) for dealing with problems such as general anxiety, tension, or depression (with the possible exception of EMDR [Shapiro, 1995] discussed in the next chapter).

Thoresen (1974), on the other hand, claims that such goals of humanistic therapists might be achieved in part by utilizing behavioral techniques. In other words, he suggests that humanistic concerns might be translated into human-action terms or into "what persons would do" (p. 308). He further challenges the apparent dichotomous perspectives which, he believes, previously tended to "pit humanist against behaviorist" (p. 308). The issue, he contends, is not behaviorism versus humanism. That, in his estimation, was a "pseudo-issue" (p. 311) promoted by extreme views of these positions. Instead, he believes, the issue might be "how best to utilize the concepts and methodologies" (p. 311) of both behavioral and humanistic psychology.

Paralleling this view, Bordin (1974) similarly maintains that to identify "pantheoretical variables," psychotherapy research should give the highest priority to the "recording of concretely defined instances of a particular kind of behavior" (p. 63). (It is interesting to note that shortly thereafter, Bergin and Lambert [1978] identified a trend developing in the field involving increasing attempts "to merge traditional insight approaches with behavioral approaches" [p. 171]). Lending support for this view from a humanistic perspective, Avila, Combs, and Purkey (1977) suggest that the study of human behavior might be approached both externally and internally depending upon the researcher's *frame of reference*. As they state, "The question is not which frame of reference is right? The proper question is, which frame of reference is most appropriate to supply the answers needed for the problem posed?" (p. 65). Prochaska's (1979) view is similar. To study psychotherapy, he suggests employing an "integrative model" (p. 15) combining internal and external perspectives to provide, in his words, "a more balanced view." Such a view, he maintains, would provide "a more complete picture of individuals by accepting their potential for inner change while recognizing the limits that environmental conditions and contingencies can place on such change" (p. 15).

It is from this perspective, therefore, that while acknowledging the reality and heuristic contribution of the intrapsychic approach to psychotherapy, this book explores an external, behavioral, or "co-oriented activity" (Orlinsky and Howard, 1978, p. 285) approach. However, the behavioral context in which this book approaches the problem of attempting to identify facilitative nonverbal therapist behaviors involves only delineating such behaviors as opposed to applying existing behavior modification techniques to psychodynamic therapy. Underlying this endeavor is the assumption that if therapeutic nonverbal behaviors do exist, they have not yet been identified (or specified) and are therefore being employed to varying degrees, indiscriminately and nonconsciously, by *all* therapists within *all* therapies. The purpose of identifying such behaviors and transactions would be to promote their more conscious and systematic application thereby increasing psychotherapeutic effectiveness and operationalism.

The need for such an empirically grounded theoretical framework to guide future research in psychotherapy is supported by Strupp (1973). In his words:

> . . . It is clear that the development of psychotherapy tends in the direction of greater specificity, explicitness, precision. This movement is inescapable if psychotherapy is to be taught, described, and explicated. Concepts must be defined more stringently, and the vagueness inherent in the subject matter must be diminished. The demands for operational definitions—or at least demonstrable empirical referents—can hardly be sidestepped. (p. 738)

Others in the field, such as Lazarus (1992) and Carkhuff and Berenson (1977), voice similar concerns about the lack of operationalism caused by focusing mainly upon intrapsychic phenomena. Commenting on this problem in relation to client-centered therapy, for example, Carkhuff and Berenson (1977) state, "None of the 'necessary and sufficient' conditions of the client-centered approach are ever operationalized beyond reflection" and none of the conditions "are ever developed beyond concepts." Furthermore, they add, because none of these concepts or constructs is defined in terms of specific behaviors "they never develop into goals or means to achieve goals for the helpee as well as helper" (p. 71). Wexler (1974) makes a similar observation. The client-centered concepts, he says, "have stimulated relatively little systematic investigation in scientific psychology; their molarity and ambiguities in the way in which they are defined have made them difficult to operationalize and investigate empirically" (p. 49). Consequently, as Strupp (1978) states, technique variables are still "intertwined with the person of the therapist" (p. 8).

The particular significance of operationalism in psychotherapy, derived from scientific theory, was outlined in the descriptive function of theory offered by Stefflre and Matheny (1968). The general tendency in psychotherapy, they maintain, is to view theory as a "conceptual model" enabling one to see happenings and to make sense of them. They add, however, that such theory makes sense "only if we are able to postulate some process which, if it operated, would result in the behavior" (p. 3). Or as Bordin (1974) puts it:

> To be fully validated, a theory and its associated pattern of psychotherapy must be able to articulate the kinds of actions of the therapist, whether verbal or nonverbal, intended as communications or as spontaneous expressions, which interact to mediate the succession of changes, culminating in the enduring patient behavior and experience sought as an end product. (p. 121)

The significance of operationalism or technique to the advancement of theory might also be compared to the function of the *mutation* in fostering genetic diversity in biological systems. Strupp (1973) elaborates from a psychotherapeutic perspective:

. . . The conclusion emerges that new departures in psychotherapy derive from changes in technical procedures, not from theoretical reformulations, however sophisticated the latter may appear. From the standpoint of the researcher, this conclusion suggests, from a different angle, that he needs to focus on the therapist's operations, that is, on empirical data of what he does rather than upon verbal descriptions of intentions, goals, and theories. (p. 88)

The difficulty in researching psychotherapy ostensibly has been, however, in specifying the probable actions, processes, or therapist behaviors, which likely contribute to therapeutic change, in order to test them empirically. Nor has it apparently always been denied by humanists that technique and behavior play a part in therapy. As Jourard (1968) observes, for example, "This is not to say there is no place for technique in the art of psychotherapy." Technique, which must be learned from a teacher, he says, is "an 'idiom' in which one expresses an initial therapeutic intent" (p. 57). Similarly, Rogers (1975) states: "In client-centered therapy, we are deeply engaged in the prediction and influencing of behavior, or even the control of behavior." As therapists, he says, "we institute certain attitudinal conditions, and the client has relatively little voice in the establishment of these conditions" (pp. lxxvi-lxxvii).

Nevertheless, according to Zimring (1974), the paucity of research in this area and the fact that so few theories have concerned themselves with "how the therapist's action produces the client's change," may have been due to "a deliberate avoidance based on the premise that attitudes are more important than technique, that technique by itself is manipulation." As Zimring goes on to explain, however, "if emphasis on technique leads to dealing mechanically with the client, then therapy should not be taught in this way" (p. 123). But on the other hand, he maintains, if the change processes or operations by which the therapeutic relationship facilitates change can be specified, such knowledge might enable therapists to be trained more rapidly and allow for greater precision of measurement in the processes that bring about change. In other words, such knowledge might lead to greater efficacy and quality control in psychotherapy.

Recapping thus far; since, as Gladstein (1974) points out: nonverbal behavior can now be "reliably classified" in therapy; that such behaviors are related to therapeutic "changes and emotional states"; that methods exist to measure them in therapy; and that "clinical opinion and data indicate" that the therapist "must utilize nonverbal communication with his client/patient" (pp. 38-40), research in this heretofore neglected area of psychotherapy (from nonverbal behavioral field as well as from the allied field of interpersonal communication) may help shed light on possible interactional change processes operating within the therapeutic relationship.

THE THERAPEUTIC VERSUS INTERPERSONAL RELATIONSHIP

If, as some theorists believe, what is therapeutic in the psychotherapy relationship is the same as that which is growth-enhancing in normal healthy human relationships (Rice, 1974, p. 315), then, according to Vaughn and Burgoon (1976), the logical conclusion seems to be that warm human relationships, in themselves, may constitute the sole therapeutic ingredient. Carrying this line of reasoning further, they maintain, it might also follow that "untrained, unskilled persons who are naturally warm, empathic, and nonjudgmental" (p. 264) might just as easily become therapist substitutes. However, that the therapeutic community does not seriously entertain such a possibility, according to Vaughn and Burgoon, is "testimony to the fact" that more is involved in psychotherapy "than is being acknowledged" (p. 264).

From a psychotherapeutic standpoint, a similar view is expressed in Rogers (1961): "It seems to me that you could have this feeling of loving humanity, loving people, and at the same time go on contributing to the factors that make people neurotic, make them ill" (p. 83). This perspective appears to correspond to Yalom's (1975) position as well. As he observes, "When, in individual therapy, we say that 'it is the relationship that heals,' we do not mean that love or loving acceptance is enough; we mean that an ideal therapist-patient relationship creates conditions in which the necessary self-disclosure, intra- and interpersonal testing and exploration may unfold" (p. 47). Extending this line of reasoning further, while acknowledging that

affective components of the therapeutic relationship have been cor-
related to successful outcome, Avila, Combs, and Purkey (1977)
nevertheless contend that successful therapy may more specifically
involve, "a concentration and crystallization of the best we know
about human relationships" (p. 21). Or, as Orlinsky and Howard
(1978) put it: "Psychotherapy at its best provides a 'pure culture' of
help—less admixed with the helper's own needs, more intense,
more extensive, more penetrating—but may not be basically different from the help that can be found in less specialized 'caring'
relationships" (p. 317).

Thus far, however, as was previously noted, the search for these
"better features" of the therapeutic relationship has mostly centered
around intrapsychic phenomena. This further appears to have
occurred despite the fact that humanists, such as Avila, Combs, and
Purkey (1977), for example, regard behavior as "the external expression of internal perceptual states" (p. 68) (a viewpoint similar to
that of Clevenger and Mathews [1971, p. 103]) from the field of
interpersonal communication). Nevertheless, the question remains:
Which pertinent nonverbal responses to internal therapist states to
"concentrate" and how to bring about their "crystallization"? Toward
this end, Orlinsky and Howard (1978) suggest that what is needed is
"a comprehensive list of input, process, and output factors that
makes sense and is subscribed to by most people in the field—no
matter what their theoretical predilections might be—so that their
efforts may become mutually intelligible and their results comparative and cumulative" (p. 319). The need for this sort of delineation
is further heightened by the studies of Truax and Carkhuff (1967);
Truax and Mitchell (1971); Lister (1970); Garfield and Bergin (1971);
Strupp (1973); and Bergin and Lambert (1978) which found that
some therapists, irrespective of theoretical orientation, are helpful to
the client while others may have growth-inhibiting effects.

Supporting this need for delineation, from the field of interpersonal communication, Vaughn and Burgoon (1976) observe: "Since
it is virtually axiomatic to members of the helping professions that
the unique relationship between a particular client and therapist is
the most important factor in treatment (Combs, Richards, and Richards, 1971, p. 5), one might reasonably ask why more has not been
done, and sooner, to determine what is at work in successful thera-

peutic relationships. What kinds of communication transactions bene-fit clients and what kinds further impair their functioning" (p. 264). While some in psychotherapy may have been reluctant to research the therapeutic relationship (Bordin, 1974, p. 2), others in interpersonal communication maintain it is possible and, in their view, would require an analysis of the "patterns of social interchange" (Danziger, 1976, p. 108) and the effects of these interpersonal transactions upon the client. That psychotherapy is basically an interindividual process seems, in Danziger's view, to be relatively obvious. However, he believes it may need reemphasizing, considering that most theorizing in this area tends to focus on intraindividual states and events. This intrapsychic theorizing, he contends, may take the form of analyzing the psychodynamics of the client or the personality characteristics of effective therapists. However, in either case, he says, "the actual ex-changes that occur between therapist and patient or between counselor and client are lost from view" (p. 117).

This criticism of psychotherapy research, as previously noted, has been levelled from within psychotherapy as well. According to Bordin (1974), the difficulty is that "any designation of treatment (e.g., client-centered, psychoanalytic, behavioral) selects for observa-tion only a relatively limited aspect of the behavior of the therapist during the treatment process, often as expressed in the content of his [verbal] communications with his patient." However, he adds, "there are also facial expressions, gestures, other bodily movements, and body positions, as well as paralinguistic cues, which may turn out to be the important events" (p. 51). It is therefore likely, as long as these nonverbal patterns of interpersonal communication in psychotherapy remain "unspecified" (Watzlawick and Beavin, 1977, pp. 58-59), that therapists will continue to employ them nonconsciously and indiscrim-inately, failing to capitalize upon behaviors which might be growth-enhancing while employing others that may be growth-inhibiting.

FACILITATIVE VERSUS GROWTH-INHIBITING BEHAVIORS

Maslow's (1965) recognition of the potential of human communica-tion to have either a therapeutic or pathogenic influence is supported by the therapist effectiveness work of Vandenbos and Karon (1971) which studied therapists who had either pathogenic or benign effects upon clients. Additionally, Maslow's (1976) classification of the Taoistic therapies, i.e., those employing the therapeutic relationship, as "non-interfering" (p. 91), may have been based on the premise that communication in these therapies is believed to be among the least growth-inhibiting of human relationships. This characteristic may also have influenced Prochaska's (1979) observation that humanists may stress sensitivity to, in his words, "do the least damage to another's experience as possible" (p. 88). Or as Rossi (1993) puts it, "both therapist and patient simply need to get out of the way of the emergent patterns of healing."

But how, Rossi (1993) asks, is this accomplished? How does the therapist learn to facilitate, but not get in the way of the patient's own "patterns of healing"? It is an art, he replies, one "that requires careful observation, sensitivity, skill, humility, and restraint by the therapist" (p. 99). From a psychoanalytic perspective, Freud may have also recognized certain therapist behaviors to have an interfering effect upon the flow of communication between client and therapist. According to Jaffe (1978), for example, Freud's therapeutic approach required the patient to recline on a couch and to verbalize, continuously and without "censorship," all thoughts "that come to mind" (p. 56). To facilitate this process of "free association," Freud sat behind the patient, out of view, and listened passively and non-directively, refraining from vocal response for the duration of the fifty-minute session. Within Freud's procedure, Jaffe maintains, the "violation of social expectancies" inherent in the technique included continuous disclosure by the patient, who was "unable to see the doctor's facial expression or gestures," and an "enforced inhibition of the doctor's customary verbal response" (pp. 56-57). Such a procedure might therefore imply a recognition, on Freud's part, of possible interfering effects of both therapist verbal and nonverbal behavior.

Similarly, Danziger (1976) maintains that one of Freud's primary reasons for sitting behind the patient and out of his view may have been so that the patient's interpersonal presentations might be "much less subject to censorship that has its origins in the momentary reactions of the analyst" (p. 106) (a function possibly similar to "unconditional positive regard," the nonjudgmental client-centered attitude). The problem with Freud's lack of face-to-face interaction, however, is that while it may have controlled for possible inhibiting effects of therapist nonverbal behavior, it may also, as the next chapter indicates, have sacrificed other therapist behaviors possibly serving to enhance the therapeutic process.

That such "uncontrolled" nonverbal behaviors, in relation to facial expression, for example, are apparently learned, nonconscious, and established mainly by convention, was revealed by nonverbal communication researchers, Ekman and Friesen (1975). They maintain that normal or everyday face-to-face behavior has developed, not necessarily for effective communication reasons, but in accordance with social norms of "politeness" and "intimacy" (p. 16). They therefore conclude that if we want to know how a person feels (as in psychotherapy), it may often be necessary to "counteract habits" (p. 16) we have learned and "unconsciously follow." Otherwise, they say, conventional face-to-face behavior may lead us to "ignore and miss many facial expressions of emotion" (p. 16).

From a psychotherapeutic perspective, Efran, Lukens, and Lukens (1990) similarly contend that one of the values of therapy, as communication, is that "some of the ordinary 'club' rules can be temporarily suspended." Therapy, they say, is an opportunity "to be pried loose from the constraints imposed by local ordinances" (p. 187). Supporting this view, as well, is the work of Carkhuff (1977), who contends that just as we may have been conditioned not to listen or hear, so must we "train ourselves to actively listen or hear" (p. 56). Bandler and Grinder (1979) concur, suggesting that therapists need to pay closer attention to their own experience to notice, what they term, "a certain dimension of sensory experience" that, culturally, we may have been "trained not to notice" (pp. 26-27).

From a sociobiological perspective, some in the therapeutic field suggest that the possible existence of "genetic selfishness" may require specific teaching to, in their words, "control some of the selfishness to be expected in interpersonal relations" (Lang and West, 1980, p. 173). Such training might therefore presumably counteract any possible genetic predisposition toward selfish, and thus, growth-inhibiting behavior. The views of Carkhuff and Berenson (1977) similarly suggest that client-centered therapists, for example, may advocate "nondirectiveness" in therapy as a possible means of protecting the client from the therapist who, they say, "knows how destructive he or she really is" (p. 72). And Rogers (1977), himself, maintains in this regard that psychotherapy may soon be able "to move ahead and identify empirically those elements that promote dissociation" in human relationships or that "bifurcate" the client's "actualizing tendency" (p. 249).

SUMMARY AND CONCLUSION

In summary, psychotherapy's quest for a higher-order theory, eclectics and integrationists believe, may be enhanced through integrating knowledge from the allied fields of information processing, nonverbal behavior, and interpersonal communication. To support this claim, comparative outcome studies reporting few differences among therapies seem to reinforce studies reporting therapist differences to account for eight times as much variance as treatment differences. This research therefore tends to argue in favor of common or universal factors, related to therapist behavior, cutting across therapies. Moreover, these findings, coupled with the fact that past gross outcome studies generally reported no observations or recordings of what the therapist actually did, likely account for the current lack of scientific grounding in the field.

With respect to therapeutic change processes occurring *within* clients, Stanley Strong, Laura North Rice, David Wexler and others suggest that this search be conducted within the allied area of information processing—once a theory is formulated to guide therapists in fostering such information processing within clients. This higher-order theory, as previously noted, further may derive from knowledge accumulated in the allied areas of nonverbal behavior, interpersonal communication, and neurology. This consolidation of knowledge should further accrue since nonverbal and interactional therapist behaviors, currently classified as "nonspecific," appear to underlie relatively large treatment effects related to "attention" and/or "placebo" factors.

The need for such an integrated theory is heightened since, consistent with the extreme humanistic view that "the relationship *is* the therapy," treatment effects in psychotherapy still appear to be attributed to the therapeutic relationship, itself, or to psychotherapy in general. Nevertheless, the potential for both growth and growth-inhibiting nonverbal behavior in interpersonal relations and in psychotherapy has been acknowledged. Whatever its origin, however, the point raised by such research is that in psychotherapy, where interpersonal communication within the therapeutic relationship appears to be of central importance, normal or nonconscious nonverbal therapist behavior may be inadequate to effect maximum therapeutic change and, in some respects, could be growth-inhibiting.

In conclusion, the review of research in nonverbal behavior which follows in subsequent chapters may help clarify which therapist behaviors could be growth-inhibiting, and why, and which ones may promote therapeutic growth. In so doing, this book explores external therapist "stimuli," or behaviors, intervening between therapist attitudes and client change thus possibly serving as interactional processes facilitating cognitive and/or psychobiological change processes within the client. The aim of such an endeavor would be to specify the therapist's procedure, and the client's therapeutic response, in more operational terms as a precondition to marshalling scientific agreement.

Chapter 4

Face-to-Face Interaction: The Behavioral, Biological, and Cognitive Relevance of Dominant Eye Contact in Psychotherapy

A principal dilemma faced by practitioners of psychotherapy is that it has been defined so broadly as to become virtually meaningless. In extending the boundaries of practice, we have lost sight of some basic therapeutic principles.

—Stephen T. DeBerry, 1990

Rational authority, derived from sustained critical reflection on verified observations, is the standard of modern culture, and science is the supreme embodiment of rational authority in the cognitive domain (as law is in the political domain), the ultimate warrant for all secular knowledge and technique.

—David Orlinsky, 1994

RAMPANT EMPIRICISM without a firm grounding in theoretical structures will result in multiple research projects with fragmented yield and low efficiency. Theoretical digressions without grounding in research data will result in arid philosophizing of little practical benefit to the treatment of patients. There is, obviously, a need for the integration of research and clinical practice. The nature of this integration is seldom carefully articulated.

—Otto Kernberg and John Clarkin, 1994

The face-to-face context of the therapeutic relationship is probably its most universal characteristic. Looking at someone's face, according to nonverbal communication researchers Ekman and Friesen (1975), is intimate. You take such liberty, they say, only if the other person gives it to you by being "a public performer, or if your social role bestows it upon you . . . or if you avowedly seek to share intimacy, looking and inviting the look of the other person" (p. 16). On the other hand, not looking at another person's face, in addition to being polite and not wanting to embarrass or be embarrassed, Ekman and Friesen maintain, is often motivated by not wanting to be burdened with the knowledge, or not feeling obligated, "to do something about how the person feels" (p. 16).

Since the opposite is true of the social role of the psychotherapist, it would therefore seem reasonable to assume that looking at the client's face should conversely signal a desire to learn more about how the client "feels"—or about his or her personal concerns—seemingly a prerequisite to activating change processes within the client. Humanists Truax and Mitchell (1971) expand upon the psychotherapeutic function of looking at, or focusing upon, the client:

> Intense focusing on the other person, of course, is central to the perceptive aspect of deep empathic understanding, since it allows us to note subtle nonverbal communications—the minute facial, postural, and gestural clues that often contradict or multiply the meaning of another person's verbal communications. This intense focusing on the other person also tends to ensure that errors in either our own perception or communication of understanding will be quickly recognized. We will be able to sense from his often subtle responses when our communications do not fit exactly and, sometimes in midsentence, we can shift to correct for errors of language or content. In short, our intense focus on the other person makes possible the moment-to-moment contact necessary for accurate empathic understanding. (p. 317)

A comprehensive overview of the function and contextual meaning of looking at another, from an interpersonal communication perspective, is also provided by Danziger (1976):

Perhaps the most useful interpretation of the human look directed at another is to regard it as a form of address. To look at another is to address him, to take him into account. The response to this address will depend on the social identity of both the source of the address and the addressee. It will also depend upon the verbal and nonverbal content of the message that is sent to the addressee. Looking at the other may be thought of as another way of calling him. It informs him that he is at the focus of the looker's attention. The person being looked at will interpret this information in the light of other aspects of the relationship. If the source of the look is a stranger, it will be interpreted as an invitation to assume a relationship, an invitation that may cause interest, embarrassment or revulsion, depending on the circumstances. At other times, the look may have the quality of a confrontation that may be accepted by attempting to outstare the other, or rejected, by looking away. But the look of the other may also indicate his interest in oneself or one's actions and, if this interest is mutual, a high level of eye contact may result. The person who looks will generally communicate the purpose of the address through other channels, by his posture, gestures, statements, and so on, and the social setting will convey further information about the way the address is to be interpreted. (p. 66)

Within this face-to-face interaction, as Danziger (1976) indicates, eye contact may be of particular significance to psychotherapy. In addressing another person by means of gaze, he says, the sender—or in this case, the therapist—is able to convey messages whose effects, depending upon the social context, may be regulatory in terms of "coordinating the behavior of two participants in a joint activity such as a conversation" (p. 69). This regulatory effect may also involve the creation of what he terms, the "stable features" of the relationship between the interactants, especially their level of intimacy. The structuring of the relationship in terms of these features, he says, "involves a pattern of reciprocity in the gaze direction of the interactants." Where such reciprocity is not achieved, he contends, the relationship is "likely to prove unstable and to be marked by poor coordination of activities and by conflict over levels of intimacy . . ." (p. 69).

These findings also seem to be supported by others in the field of interpersonal communication, Ellsworth and Ludwig (1972), for example, who regard visual behavior as "one of the major regulators of the flow of conversation" and of "the sequencing and pacing of speech" (p. 376). In addition, Exline and Winters (1965) maintain that one learns from the behavior of the other's eyes "something of the other's desire, willingness, or ability to relate emotionally to another" (p. 320). Similarly, from the field of nonverbal behavior, Argyle and Cook (1976) conclude that mutual gaze appears to have a special significance—being experienced as "a special kind of intimacy, mutual access, and a meeting of minds" (p. 170). And the work of Rosenhan (1979), which concludes that "eye contact and verbal contact reflect concern and individuation; their absence, avoidance, and depersonalization" (p. 231), also seems to support these findings.

Conversely, with respect to the effect that an absence of eye contact can have upon the therapeutic relationship, Siegel and Sell (1978) report that one of the characteristics of a *poor* therapist is infrequency of eye contact. Similarly, Gelso (1979) found in his study that "nonexpert" therapists maintained eye contact "during less than 25% of the interaction" (p. 14). The work of Kendon and Cook (1969) also found that subjects preferred others who gave long glances and evaluated less favorably those who looked frequently but in short glances. The study of Di Francesco (1977) further appears to support these findings by concluding that maintained or prolonged eye contact is instrumental in the conveyance of positive affect to the client and that a therapist maintaining eye contact, while delivering a message of empathy, was perceived as more congruent than when limited eye contact was employed.

In view of such findings, therefore, and because eye contact is a common or universal factor in psychotherapy, the rest of this chapter will explore its possible relevance and role as an interactional stimulus in facilitating cognitive and/or psychobiological change processes within the client.*

---

*Some of the information contained in the rest of this chapter, and parts of Chapters 3, 5, and 7, are abstracted from my 1989 book, *A Behavioral and Biological Approach to Counseling and Psychotherapy: The Dominant Eye Phenomenon* (New York: Carlton Press), which was based on a doctoral dissertation proposal.

EYE CONTACT RESEARCH
IN PSYCHOTHERAPY

Although it is generally recognized that communication is a "total organismic process" (Birdwhistell, 1970) and that specific nonverbal cues usually derive their meaning from the situation or context in which they occur, often in combination with other nonverbal or verbal cues, some researchers nonetheless believe that there is justification for examining "isolated variables" (Cegala, Soluvitz, and Alexander 1979, p. 99). Eye behavior, for example, Cegala, Soluvitz, and Alexander point out, seems to be "unique" among nonverbal variables. Unlike other nonverbal behaviors, they contend, eye behavior is used for both decoding (receiving) and encoding (sending) information and may further occur during speaking or listening. The complexity of this behavior, they maintain, has provided researchers in the past with a rationale for studying such specific behaviors, provided other situational variables are described and "reasonably controlled" (p. 99).

With respect to the physiology underlying eye behavior, Long (1992) maintains that the visual system is "awesomely complex" (p. 36). As a result, Kosslyn and Koenig (1992) caution that it is easy to become overwhelmed with the wealth of research on the neural bases of vision. Nevertheless, they say, "Fortunately, once one has a particular problem in hand, and is actively looking for relevant information, this literature falls into place" (p. 53). Much of what is known about the neural systems underlying vision comes from work with monkeys. However, because this type of primate's visual abilities are similar to humans, and the neuroanatomy of their visual systems similar as well, Kosslyn and Koenig therefore maintain that it is "relatively safe to extrapolate from them to humans" (p. 53).

While some research has already been conducted on eye behavior in psychotherapy and in the field of interpersonal communication, previous researchers have nevertheless defined eye contact globally as involving, for example: looking into the "line of regard" (Lambert and Lambert, 1964); engaging in "mutual glances" of eyes (Exline and Winters, 1965); or maintaining "mutual gaze" (Argyle and Cook, 1976). Eye contact in this book, on the other hand, will refer more specifically to the therapist contacting the *motorically dominant eye* of the client (about which more will be said in a later section pertaining to eye dominance).

An Overview of Eye Contact Research

According to Maloney (1976), the "power coming from the eye" (p. viii) to project either good or evil through eye contact is a long-held folk belief. This anthropological belief, he says, arises in part from "the notion that each person has an inner energizing force which interacts with the world about him, so that the psychic power of the mind can be projected" (p. viii). Similarly, Rossi (1993) maintains that throughout human history and in most cultures and times, there have always been ritualistic practices where the medicine person or spiritual authority achieved healing effects by "a glance (the healing or evil eye)" which succeeded in activating "state-dependent expectations of healing" (p. 207). That this phenomenon does not appear to be superstition that can be dismissed with jokes, according to Maloney (1976), is further evidenced by the fact that the belief is reportedly diffused "over half the world" (pp. xv-xvii). In Maloney's view, therefore, for it to be so widespread, there "must be reasons" (p. xvi).

With respect to possible "reasons," research in interpersonal communication reported by Ellsworth and Ludwig (1972) found observed physiological effects of this variable which they describe as follows:

> Kleinke and Pohlen (1971) found that subjects paired with a steadily-gazing confederate had significantly higher heart rates than subjects paired with a confederate who averted his gaze. Similarly, Nichols and Champness (1971) reported G.S.R. increases for direct eye contact. In this case, the emotional arousal may be taken as a basic element which may produce or interact with more cognitive elements. In some of our own current research, we have found these to be key studies in linking research on visual behavior with theories of emotional attribution in order to explore the attribution process in social interaction. (p. 389)

Similarly, physiological effects of eye contact, in terms of decreased EEG, were found by Gale et al. (1972)—research which again may signal the need for greater scrutiny of this variable in psychotherapy.

Adding to this visual knowledge, Kosslyn and Koenig (1992) point out that a study by Perrett and colleagues (1985) identified specific cells in the brain (the inferior temporal lobe) which respond "to eyes per se" (p. 89). Physiological evidence arguing for closer investigation of eye contact in psychotherapy is also offered by Rossi (1993) who contends that the relationship between light (daylight and/or artificial light) and endogenous depression, for example, may be attributable to the "separate neural channels linking the retina of each eye directly to the suprachiasmatic nuclei in the hypothalamus (Bloom, Lazerson, and Hofstadter, 1985)." These suprachiasmatic nuclei in the brain, Rossi further points out, "act as pacemakers for the entire endocrine system" (p. 205).

As a sociological phenomenon, eye contact has further been described by Exline and Fehr (1978) as a nonverbal behavior whose "basic designatum" is that of "attention" toward the "focal point of the look" (p. 132). They elaborate:

> A number of investigators explicitly recognize the linkage between eye behavior and attention. Hore (1970) compared Ss with respect to "visual attention," Hersen et al. (1973) spoke of spouses "attending to" one another, and Williams (1974) compared schizophrenic patients, nonschizophrenic patients, and normals as to their "selective attention." . . . In each of the above cited studies, the investigators equated eye contact with attention. (p. 133)

And since, as previously mentioned, nonspecific behaviors related to "attention" or interest in the client may be associated with therapeutic change, eye contact might therefore warrant further investigation.

With respect to research of the therapeutic relationship in particular, the rationale for selecting eye contact as a relevant variable is supported by evidence in the study of "gaze" (Argyle and Cook, 1976) which has been accumulating suggesting a possible relationship between mutual gaze and the facilitative attitudes. Argyle and Cook (1976) suggest, for example, that eye contact can serve as an "affiliative signal" (p. 4) in human interaction. The study of Exline and Winters (1965), which found that eye contact can indicate a willingness to share affective involvement with another person and the work of Mehrabian (1972), whose data show that people look more at those they like, seem to support this contention. For example, Exline and Winters (1965) allowed both male subjects and female subjects to interact with two same-sex confederates. After asking subjects to disclose which of the two confederates they liked more, subjects were allowed to speak to both together. Results indicate that both males and females exhibited a significant increase in mutual gaze with the liked confederate as compared to mutual glances shared with the less liked confederate.

However, Exline and Fehr (1978) maintain that the "attentive look alone" does not specify the nature of the involvement, and that additional information about the context (other verbal and nonverbal cues) is generally required to determine the "affective tenor" of the interaction. Nevertheless, they say, the absence of a high degree of visual attention often is taken as evidence of "a disinterest in, or unwillingness, to become involved with another" (p. 133). These findings would further appear to parallel those of Ellsworth and Ludwig (1972) who conclude that while eye contact does not always involve interpersonal *attraction*, interpersonal *involvement*, on the other hand, "is always involved" (p. 397). As mentioned earlier, since interpersonal involvement with the client in the therapeutic relationship is considered basic to therapeutic change, outcome research of eye contact in psychotherapy would therefore seem justified.

With respect to existing process research of eye contact in psychotherapy, Tepper and Haase (1978) report, from a study of verbal and nonverbal communication of facilitative conditions (therapeutic attitudes), that nonverbal cues accounted for significantly greater message variance than did verbal messages. In addition, eye contact proved to be a significant contributor to final judgments of facilitative conditions by independent client and therapist observers viewing videotaped therapy sessions of therapists portraying different combinations of nonverbal behavior. In a similar study, Tipton and Rhymer (1978) studied the effects of varying levels of therapist eye contact on client-focused and problem-focused therapy styles. Judgments by independent observers of therapist effectiveness on three dimensions—genuineness, competence, and self-confidence—showed progressively higher ratings for both therapy approaches on all dimensions from a low, medium, to high gaze condition. Again, with respect to operationalizing the therapeutic process, the results of these studies may argue in favor of prospective outcome study of eye contact in psychotherapy.

Along similar lines of reasoning, from the field of interpersonal communication, Kendon (1967) suggests that direction of gaze may play a "crucial role" (p. 23) in the initiation and maintenance of social encounters. In citing the sociological work of Goffman (1964), Kendon observes that where an individual looks may be an indicator of his social accessibility. He further explains: "This is because whether or not a person is willing to have his eye 'caught', whether or not, that is, he is willing to look back into the eyes of someone who is already looking at him, is one of the principal signals by which people indicate to each other their willingness to begin an encounter." In this respect, he adds, "It seems that it is through the mutually held gaze that two people commonly establish their 'openness' to one another's communications" (p. 23). In other words, as Knapp (1978) reports from his nonverbal behavioral research, eye contact signals that the "communication channels are open and an obligation to communicate exists" (p. 212) while simultaneously signifying "a free flow of communication and mutual openness" (p. 307). Finally, the study of Hess (1975a), which concludes that during eye contact, "pupil size serves as a signal between individuals" (p. 110), usually at a nonconscious level in interpersonal interaction, again seems to argue for greater scrutiny of this variable in psychotherapy.

From a sociological perspective, Goffman (1964) also maintains that when two or more people interact, they position themselves in an "eye-to-eye ecological huddle" (p. 95) by which the participants maximize the monitorings of each other's perceivings. He also suggests that it may be through the maintenance of mutual gaze that the participants express their continued commitment to the social interaction. In quoting George Simmel, Goffman (1964) expands upon this phenomenon which appears to be nonconsciously and culturally imbedded in interpersonal interaction:

> Of the special sense organs, the eye has a uniquely sociological function. The union and interaction of individuals is based upon mutual glances. This is perhaps the most direct and purest reciprocity which exists anywhere. This highest psychic reaction, however, in which glances of eye to eye unite men, crystallizes into no objective structure; the unity which momentarily arises between two persons is present in the occasion and is

dissolved in the function. So tenacious and subtle is this union that it can only be maintained by the shortest and straightest line between the eyes, and the smallest deviation from it, the slightest glance aside, completely destroys the unique character of this union. (p. 93)

Consistent with these early observations, Long (1992) states that in the visual research which helped David Hubel win the 1981 Nobel Prize, Hubel and his colleagues discovered neurons in the retina to be "fussy" or selective of the stimuli to which they respond. In other words, Long says, individual retinal cells "fired only when a line of light was presented at a certain angle" (p. 35). In this regard, as well, as previously noted, Kosslyn and Koenig (1992) describe the results of an experiment by David Perrett (1985) and his colleagues that identified specific cells in the temporal lobe which, according to Kosslyn and Koenig, had a "remarkably specific taste in stimuli" (p. 81), responding only to heads in specific orientations or to eyes in specific positions or directions of gaze. Given their strategic location in the brain, and the fact that these cells are tuned for "particular vantage points," therefore lead these researchers to conclude that they may "pass information" (p. 81) to other parts of the brain.

In other words, if, as Kosslyn and Koenig (1992) maintain, these visual cells or "perceptual units" are "matched against" or connected to "stored memories in the pattern activation subsystem" (p. 81) of the brain, this neurological finding could therefore suggest that the eyes may function to stimulate information processing centers of the brain by promoting access to stored information and activating pattern recognition and/or correlative functions in the brain. This may also account for why human beings, in general, often nonconsciously tend to avert eye contact when attempting to conceal or avoid disclosing information. This biological finding may underlie, as well, the therapeutic effects reported by Shapiro (1995), recipient of the 1994 Distinguished Scientific Achievement Award in Psychology from the California Psychological Association for her work on eye movement desensitization and reprocessing (EMDR). This *client* eye-manipulation technique, reportedly able to promote *cognitive restructuring*, or the reprocessing and desensitizing of traumatic memories, has resulted in a reduction of anxiety, intrusive memories, flashbacks, and nightmares. One explanation for her technique, Shapiro (1995) further reports, is a possible "link between its effects and those of the rapid eye movement (REM) stage of sleep" whose effects, in turn, she states, may help "process information, including emotional, stress-related, and survival material" (p. 24).

Further supporting the possible therapeutic effects of eye contact in psychotherapy, from the field of interpersonal communication, is the work of Tomkins (1963) who concludes that "there is no greater intimacy than the interocular experience" (p. 180). This opinion is also echoed by Key (1975) who suggests that "eye contact is one of the closest possible relationships" (pp. 85-86). Eisenberg (1975) also contends that the better the eye contact, the better the listening. Avoidance of eye contact in interpersonal relations, she states, "seriously reduces the extent to which the other listens" (p. 142). This research, and that on the sociological and physiological effects of eye contact, may also support such common, related idioms as, "seeing eye-to-eye" and "being on the same wavelength" (Orlinsky and Howard, 1978, p. 317). The work of Sarles (1975), for example, suggests that human interaction may involve shared rhythms, that the heart or pulse rate may be susceptible to being shared, and that eye contact may be sufficient to initiate such shared rhythms. On checking pulses of people at rest, for example, Sarles found that their pulses "jumped together in a kind of momentary synchrony when they came into mutual eye contact" (p. 27).

The significance of these findings to psychotherapy might therefore lie in their possible relation to the attitudinal construct, *empathy*, described by Orlinsky and Howard (1978) as implying "a significant attunement or resonance of meanings between the patient's and therapist's messages" (p. 308)—a view seemingly paralleling that of Phillips and Metzger (1976) when they state, "Our real mirrors are indeed the eyes of others" (p. 121). In this regard, as well, the work of Spitz (1965) also suggests that the eyes may be the *stimulus for an innate releasing mechanism* in infants. Spitz found, for example, that during the first two months of life, the stimulus necessary to elicit smiling in infants was a pair of eyes. The study of Robson (1967) similarly suggests that early mutual gaze between mother and infant may act as a releaser of maternal responses, thus possibly strengthening attachment to the infant. In conclusion, such findings would appear to lend support to the visually based anthropological belief, or "power" (Maloney, 1976, p. viii), supposedly inherent in eye contact.

Recapping thus far, then: if eye contact is one of the principal signals by which people indicate to each other their willingness to begin an encounter; and if it is through their mutually held gaze that two people commonly establish their openness to one another's communications; and further if, as Argyle and Cook (1976) suggest, mutual gaze is one possible means by which we perceive "intersubjectivity" or "an awareness of the thoughts or intentions of the other" (p. 14); then further study of the effects of eye contact in psychotherapy would appear warranted in the delineation of therapist behaviors possibly serving to enhance therapeutic effectiveness.

THE SIGNIFICANCE OF EYE CONTACT IN THE THERAPEUTIC RELATIONSHIP

While the study of eye contact has not yet been systematically applied to therapy outcome, some therapists nevertheless appear to recognize its possible relevance. Humanist Carkhuff (1977), for example, makes reference to what he terms "eyeing" (p. 36). His use of eye contact, he states, is for the purpose of communicating the therapist's "full and undivided attention" during the initial stages of therapy which he calls "attending" (p. 36). In Carkhuff's words:

> Perhaps the key way of attending personally involves how we use our senses, particularly our eyes. We communicate attentiveness when we maintain eye contact with the helpee. The helpee is aware of our efforts to make contact with her psychologically through our efforts to make contact with her visually. (p. 36)

In addition, as previously stated, evidence suggesting the need for further exploration of this variable comes from eye contact studies which suggest parallels with the Rogerian intrapsychic constructs and which may therefore offer possible behavioral avenues for communicating these attitudes. For example, Argyle and Cook (1976) report that "people who look more are seen as more truthful and credible" (p. 91). The study of Exline and Eldridge (1967), which found that "people thought someone more likely to mean what he said if he looked at them" (p. 91), would similarly seem to support this finding. In this study, the authors asked subjects to rate the believability of a confederate and the confidence they had in the validity of the information contained in his statement. The results indicate that ratings of confidence in the confederate, or his believability, were significantly higher when he looked steadily at listening subjects as opposed to away from them. This study implies, as suggested in a later statement by Exline and Fehr (1978), that "the subject's attribution of different degrees of credibility and confidence to the confederate was based on the difference in the behavior of the confederate which implied the degree of his involvement with the judge—namely, the direction of his gaze" (p. 136). Within a therapeutic context, this might therefore suggest a possible means for communicating the therapist attitude, *genuineness* or *congruence*, through eye contact.

Supporting this hypothesis from the therapeutic field are the studies of Kaul and Schmidt (1971) and Roll, Schmidt, and Kaul (1972) which suggest, for example, that therapist style such as gesture and facial expression may be as influential on perceived trustworthiness as are verbal cues. The conclusion of Strong (1978) also suggests that "therapist behavior in the initial stages of therapy can affect clients' perception of therapist credibility" (p. 108). Similarly, the study of Tepper and Haase (1978) indicates that nonverbal cues, including eye contact, were significant "to the eventual judged level of empathy, respect, and genuineness" (p. 41).

In possible relation to the Rogerian construct, *unconditional positive regard*, the studies of Mehrabian (1968) and Efran (1968), which found that people look more at people of higher status, might suggest eye contact to be one possible variable, nonconsciously in play, facilitating the communication of unconditional self-worth toward the client. In other words, if a greater frequency of eye contact is directed toward people whom we consider to be of higher status or of considerable worth, eye contact may therefore be a possible behavioral gesture nonconsciously helping the therapist communicate his considering the client to be a person of considerable (or unconditional) self-worth. In this regard, the study of Exline, Ellyson, and Long (1975), which concluded that individuals who are looked at most see themselves, and are seen by others, as the most powerful members of the group also seems to support these findings. Moreover, that communicating such an attitude to the client may help effect change in self-attitudes and behavior, seems to be supported by social psychological studies employing the "attribution" (Strong, 1978, p. 112) method of research. Strong points out, for example, that the study of Miller, Brickman, and Bolen (1975), although not in the clinical area, nevertheless may lend support to the contention of Rogers (1961) that as therapists communicate self-worth to clients, they generally begin to perceive themselves in this way and tend to behave in accordance with this "revised view" (p. 113).

That some therapists appear to recognize the possible effects of nonverbal behavior in facilitating the communication of therapeutic attitudes, is also evidenced by the words of Strupp (1973):

> The importance of the therapist's attitude as communicated non-verbally or by minimal verbal cue, can hardly be over-estimated. The message to the patient is that of simple acceptance and worthwhileness as a human being, regardless of the symptoms and personality characteristics about which the patient and others (including the therapist) may have misgivings or regrets. In this way, the therapist helps the patient toward greater self-acceptance and self-esteem. (p. 38)

Similarly, Rogers (1975) appears to recognize the therapist's need to express him- or herself behaviorally when displaying facilitative attitudes. What it means to be "congruent" in a given instance, he says, "is to be aware of what is going on in your own experiencing at that moment, to be acceptant toward that experience, to be able to voice it if it's appropriate, and to express it in some behavioral way" (p. 20). Just what therapist behaviors or nonverbal transactions help communicate therapeutic attitudes, however, Rogers and Strupp do not say. In this respect, however, the study of Haase and Tepper (1972), which found verbal responses to be more empathic when eye contact was present, may suggest this variable to be one such behavior.

It might also follow, then, that if therapeutic behaviors *do* exist, their nonconscious, indiscriminate application might possibly be one factor contributing to variations in therapist effectiveness. As a possible explanation for such variations and as evidence supporting the hypothesis that some nonverbal therapist behaviors, eye contact, for example, may be being used indiscriminately, Argyle and Cook (1976, p. 47) report from the field of nonverbal behavior that in normal human interaction, people fixate a widely scattered series of points within the other's face. This finding, together with the work of Lord (1974) and Lord and Haith (1974), which suggests that people may react differently to actual eye contact, as opposed to face gaze—even when they cannot discriminate it "psychophysically" (Lord, 1974, p. 1116)—suggests that indiscriminate fixation by therapists could therefore account for some of the inconsistent effectiveness across therapists. When such fixation does occur, Argyle and Cook (1976) report that it does so for "relatively short glances" and for "limited proportions of time" (p. 171). By extrapolation, due to the "nonspecific" status of nonverbal behavior, this could also be the case in psychotherapy. (It is recognized, however, that other variables besides eye contact potentially account for additional variation in therapist effectiveness. Consequently, other such possible behaviors, supported by pertinent research in nonverbal behavior, are discussed in Chapter 7.)

The conclusions of Orlinsky and Howard (1978), in their review of outcome studies of therapist attitudes, also lend support to the hypothesis that therapist behaviors help communicate therapeutic attitudes. As they explain:

> The results are far too variable to support the hypothesis that warmth and empathy are necessary and sufficient conditions of good outcome. . . . if they do not by themselves guarantee a good outcome, their presence probably adds significantly to the mix of beneficial therapeutic ingredients, and almost surely does no harm. That these factors interact differentially with other aspects of therapist style is suggested by Mintz et al. (1971), who found that an "optimal empathic relationship" was positively related to outcome only when therapist directiveness was minimal. . . . (pp. 293-294)

Conversely, when therapist directiveness is "minimal," presumably *client* directiveness is maximized (thus possibly supporting the thesis of Chapter 5, "intensive experiential exploration," as the second major universal factor in psychotherapy).

Other indications that the study of eye contact may be warranted in psychotherapy comes from studies of so-called deviant behaviors. Research of behaviors sometimes associated with clients requiring therapy, i.e., people who are depressed, schizophrenic, lying, guilty, or embarrassed, has indicated an avoidance of eye contact associated with these behaviors (Argyle and Cook, 1976, p. 67). In this regard, Key (1975) maintains that avoiding eye contact, or looking away, contributes "to maintaining psychological distance" (p. 86). It might not seem illogical to suggest, therefore, that: if deviant behaviors are associated with an avoidance of eye contact; and if avoidance of eye contact fosters psychological distance; and, further, if psychological closeness or intimacy is associated with therapeutic change; then facilitating change of deviant behaviors might possibly involve, among other things, an increase in eye contact.

Supporting the use of visual phenomena in the remediation of emotional and psychological concerns is the work of Hess (1975b) who concludes from his studies of pupilometrics, for example, that the eye may possibly help provide access to the "innermost workings of the mind" (p. 3). Along similar physiological lines, Gregory (1977) reports that the neural system responsible for vision begins in the retinas of the eyes, which he describes as "outgrowths of the brain containing typical brain cells as well as specialized light sensitive detectors" (p. 44). The function of this physiological organization which may be of relevance to psychotherapy is the reported ability of the eye to process some of the data of perception, by itself, thus making it, as Gregory states, "an integral part of the brain" (p. 61).

While the physiological eye may be becoming demystified, Key (1975) points out that the "perceptual eye" (p. 87) has only begun to be scientifically explored. Moreover, as previously suggested, this perceptual eye may be of relevance to psychotherapy as well. With respect to therapist facilitative ability, for example, the affiliative properties of eye contact may possibly be of significance to the remedial work of Jourard (1971), who found that his subjects tended to vary the amount of self-disclosure to colleagues with their degree of liking for their colleagues. In other words: if eye contact is associated with interpersonal attraction, and if interpersonal attraction increases the amount of self-disclosure (Reece and Whitman, 1962), and if self-disclosure is a vehicle for reducing neurotic and psychotic tendencies (Jourard, 1971, p. v), it may therefore be possible to devise a therapy based upon such nonverbal therapist behaviors rather than solely upon the relatively less operational therapist attitudes.

As for safeguards related to preventing potential abuse of these proposed therapist behaviors outside therapy, Fisher's (1978, p. 140) explanation—that knowledge of the situation, or the context in which behavior occurs, enables one to detect discrepancies between outward behavior and internal states of functioning—should be reassuring. Similarly, the conclusions of Argyle and Cook (1976) in this regard suggest that an increase in gaze, outside the therapeutic context, would not have the same meaning and would therefore "not necessarily alter intimacy" (p. 66). These observations by Fisher, Argyle, and Cook might also hopefully help reduce fears of manipulation which in the past may have tended to discourage exploration of the therapeutic relationship. On the contrary, as the rest of this book suggests, the issue is not one of manipulation, but one of facilitation through noninterference.

Despite the apparent general reluctance to investigate the therapeutic relationship, it appears that support for such research nevertheless exists. The work of Strupp (1973), for example, was undertaken to help "sort out the various influences impinging on the interpersonal process called psychotherapy" (p. 23). The conclusions of Orlinsky and Howard (1978) appear similarly oriented. In their view, "the core problem of psychotherapy research is the determination of causal relations between sets of process and outcome variables." However, at this time, they state, "such causal attribution is supported mainly by circumstantial evidence, practical assumption, and intuition" (p. 319). The need for research of the therapeutic relationship, according to Strupp (1973, p. 28), arises from the lack of precise knowledge of what makes therapy effective. In this regard, he suggests that scientific search be directed at delineating "the variables that make a particular treatment effective or ineffective" (Strupp, 1978, p. 7).

Strupp (1973) further suggests the designated area where this search might begin. As a sensitive human being, he says, "the therapist is a highly complex scientific instrument, whose operational characteristics are still in great need of exploration and specification" (p. 29). Such a description of the therapist would also appear to parallel that of Schwartz (1978) who describes the therapist as a "psychobiological intervention system" (p. 78). The noteworthy significance of these definitions, in short, lies in the similarity of their orientations—toward greater behavioral and biological exploration of interactional change processes occurring within the therapeutic relationship.

THE SIGNIFICANCE OF EYE DOMINANCE IN PSYCHOTHERAPY

The rationale for including client eye dominance in the study of eye contact in psychotherapy (Leger, 1989) centers around recent studies of this variable indicating that while the right and left eyes of visually normal individuals may be similar in most respects, there is evidence to suggest that "the eyes do not function in an equivalent fashion" (Porac and Coren, 1979, p. 55). It has further been shown that, of members in any bilateral pair of structures in the body, be they hands, legs, or brain hemispheres, often one member is preferred over the other in behavioral coordinations, or seems to exhibit "physiological superiority" (Porac and Coren, 1976, p. 880). With respect to eyes, the superior bilateral member has been termed the *dominant eye* and has been described by Porac and Coren (1976) as follows:

> The dominant eye has often been defined as the eye whose input is favoured in behavioral coordinations in which only one eye can be used, the eye preferred when monocular views are discrepant, or the eye manifesting physiological or refractive superiority. Although its functional significance has not yet been ascertained, patterns of ocular dominance have been shown to be related to a large number of perceptual, performance, and clinical phenomena. (p. 880)

In addition to these functional differences between the right and left eyes, there appear to be physiological differences as well. Kovac and Horkovic (1970) cite the Vinar Test, for example, which, with the aid of ophthalmologic techniques, involves anatomical measurement of neural and connective tissue on the ocular background or retina of the eye. The eye in which the neural representation is better developed than the connective tissue, they report, "is considered to be dominant" (p. 7). Additionally, the physiological study of Siegel and Grinvald (1992) supports the existence of ocular dominance columns of neurons in the brain. Their study revealed, for example, that by alternately activating each eye of a monkey through showing the monkey movies, while it wore glasses with shutters that opened and closed independently over each eye, the firing of different neurons in different stripes of brain cells occurred in a manner consistent with ocular dominance. Ornstein (1993) expands upon this phenomenon's apparent developmental history:

> . . . It is only through continuous exercise, effort, and stimulation that the highly specialized areas of the cortex of the adult brain develop to their full extent. In the adult visual cortex, there are modules of cells called ocular dominance columns. The cells in one set of columns respond only to input from the nerves of the left eye; the cells in the other set respond only to input from the right eye. These columns alternate along part of the visual cortex. But at birth, there is no such pattern; all the neurons in that area of the brain respond equally to visual stimulation from either eye. This is not simply a matter of incomplete or immature development that the passage of time in the individual animal's life will automatically rectify. . . . If the visual cortex neurons receive no input, no dominance columns will emerge. . . .
>
> It happens this way: neurons that are active at the same time become joined. So neurons connected to the left eye, in firing together often, become strongly joined to each other, and they lose many of the connections to neurons from the right eye, which are less synchronized with them. (pp. 182-183)

Finally, neurological findings have been reported supporting the existence of "two completely separate visual worlds" (Sage, 1979, p. 51) residing in each hemisphere of the brain. Such biological visual differences are apparently a product of the phenomenon of lateral dominance (Coren, 1992, p. 169) which is believed to result from the unequal growth of brain hemispheres—one hemisphere eventually establishing dominance, thereafter determining handedness, eyedness, etc. The significance of this neurological and visual organization may further illuminate observations from the psychotherapeutic field. Mahoney (1991), for example, reports using a technique in which he encourages clients to use a mirror as a medium for initiating or continuing dialogues. In response to this technique, Mahoney states, "some individuals will experience strong reactions to eye contact with themselves, and many report a 'felt difference' depending on which of their eyes they focus upon" (p. 307). This strategy of opening and closing eyes (or of shifting focus from one eye to the other), he says, "can evoke significant reactions in some clients" (p. 308). In any event, in view of the apparent functional and anatomical differences between the right and left eyes, there is reason to believe that in psychotherapy research, dominance of one eye over the other could "obscure the effects of the variations in stimuli in which the researcher is interested" (Selltiz, Wrightsman, and Cook, 1976, p. 82).

In addition, research involving eye dominance and visual field suggests that when eye contact does occur, human beings generally contact the lateral counterpart of their own dominant eye, i.e., dominant right-eyed people contact the right eye of others with whom they interact, while dominant left-eyed individuals contact the left eye. It therefore follows that since eye contact is currently a nonspecific variable in psychotherapy, should client and therapist differ with respect to eye dominance, this difference could conceivably affect therapeutic outcome and thus possibly contribute to varying effectiveness among therapists (not to mention the possible effects such a difference in eye dominance could have on normal interpersonal communication). For this reason, and because contacting the dominant eye of the client has been a clinically effective, integral part of my therapeutic practice and interpersonal interaction for the past twenty-five years, it is explored in greater detail in this section.

Porac and Coren (1976) admit, however, that eye dominance has been marked with definitional as well as theoretical disagreement. This confusion may further be due to the human visual ability to identify objects in a wide range of circumstances. This ability, according to Kosslyn and Koenig (1992), apparently arises from "the joint action of a number of subsystems working in concert" (p. 54) within the brain. As Long (1992) points out, as much as "a third of the highest level of our brain, the cerebral cortex, is devoted to visual processing." Our eyes, he says, "funnel two million fibers into the optic nerve, while the auditory nerve, the conduit for hearing," by contrast, "carries a mere 30,000 fibers." Sight, Long therefore maintains, "mediates and validates the other senses" (p. 8).

With respect to its physiological characteristics, Kosslyn and Koenig (1992) describe the visual channel as follows:

> A remarkable fact about the retina is that it is actually part of the brain that has been pushed forward during development. The left side of each retina is an extension of the left side of the brain, and sends fibers only to the left cerebral hemisphere, and vice versa for the right. It is not that the left eye sends information only to the left part of the brain and the right eye sends information only to the right part of the brain. Rather, each eye sends information to both halves of the brain, but the left half of each eye sends information only to the left cerebral hemisphere and the right half of each eye sends information only to the right cerebral hemisphere. (p. 96)

EYE CONTACT AND INFORMATION PROCESSING

As for the possible relationship between eye contact and information processing, Kosslyn and Koenig (1992) report that researchers have located two distinct pathways in the brain for processing information: the "ventral system," which processes "object properties" such as shape and color, and the "dorsal system," which accommodates "spatial properties" such as location and size. These pathways were identified when researchers implanted electrodes in the brain cells of these two regions in monkeys and found that the cells fired to different kinds of stimuli. Cells in the ventral system fired most vigorously when specific shapes were shown to the animal, while cells in the dorsal system, which are sensitive to spatial properties, fired when objects were in different locations. The firing of these cells, according to Kosslyn and Koenig, was further influenced not only by the location of the object but also by the position of the eyes. In other words, some of these cells fired only when the animal saw "a face or hand," and some, they say, fired only for a face when the eyes were "pointed in a certain direction" (p. 56).

This physiological visual complexity appears to parallel Porac and Coren's (1976) reports of the functional complexity of eye dominance, as well, or the existence of types or "functions" of this phenomenon. They therefore recommend, when employing this variable, specifying its functional context. In this respect, the function which would appear to be most relevant to client-therapist eye contact is "motoric efficiency" (Porac and Coren, 1976, p. 882) which they define as the eye which "shows no deviation or phoria during binocular fixation" or the eye that "continues to maintain fixation" (p. 882) during binocular vision. Within a therapeutic context, this function would appear to be of significance since it would seem reasonable for the therapist to contact the eye which maintains "fusional control," during binocular vision, as opposed to the nondominant eye.

To measure this particular type of dominance, Kovac and Horkovic (1970) suggest, as a test of motoric efficiency, the *blink test*, wherein the dominant eye during binocular fixation is defined as either the eye which is "more difficult to wink or the eye that cannot be winked without some lowering of the contralateral eyelid" (Porac and Coren, 1976, p. 882). In this test, the client would be asked to alternately blink each eye and to estimate which one is easier to close. The eye more easily blinked without some lowering of the contralateral lid is considered to be the nondominant eye during binocular fixation. (It was also suggested to me by Arnold Lazarus, after our meeting in Anaheim in 1990, that handing the client a kaleidoscope, and noting the eye through which he or she sights, might also reveal this form of eye dominance.)

Supporting this method of determining eye dominance is the study of Palmer (1976), whose data suggest, in subjects only able to wink one eye, that the *nonwinking eye* was used as the dominant one in tests of monocular and binocular sighting. (The study of Coren and Porac [1978] further indicates that self-report methods are valid and reliable procedures for the assessment of various forms of lateral preference.) It should also be noted that in some individuals, eye dominance can often be visually recognized—with practice. As Kovac and Horkovic (1970) note, the dominant eye usually has a larger "size of the eye segment not covered by the eyelid"—the larger open segment of the eye presumably enabling "more visual information to be received"

(p. 8). In this respect, the dominant eye therefore also generally presents as the one with greater intensity and/or visual acuity.

The argument for including eye dominance in client-therapist eye contact may also be strengthened by the conclusions of Porac and Coren (1976). They state, for example, that in diploptic situations, when both eyes are open, " input from only one eye may be used." They further point out that during binocular fixation, the eyes nonconsciously adopt "a strategy of monocular viewing" (p. 881) with input from the nondominant eye giving way to input from the dominant one. Evidence also indicates that the dominant eye may only be "motorically superior" but that its movements, according to Porac and Coren, may provide "the primary information for the computation of visual direction" (p. 890). If so, then it may seem reasonable to suggest that a more effective form of eye contact may therefore involve contacting the dominant, as opposed to nondominant, eye. (This has also proven to be the case in my clinical practice.) Stated in the terminology of "folk" psychology, then: if the eye is supposedly the "window to the soul" or the "gateway to the mind" (Bakan, 1971, p. 64), the dominant eye may provide the clearer window or the more effective gateway. In any event, in view of the apparent functional and anatomical differences between dominant and nondominant eyes, specification of the particular client eye, contacted by the therapist, should provide an additional measure of control in prospective outcome research involving eye contact in psychotherapy.

In conclusion, that this sort of integration of biological phenomena with psychotherapy is consistent with rising interest in nonverbal behavior in therapy (Kiesler, 1979, p. 46), as well as present psychobiological trends in the field, is evidenced by the words of Schwartz (1978):

> We are presently witnessing a revolution in our thinking concerning the relationship between biology and behavior. This conceptual revolution has profound implications for methods, theories, practice, and even licensing of psychotherapy and behavior change procedures. . . . The psychobiology of psychotherapy and behavior change is one expression of the present scientific revolution attempting to integrate theories of

mind and brain, behavior and body (e.g., Schwartz and Shapiro, 1976; 1978).

Not surprisingly, basic knowledge linking the biological and
behavioral sciences is advancing at a more rapid rate than
the systematic application of this knowledge and consequent
techniques to psychotherapy and behavior change. (p. 64)

There therefore appears to be a need for greater systematic application of psychobiological, nonverbal, and interactional knowledge of
face-to-face behavior to psychotherapy. Moreover, as the empirical
evidence cited herein suggests (supported by my clinical practice),
dominant eye contact may be the most significant facilitative behavioral variable in face-to-face interaction ostensibly promoting access
to stored information and activating correlative functions in the
brain to reprocess this information.

Concluding this chapter, Lynch (1985) offers the following
account of his experience with eye contact as a therapeutic variable,
based upon his psychotherapeutic work with hypertensive clients:

At times I have found myself trembling when meeting the eyes
of a patient—looking at me, searching, hoping earnestly to discover for the first time the emotional meaning of his elevated
blood pressure, rapid heart rate, or freezing hands. At such
moments I have felt Schrodinger's reality—deeply felt it—for
surely there is far more to their eyes than optical sensors whose
only function is to detect light quanta. And I have trembled then
precisely because I have caught a glimpse of the infinite universe
behind those eyes and the reality of a universal Logos uniting us
in dialogue. And it is at such moments, in the quiet sharing of
reason and feelings in dialogue, that I have felt most alive and
human. (p. 310)

SUMMARY AND CONCLUSION

In summary, the face-to-face nature of the therapeutic relationship is probably its most universal characteristic. Within this context, possibly stemming from the widely held anthropological belief
or "power" supposedly inherent in eye contact, eye behavior presents as one of the most researched variables in the allied fields of

interpersonal communication, nonverbal behavior, and the neurological bases of vision. This research further suggests this variable's implication in the communication of the therapeutic attitudes—empathy, congruence, and unconditional positive regard—which tends to complement knowledge derived from sociological perspectives as well.

For example, studies on the neurological bases of vision suggest that the eyes may function to stimulate information processing centers of the brain by promoting access to stored information and activating pattern recognition and/or correlative functions (thus possibly underlying the therapeutic results reported by Shapiro [1995] through eye movement desensitization and reprocessing [EMDR]). These findings, coupled with the observed physiological and functional differences between the right and left eyes, termed eye dominance, may therefore support contacting the client's dominant eye as a means of promoting more effective access to stored information and stimulating pattern recognition and/or correlative functions.

In conclusion, these findings, in turn, may link scientifically with the second major universal characteristic of the therapeutic relationship—intensive experiential exploration—discussed in the next chapter.

Chapter 5

Intensive Experiential Exploration:
The Psychobiological Significance
of Client Verbalization
and Self-Disclosure in Psychotherapy

... The bond between therapist and patient is not of love—rather, we might say that love is not required—but of desire for shared discovery.

—Carl Goldberg, 1992

Is the hypothetical master story in the patient's head like a daydream, its specific content already fixed? Or is it merely an abstract schema that will generate many stories depending on how the conceptual "slots" are filled in? Is it not a story at all, but simply a (mysterious) disposition to respond to certain kinds of events in a certain way?

... Psychotherapy research offers very little in the way of answers to questions like these.

—Marshall Edelson, 1994

Empirical research in information processing and psychobiology, according to Toukmanian (1992), has enhanced the field of psychotherapy by introducing the possibility of studying therapeutic change from the point of view of "client's internal mental operations." This is a dimension, she says, which has received little attention, but which nevertheless requires greater emphasis in order to delineate the "mechanisms underlying client change" (p. 99). Currently, as Edelson (1994) explains:

The patient's mind is a "black box" into which we cannot look directly. This story in that black box to some extent determines what patients make out of what they perceive and how they then respond to it. There is no direct causal connection between incoming information and outgoing response. What is in the black box mediates the relation of perception and response.

. . . Patients are more or less unaware of the stories in the black box, which produce manifestations when triggered by information from their internal or external world. These manifestations are their responses to that information, including the inferences they make from it about their internal and external world and therefore their interpretation of its meaning or significance. Their response in one form or another constructs out of their experience, or realizes in some experience, more or less disguised transformations of the stories in the black box. (pp. 71-72)

Despite the apparent limited knowledge concerning the client's internal functioning (which parallels, by analogy, the limited knowledge of electricity, in physics, cited earlier), Mahoney (1990) maintains that client change processes are nevertheless routinely engaged in successful psychotherapy, and that the key activity in doing so, as well as in adapting and progressing in life in general, is exploration. The initiation of psychotherapy, he states, "is a clear expression of such exploratory activity." The client is ultimately best served, he adds, "by a therapist who encourages and facilitates general exploratory activities" (p. 165). Supporting this view, in his study on the helping and hindering processes in client-centered/experiential psychotherapy, Lietaer (1992) similarly concludes that both clients and therapists perceived "self-exploration and experiential insight" as the "salient ingredients of their therapy sessions" (p. 147). In this regard, the empirical work of humanists Truax and Carkhuff (1965), as cited by Papouchis (1990), also supports the contention that the greater the degree of self-exploration, the greater "the potential for constructive personality change" (p. 159).

The particular significance of this apparent universal factor in psychotherapy is highlighted by Truax and Carkhuff (1967), who state that in addition to the three Rogerian attitudes cited earlier, "depth of self-exploration is viewed as a fourth major ingredient of effective therapeutic encounters" (p. 3). Mahoney (1991) espouses a similar view, stating that there is strong agreement across theoretical lines that "optimal psychotherapy involves encouragement toward self-examination" (p. 16). Derlega et al. (1991, p. 11) also cite the study of Lansford (1986), which concludes that the client's ability to discuss concerns in the therapy relationship contributes to overall therapeutic outcome in psychoanalytic therapy.

From a constructivist point of view, Neimeyer (1990) similarly contends that therapy is therefore "more a *creative* than a *corrective*" (p. 161) experience. Rather than directly challenging the validity of the client's beliefs, Neimeyer suggests that the therapist help the client explore and invent new and more viable alternatives. Thus, he believes psychotherapy is "typically more invitational and exploratory than it is directive and disputational" (p. 161). The view of Gendlin (1962, 1970, 1974) appears to support this sort of client-centered self-exploration as well. For example, describing what appears to be an integrative and eclectic experiential method, Gendlin (1974) states:

The experiential method . . . is a way of using many of the different therapeutic approaches. It is a method of methods. It enables me to show just how client-centered therapy ought to be part of every therapist's way of working. It is a systematic way of using various vocabularies, theories, and procedures, among them client-centered therapy. . . . My rendition of client-centered therapy . . . is really a reformulation of it in experiential terms. (p. 211)

From the therapist's point of view, these perspectives seem to support that of Hill (1994) who suggests that the therapist must put "aside his or her own needs . . . in the service of the client's needs and growth for the time of the work" (p. 92). Derlega et al. (1991) agree and maintain that in therapy, the therapist may or may not give advice. However, they note that there is generally an emphasis on the client's participation in, and responsibility for, his or her "cure" and an understanding that "the client and therapist *together* will find the path to improvement" (p. 27). Further expanding upon this asymmetric characteristic of therapeutic interaction, Derlega et al. state:

Although personal relationships between adults are generally symmetrical, the therapy relationship is asymmetrical. In a symmetrical relationship, each partner is similar in terms of power in the relationship and resources that she or he can provide to the relationship. Thus, each is expected to participate in the relationship in similar ways, for example, by offering similar amounts and levels of intimacy of self-disclosure or amounts of social support. . . . In asymmetrical relationships, there is a clear difference in power and in resources provided by each partner in the relationship. (p. 2)

Rogers (1942) may have also recognized this need for *asymmetry* within the psychotherapeutic relationship, when he developed his "nondirective" therapy over fifty years ago (which subsequently evolved into client-centered and, more recently, person-centered therapy). At that time, he observed that unless he, as therapist, had a particular need to promote himself as the "expert" on the client, therapy would be better served by allowing the client direction in the process. Or, as Goldberg (1992) notes, by not presenting oneself as "all knowing and all powerful," the therapist gives "the power of transformation" to clients, permitting them to be changed "by their own chosen ordeal" (p. 74). These observations also parallel and illuminate the following nondirective, nonverbal, or client-centered encounters experienced by Maslow (1970), Garfield (1992), and Lazarus (1993b). First, Maslow's (1970) experience:

Sometimes therapeutic results occur without the therapist saying a word. In one instance, a college girl wanted advice about a personal problem. At the end of one hour, during which she talked and I said "not a single word," she had settled the problem to her own satisfaction, thanked me gratefully for my advice, and left. (p. 246)

Garfield (1992) describes a similar therapeutic occurrence:

A young man wanted to discuss a problem that involved his relationship with his girlfriend. When he came into the office he was acutely upset, and as he described his relationship with her, he began to talk very quickly and quite emotionally. My interactions were limited primarily to listening, nodding, and trying to be empathic. The few times I tried to offer some therapeutic wisdom to the client, he ignored me and continued with his emotional outpouring. As he described his difficulties, the solution to his problem, which he was unable to face earlier, became clear to him. He now saw clearly that his planned marriage was not a good decision. Although he had strong feelings of guilt about this, these seemed to be fully expressed in the session, and he ended with a great sigh of relief. Before I could offer another bit of therapeutic wisdom, he thanked me profusely and quickly departed. (p. 186)

And that of Lazarus (1993b), who describes his particular nonverbal or client-centered experience as follows:

Mr. West, a 42-year-old stockbroker, sought help with problems regarding work options, conflicts with his wife, and feelings of personal insecurity. Any active interventions on my part—e.g., attempting cognitive restructuring, suggesting a role-playing sequence, or venturing to provide homework assignments—met with a puzzled facial expression and less than enthusiastic cooperation. Even empathic reflection seemed to occasion a sense of impatience in Mr. West. It dawned on me that he wanted a good listener—period. Accordingly, I would hear his tales of woe, nod my head intermittently, and force myself to refrain from offering any observations, reflections, advice, or suggestions. I was intrigued when he would stress how helpful an earlier session had been, one in which I had said virtually nothing. "You really helped me put things in perspective. . . ." (p. 406)

Since in these three instances, verbal interventions by the therapists were at a minimum, therapeutic change might therefore have been attributed to client self-exploration facilitated mainly by the therapists' nonverbal behavior.

Indirect support for this hypothesis may also be found in comparative process studies which, Stiles, Shapiro, and Harper (1994) maintain, confirm that the therapist's verbal behaviors "differ sharply and systematically across theoretical orientations" while, at the same time, comparative outcome studies show "no differential efficacy" (p. 40).

This apparent lack of empirical therapeutic support for therapist verbal behavior may further be due to the fact that, as Efran, Lukens, and Lukens (1990) point out, "Evaluations by the listener, even sympathetic ones, get in the way of experiential reports." They signal what the listener "expects to hear," they note, and therefore "distort the process." What is required from the listener to facilitate client self-disclosure, Efran, Lukens, and Lukens maintain, is "relaxed attention—not sympathy or judgement" (p. 172).

THE SELF IN PSYCHOTHERAPY

While asymmetry within the therapeutic relationship (about which more will be said in Chapter 6) may be how the client's self-exploration is facilitated, the *what* of this exploratory process, according to Mahoney (1991), is the "self." In his words:

> As psychology and psychotherapy have entered the second century of their own identity development, some interesting insights have emerged. One of those insights is that *all psychotherapies are psychotherapies of the self.* They always have been, even when their theorists and practitioners have sometimes ignored or denied the importance of the self. By necessity, all psychological services are experienced uniquely by individual service seekers. Thus, psychotherapy has always been modulated through self systems. . . . (p. 235)

Furthermore, not only psychotherapists but others working primarily in the biological sphere appear to recognize the significance of the self. For example, Edelman (1992) describes the development of selfhood and its environmental contingencies as follows:

> Human individuals, created through a most improbable sequence of events and severely constrained by their history and morphology, can still indulge in extraordinary imaginative freedom. They are obviously of a different order than nonintentional objects. They are able to refer to the world in a variety of ways. They imagine plans, propose hopes for the future, and causally affect world events by choice. They are linked in many ways, accidental and otherwise, to their par-

ents, their society, and the past. They possess "selfhood," shored up by emotions and higher-order consciousness. And they are tragic, insofar as they can imagine their own extinction. (pp. 170-171)

The consequences of the omission of the self, or of the client's "experiential structures," in psychotherapy, is further highlighted in the cognitive-mediation approach of Martin (1992) (based upon the personal construct theory of George Kelly). As Martin explains:

> In most extant theories of, and approaches to, counseling and psychotherapy, the exact manner in which therapy is thought to lead to client growth and change is not specified in sufficient detail to remove vestigial shrouds of mysticism that have enveloped many popular (and professional) conceptualizations of therapy. By denying human [client] capacities for active agency (supported by individual knowledge and experiential structures developed through unique personal histories), many earlier "scientific" theories of therapeutic change left a frustrating gap between change as promoted through therapeutic interactions and change as maintained and perpetuated in the everyday lives of clients. (p. 129)

Furthermore, this "capacity for active agency" within the client may hold the key to bridging this "frustrating gap" in psychotherapeutic theory as discussed in Chapters 6 and 7.

Meaning and the Formation of Self

The question remains, however, how to bridge this "frustrating gap" in psychotherapeutic theory? Toward this objective, Harre and Gillett (1994) observe that understanding human agency requires an interpretation of the behavior of the other "according to some appreciation of the self-positioning of the subject within the complex structure of rules and practices within which that individual moves" (p. 20). In other words, the behavior of an individual is best understood through grasping "the meanings that are informing that person's activity" (p. 18). Furthermore, they contend, these meanings become discernible in the course of discourse wherein human beings constitute their *selves* as embodied moral units. That is, by using the indexical word *I*, Harre and Gillett state, we create our "moral individuality" (p. 29) for anyone we might address.

Despite the apparent "giveness" of this self-formation process, Edelman (1992) nevertheless points out that the self (and consequently the mind) have traditionally been omitted from the study of biology. What has been sacrificed in the process, he says, is "the notion of meaning" which he describes as "interactional." The environment, he contends, plays a role in determining a "speaker's words." Moreover, the unpredictability of dialogue during a dyadic encounter (or the fact that it is generally unpreconceived by either speaker prior to their discourse) may be influenced by what Edelman describes as an environment which is "open-ended." In such encounters, he says, the "actual body of the speaker plays an equally great role in determining meaning" (pp. 224-225). Or as Friedman (1992) puts it, we come to awareness of ourselves as selves not just through our individuality but "in our dialogue with other selves—in their response to us and in the way they call us into being." (p. 5).

The meanings or values which define the individual humanity of clients (which humanists believe to be sacrificed in reductionistic science) are further defined as "touchstones" of the "human image" by Friedman (1992):

> Real values, the values that are operative in our lives, are brought into being through our ever-renewed decision in response to the situations we meet. These values become touchstones of reality for us. We carry them forward not as abstract principles but as basic attitudes, as life-stances that we embody and reveal in ever new and unexpected ways. They remain with us, latent in the deepest levels of our being, ready to be evoked and given form by the situations that call us out. These basic attitudes are the images of the human that unite one moment of lived dialogue with another, for it is not abstract consistency of principles or ideals but faithfulness in responding to the present with the touchstones that live in us from the past that gives unity and integrity to our lives as persons. (p. 17)

In this respect, the "gap" caused by the omission of these "touchstones" or meanings, (and, consequently, the self of the client) in process-outcome research, may have been due to what Friedman

(1992) terms, the tendency of humanists to pursue self-realization as an end in itself rather than as a "by-product" of "genuine dialogue with others" (p. 17). (This topic is therefore addressed in greater detail in Chapter 6 concerning language.)

As for the nature of the self, itself, Combs, Richards, and Richards (1976) characterize it as a "stable organization" which resists change. However, this does not mean that once it is established no further change is possible. On the contrary, they say, "the phenomenal self is in a constant process of change throughout its existence, particularly as a consequence of what a person perceives about the reactions of others to himself" (p. 187). Indeed, as Rogers (1975) points out, psychotherapy research has shown that what probably changes most in individual therapy is "the person's concept of himself." As therapy progresses, he notes, the client "moves toward being a more confident self, more acceptant of himself; self-hatred decreases." As the client feels more genuinely confident of who he is and his capabilities, Rogers adds, he utilizes "his past, his conditioning, and the biological basis of his being in more constructive ways" (p. 76).

With respect to possible processes constructing and transforming the self, Toukmanian (1992) suggests that the mental activity which performs this critical integrative cognitive function is *perceiving*. (Her construct of the schematic structure may further parallel that of Friedman's (1992) touchstones described above.) Citing the work of U. Neisser, Toukmanian (1992) elaborates:

> Neisser (1976) contends . . . that perceiving is the most fundamental cognitive act and maintains that the constructive nature of mental activity is the direct function of *schemata*, the dynamic structures of cognition that develop progressively through people's continuous interactions with the environment. From this perspective, perception is seen as a constructive developmental process that, at any given moment in time, reflects the perceiver's cognitive capability to detect, integrate, and give meaning to information on the basis of his or her past transactions with the world. These transactions, according to Neisser (1976, p. 11),"do not merely inform the perceiver, they also transform him" and as such they are seen to be the perceiver's own creation or construction of his or her experience of "reality." (p. 78)

This personal "construction" of reality, forming the basis of self, further becomes the "lens" through which clients view and interact with the world.

When this lens becomes distorted or too far removed from reality, however, personal concerns may develop within and between individuals. This consequently leads Fisher (1990) to assert that alienation from self and others encompasses "the root of psychopathology" (p. 9), or what Rogers (1961) terms, neurosis or "incongruence." Facilitating the client's personal awareness of this discrepancy between self-constructs or meanings, and reality, Martin (1992) further maintains, is the function of psychotherapy. This is achieved, he contends, through a recognition of the client's "implicit theories" about a concern, or problem, and the ways in which the thoughts, behaviors and emotions associated with them interact with his or her "experience of the concern or problem" (p. 127). This he terms, "personal theory revision," upon which he elaborates:

> Personal theory revision begins with recognition of the inadequacies of current personal theories and associated patterns of thinking, feeling and acting in relation to one's goals. Personal theory revision then entails subsequent initiation of serious, personally motivated attempts to alter one's personal theories (experiential, mnemonic, and knowledge structures) to promote one's goals more adequately. (p. 127)

Moreover, how this "alteration" of personal theories or self-revision is likely achieved is the focus of the remainder of this book.

Self-Disclosure as a Universal Variable: Disclosing Clients to Themselves

Accomplishing this task of altering one's "personal theories," as previously stated, appears to involve, among other things, exploring the self through self-disclosure. Furthermore, since all major psychodynamic therapies involve dialogue about the self of the client, client verbalization or self-disclosure may be viewed as the second major universal variable (in addition to face-to-face interaction) to be discussed in detail in this book. The particular significance of this variable is noted by Jourard (1974) when he observes that humanistic psychology, itself, can be defined as an effort to "disclose man and his situation to 'himself,' to make him more aware by any and all means," what forces influence "his experience and hence his action" (p. 359).

Josephs (1990) expresses a similar psychoanalytic view in the following:

> For the patient, verbal self-disclosure is a crucial element of "the talking cure." Finding the right words to represent, evoke, and express the experiential self constitutes the integrative process through which the patient gains a sense of his own reality, wholeness, authenticity, and genuineness as a person. In addition to serving a communication function in the service of psychic intimacy, the patient's verbal self-disclosure serves as a vehicle of seeing the self in perspective in listening to one's own self-perceptions said out loud. The process of self-articulation in verbal self-disclosure serves to develop a better integrated as well as a more clearly defined sense of self. (p. 76)

For this reason, and because each act of self-disclosure in psychotherapy is, according to Josephs, "an act of self-creation" (p. 88), the therapist's theoretical perspective, he contends, is vital in determining the manner in which the client's "self-disclosure is registered and represented" (p. 85).

Josephs (1990) further notes that self-disclosure is always an "intersubjective" process since the self that the client conveys in therapy is rarely identical to the self that the therapist "receives, registers, and reflects back." This discrepancy is inevitable, he says, because "empathy, our tool for grasping the self of the other, is an imperfect instrument that can aim at approximation, but can never achieve absolute identity" (p. 88). However, while perfect empathy may not be necessary to achieve therapeutic change, client self-disclosure nevertheless appears to be and has been used to describe the degree to which individuals reveal information about their "thoughts, feelings, and experiences to another" (Derlega et al., 1991). It has further been defined by these same authors as *"any information exchange that refers to the self, including personal states, dispositions, events in the past, and plans for the future"* (p. 146). This definition is also similar to that of *therapeutic dialogue* described by Lynch (1985) as consisting of communication between individuals involving "the sharing of thoughts, physical sensations, ideas, ideals, hopes, and feelings." In sum, Lynch says, therapeutic dialogue involves the "sharing of any and all life experiences" (p 10).

While self-disclosure may lie "at the heart of psychotherapy, the talking cure" (Stricker, 1990), the essential secrets, Stricker says, are nevertheless not being withheld primarily from the therapist, but from the "self" (p. 277). The therapist, he maintains, is merely "a conduit, a way station who encourages and allows the patient to explore ideas, risk disclosures, and come to understand that these secrets are not destructive, can be tolerated by others, and perhaps even can be tolerated by the self." Therefore, Stricker states, the main self-disclosure sought in therapy is not primarily to, or for, the therapist, but to, or for, "the self" (p. 277).

In this sense, therefore, not only is client disclosure essential to successful therapy, Derlega et al. (1991) maintain, but deficits in the ability or opportunity to "disclose to others or receive confidences from them" (p. 129), they state, may contribute to the problems that led the person to seek therapy in the first place. In their words:

> Although some professionals propose that therapist self-disclosure is not appropriate (e.g., Greenson, 1967), client disclosure and self-expression seems absolutely necessary (e.g., Stiles, 1987). In fact, substantial research has focused on ways to foster client disclosure during therapy (e.g., McCarthy, 1979). There are various steps that a therapist can take to encourage client disclosure, including asking direct questions and reflecting the client's previous statements, thereby inviting more disclosure. Nonverbal behaviors such as leaning forward, making eye contact, nodding, and in general fully attending to what the client is saying are also considered facilitative of client expression of feelings and beliefs. (p. 181)

With respect to this exploratory characteristic of effective psychotherapy, achieved through extended periods of client self-disclosure, Wachtel and McKinney (1992) observe that Freud also appeared to recognize early in his practice that "singular flashes of insight" were unlikely to lead to permanent change and that something "more arduous and less dramatic was usually required" (a process generally referred to as working through in psychoanalysis). This observation has been generally confirmed in clinical practice, Wachtel and McKinney contend, so that "therapists reading or talking about working through feel they know precisely what is being referred to" (p. 339). In this regard, Papouchis (1990) offers the following description of the relevance of this phase of therapy involving client disclosure:

> Increased self-disclosure on the part of the adult patient has been seen by practitioners of psychoanalytic psychotherapy as a sign of therapeutic progress. The progressive self-exploration in which adult patients examine their motives, relationships with others, fears, and life choices, as well as their belief systems and values, has traditionally been viewed as a fundamental aspect of the process of increased engagement in psychotherapy. . . . Similarly, they have used the adult patients' ability to speak more openly about their emotional experiences, whether they are painful or humiliating, as a barometer of therapeutic progress and as a sign of a more trusting, viable therapeutic alliance. Thus, the adult patients' ability to become increasingly more self-disclosing, to reveal more intimate and important details of themselves to the therapist and significant others, has been a widely accepted tenet of psychotherapeutic work. (p. 159)

It is further through self-disclosing in this client-directed manner that the self is supposedly revised and reconstructed, especially if it is too far removed from reality and poses inter- as well as intraindividual conflict, neurosis, or incongruence. Sanford (1990) expands upon this form of client growth resulting from the change of self-attitudes in psychotherapy:

> According to the hypothesis on which client-centered therapy is based, the person who is listened to learns to listen to him- or herself and to others; the person who is trusted and respected learns to trust and respect him- or herself and others; and the person who is accepted as responsible for himself becomes more responsible as a person and as a member of society. As a more

fully functioning person, he or she will be less likely either to follow someone blindly or to impose personal values on others. (pp. 83-84)

In other words, as Reamy-Stephenson (1990) observes, "Self-disclosure works to normalize the human dilemma" (p. 290).

Self-Disclosure: The Search for Biological Grounding

If self-disclosure is therapeutic, how, then, does it "fit in the brain?"—a question seemingly fundamental to any proposed operational theory of therapeutic change. As Wachtel and McKinney (1992) note, while the experience of client disclosure and working through may be a familiar one, the process involved, is "not nearly so clear" (p. 339). Nevertheless, in their attempt to clarify the underlying psychobiological mechanisms of human discourse, Harre and Gillett (1994) maintain that the possibility that neurological mechanisms are alterable as a consequence of social environment has, in their words, "received considerable support from recent cognitive neuroscience." They further contend that if we accept the broad Aristotelian theory of mind—"that in performing discursive, symbolic activities, the mindful agent makes use of the properties of brain mechanisms"—then it may seem logical to suggest that "social influences shape brain function" (p. 81). This is so, they state, because the brain is the "repository of meanings" since it functions as the physical medium through which mental content is realized and exercised in discursive activity. In this respect, therefore, Harre and Gillett state, "it is no different than the neuromuscular system, which is 'shaped' by playing tennis" and thereby becomes the "appropriate instrument" (p. 81) with which the athlete plays his or her match.

Paralleling this discursive view from his psychobiological perspective, Lynch (1985) observes that human beings are distinguished from all other living creatures by their ability to interact with the environment by "speaking." He elaborates:

Whether man or woman or child, we can share our desires, thoughts, plans, and . . . feelings with each other through dialogue. Coupled with this is another simple yet sublime truth: that while we speak with words, we speak also with our

flesh and blood. . . . Study after study reveals that human dialogue not only affects our hearts significantly, but can even alter
the biochemistry of individual tissues at the furthest extremities
of the body. Since blood flows through every human tissue, the
entire body is influenced by human dialogue. Thus, it is true that
when we speak we do so with every fiber of our being.

This "language of the heart" is integral to the health and
emotional life of every one of us. Yet this vital truth has been
largely obscured by a scientific-philosophical perspective we
all share and that leads us to think about the human body in
terms of its mechanical functions. (pp. 3-4)

In this regard, the probable "biochemical" changes occurring during
mental activity (such as those induced by both therapeutic as well as
dysfunctional dialogue) are described by Rossi (1993):

Under mental "stress," the limbic-hypothalmic system in the
brain converts the neural messages of mind into the neurohor-
monal "messenger molecules" of the body. These, in turn, can
direct the endocrine system to produce steroid hormones that
can reach into the nucleus of different cells of the body to
modulate the expression of genes. These genes then direct the
cells to produce the various molecules that will regulate metabolism, growth, activity level, sexuality, and the immune
response in sickness and health. There really is a mind-gene
connection! Mind ultimately does modulate the creation and
expression of the molecules of life! (p. xvi)

Consistent with this line of reasoning, if the immune system and
nervous system are linked in this way, then according to Solomon
(1990) "certain hypotheses should hold true." He expands upon
these hypotheses in relation to the biological effects of both the
distress-related, and positive, experience:

First, emotional upset and distress should influence the inci-
dence or severity of diseases resisted or mediated by the
immune system such as cancer or autoimmune diseases.
Second, severe emotional and mental disorders should be
accompanied by abnormality in the immune system. Third,
hormones regulated by the central nervous system, such as

neuroendocrines, should influence the workings of the immune system. Fourth, any experimental manipulation of relevant parts of the central nervous system should have immunological consequences. Fifth, events that affect behavior, such as stress, conditioning, or different types of childhood experience, should also have immunological consequences. Sixth, cells involved in the immune system should also be responsive to hormones connected with the nervous system and to the nervous system's chemical messengers. Seventh, any activation of the immune system should be reflected in activity by the central nervous system. As research continues, far more implications of bidirectional interactions between the central nervous and immune systems will be recognized.

All of these hypotheses have supporting evidence. (p. 177)

This biochemical knowledge further parallels the work of Lynch (1990), who asserts that communication "is vitally linked to our bodies" and is probably, in his estimation, "the single most important force that influences our health or lack of health." For example, he says, a wide range of cardiovascular diseases can now be addressed clinically by focusing on "links between the cardiovascular system and communication" (p. 75). Citing support for this view from his psychobiological research, Lynch (1985) states:

> . . . Centuries of religious, philosophical, literary, and poetic wisdom that had suggested links between words and the human heart contained the core of an astonishingly fertile truth, and one central to medicine. Once aware of this truth, we tested for it in a variety of cases and research studies. We examined thousands of individuals, from newborn babies crying in their cribs; to preschool children reciting their ABCs; to grade-school children reading from textbooks; to nursing and medical students describing their daily work routine; to hypertensive patients in our clinic, and those waiting anxiously for cardiac by-pass surgery; to schizophrenics in psychiatric wards; to elderly patients in nursing homes describing their loneliness, and in patients close to death. In each and every one, the link between language and the heart was clear and undeniable. (p. 5)

This "link" between language and the heart may therefore support the contention that psychotherapy should be more *exploratory* than disputational. As Lynch (1990) states of his hypertension research, for example, any direct attempts to break through client defences would, in his words: "only cause a patient's blood pressure to rise even higher—up to dangerously high and possibly physiologically intolerable levels—so that further dialogue would become virtually impossible" (p. 83). Thus, he views blood pressure elevations as a form of "internal blushing"—useful in the pacing of his therapy with clients (about which more will be said later in this chapter).

Lending support to Lynch's work concerning the biological bases of speech (or the effects of language and discourse) are the views of Harre and Gillett (1994). In citing the neuropsychological work of A.R. Luria, they observe that discourse and usage, particularly of the tools available in natural language, "penetrate deep into the organizational structure of the brain." In other words, they say, in the course of acquiring discursive and manual skills, "brain structure is transformed to provide the machinery that an active human agent puts to work in exercising those skills in a multiplicity of tasks of everyday life" (p. 86). This further occurs, Harre and Gillett con-tend, because the organizing power of speech, as a form of communicative activity, appears to influence "the way the brain sets up its information processing functions" which can then be employed to perform tasks that are "quite remote from the discursive activities that were involved in their creation" (p. 87).

Thus, Harre and Gillett conclude that to explicate the change processes involved in such *transformational dialogue*, "we need to deepen inquiry in two directions, one discursive and the other based on 'information' processing theory, that is, in a theory of brain function" (p. 58). (Toward this end, the next chapter on language explores the possible role speech or language-production may play in both contributing to, and remediating, neuroses and incongruence.)

AFFECT, CATHARSIS, AND SELF-DISCLOSURE

Consistent with this discursive perspective, and in addition to self-disclosure, such terms as *catharsis, ventilation,* and *working through* have generally been used to describe the client's verbal and affective expression. Since these terms often denote a similar experiential process in psychotherapy, their literature should therefore be reviewed as well. Catharsis, for example, as Prochaska (1979) states, has "one of the longest traditions" as a process of inducing therapeutic change. The ancient Greeks, he says, believed evoking emotions to be "one of the best means of providing relief and improvement" (p. 9). And Garfield (1992) similarly agrees that besides the central role of the therapeutic relationship in psychotherapy, other potential variables, such as "release, catharsis, or abreaction" (p. 186) appear to be important.

While catharsis may be necessary in psychotherapy, the amount of relief or release, according to Efran, Lukens, and Lukens (1990), does not appear to be related to "the amount of energy expended." As they explain:

> The relief relates, instead, to whether the blockage has been eliminated. People believe strongly in cathartic or steam-kettle approaches because, more often than not, the expressive process leads to collateral shifts in social process—while the person emotes, positions are softened or changed, realignments occur, permissions are given, and bonds are formed. In other words, it is the action implications of catharsis that are critical—not the energy expenditure or whether or not something has been gotten off one's chest. . . . It is easy to lose sight of the critical social alignments that are taking place and to focus instead on the signs of emotional display that accompany them. (p. 163)

Following emotional release, Efran, Lukens, and Lukens (1990) further explain, clients generally report that they feel better. The tendency therefore, they say, is to think that "crying, laughing, or tantrums have healing powers." However, Efran, Lukens, and Lukens contend, "these are simply the outward signs that people have been released from an emotional contradiction." Escaping from the bonds of contradiction, they say, is "what feels good" (p. 165).

Referring to the human neurological work pioneered by Penfield and Roberts (1959), Harris (1969) appears to support this view of emotional catharsis by pointing out that the feelings associated with past experiences have been shown to be "inextricably locked" (p. 11) to these experiences stored in the brain. Gardner (1993) presents a similar view by observing that in therapy, "Enunciation of the once-suppressed memory, along with release of the affect that normally accompanies it," appears sufficient to "eradicate the symptom" (p. 58). Or, to paraphrase a leading proponent of humanistic movement, James Bugental, who, in response to a question at the 1990 "Evolution of Psychotherapy" conference in Anaheim, California, concerning the significance of emotion in psychotherapy, replied: "Emotion is like the blood in surgery"—an important by-product, but not the main focus of "the operation." And the "operation," according to Wexler (1974), is "the client's activity of distinguishing and synthesizing facets of meaning that create reorganization and change" (p. 81).

In this respect, Zimring (1974) therefore observes, traditional psychotherapy has operated under the false assumption that emotions and feelings exist as "internal objects that can cause behavior and experience." In other words, he says, it has often been assumed that it is "the anger within a person that causes him to slam a door, whether or not he is aware of the anger." However, he notes, one would not make the same assumption about the physical world, i. e., "assume that there is a concept of gravity within a drop of water that causes it to run downhill" (p 123). Rossi (1993) expands upon this view:

> *Sensations, perceptions and emotions* are frequently the initial mind-body modalities signaling that something is coming up to consciousness. Sometimes we may feel embarrassed or depressed even before we know why. Some people may then experience *imagery* that presents a meaningful metaphor about our emotions on the way to a more *cognitive* pattern of *awareness* about what is being experienced. These cognitive or thought processes are usually a record of our personal history and *identity*. Ideally, new experience leads to an appropriate updating of our old records and identity along with innovative patterns of *behavior*. (p. 94)

SELF-DISCLOSURE AS THERAPEUTIC

While catharsis may be a more generic term encompassing self-disclosure, self-disclosure, in particular, has been termed therapeutic and is believed to help "reduce psychotic and neurotic tendencies"

(Jourard, 1971, p. v). From the beginning of the modern psychother-apeutic era, Jourard contends, psychoanalysis has involved overcom-ing "a patient's reluctance to let his analyst know him" (resistance) and becoming "an encourager and listener of another's intimate disclo- sure" (p. 358) (working through). The possible significance of this universal factor to the psychotherapeutic process can thus be summa-rized as follows: If the interpersonal interaction between client and therapist supposedly "produces statements by the client" (Zimring, 1974, p. 125), and if self-disclosure is therapeutic, it might also follow that any procedure which facilitates such disclosure might be of relevance to operationalism in psychotherapy. This may therefore be where research of therapist nonverbal behavior, facilitative of client disclosure, could enhance knowledge of therapeutic interac-tional processes intervening between therapist attitudes and client change—interactional variables which may, in turn, activate psy-chobiological and cognitive change processes within the client.

As for the properties of therapeutic disclosure, Anderson (1974) suggests from an information processing perspective that "not only feelings, but also all kinds of neglected, ignored, or rejected informa-tion, that can spell trouble for the individual or for the interpersonal network" (p. 41), might be so classified. He goes on to say that any focus by the therapist on these aspects of information might be seen as an effort to open the client's attentive resources to "a richer, more varied information field" (p. 41). If so, this may therefore suggest that the therapist should attend primarily to the process of facilitat-ing client verbalization and disclosure as a means of revealing, *to that client*, information which might be blocking inter- as well as intraindividual communication (a process which client-centered or nondirective therapy, by its name, seems to imply).

Toukmanian (1992) further summarizes the existing state of information processing research involving the processes which this sort of psychotherapeutic procedure may activate:

> For more than a decade, diverse concepts advanced within the general framework of the information processing paradigm have been used in an attempt to clarify and/or describe the components and procedures of existing methods of psycho-therapy in the language of cognitive psychology (e.g., Gold-

fried and Robins, 1983; Ingram and Hollan, 1986; Turk and Spears, 1983; Wexler and Rice, 1974; Winfrey and Goldfried, 1986). The potential of this paradigm as a conceptual tool or as a "methodology for theorizing" (Anderson and Bower, 1973, p. 136) about the change processes occurring within the client's perceptual-processing system and about ways in which therapists affect these processes on a moment-to-moment basis in experiential therapies has, however, not yet been fully explored in the realm of therapeutic psychology. (p. 77)

Toward addressing this apparent omission, the rest of this chapter therefore explores the possible relevance of this cognitive science and neuropsychological knowledge, to psychotherapy, as the area of inquiry generally designated as psychobiology.

PSYCHOBIOLOGICAL BASES OF THERAPEUTIC SELF-DISCLOSURE

With respect to the possible source of disclosure or "information field" in the client, and citing the human neurological studies pioneered by Penfield and Roberts (1959), Harris (1969) contends that evidence seems to indicate "that everything which has been in our conscious awareness is recorded in detail and stored in the brain and is capable of being 'played back' in the present" (p. 5). Expanding upon this perspective, Anderson (1974) further reports that "much evidence" exists to suggest that information processing functions, such as perception, "occur temporally and in stages—at least four of which can be specified experimentally" (p. 26). Supporting this temporal organization from a psychobiological perspective, Harris (1969) similarly observes that Penfield and Roberts' (1959) experiments indicate that whenever human beings pay conscious attention to something, they simultaneously record it in the brain in a sequential and "continuous" (p. 9) manner. In this respect, Harris maintains, memories appear to be "laid down in temporal succession" (p. 10) since complicated memory sequences have been evoked, in a time-ordered sequence, by electrically probing the brain of conscious individuals during surgery.

The experiments which yielded this psychobiological knowledge were derived from the following neurological procedure described by Dennett (1991):

> Sometimes during surgery it is important for the patient to be awake and alert, under only local anesthetic (like getting Novocain from the dentist). This lets the neurosurgeon get immediate reports from the patient about what is being experienced while the brain is being probed. This practice was pioneered by Wilder Penfield (1958), and for more than thirty years, neurosurgeons have been gathering data on the results of direct electrical stimulation to various parts of the cortex. (p.154)

Such experiments, Harris (1969) further contends, may make it seem plausible that "each of the memories we can recall has a separate neuron pathway" (p. 10). He therefore suggests that the brain may, in some respects, function like "a high fidelity tape recorder" (p. 11) (or computer) which stores past experiences and feelings and whose recordings, according to the above described neurological experiments, are "astonishingly complete" (p. 54). These recorded experiences and the feelings associated with them, Harris further notes, are "available for replay today" (p. 11). Or as Davis (1994) puts it:

> From the moment of our birth, each of us lives through a unique set of experiences, and our brains process each and every one of them. Each sensory experience, each person we see, each sound we hear, each pain or pleasure we feel, the brain processes and stores. As it does so, it builds up its network of interconnected cells and neuron clusters. . . . As it responds to its particular set of experiences, different from every other person's set of experiences, each brain creates a network that is slightly different in structure and connections from every other. (p. 209)

These views also appear to be supported by Harre and Gillett (1994) who contend, based on Penfield and Robert's work as well, that throughout life, the brain stores experience in terms of "meanings." These meanings, they believe, structure the experience as well as the responses made by the individual to "aspects of the events experienced" (p. 81). If so, then replaying memories of experiences and meanings through facilitating client dialogue and verbalization might, in effect, be tapping into the source of therapeutic self-disclosure in psychotherapy, thereby unblocking communication and allowing clients to access their own internal resources for therapeutic change (about which more will be said in Chapter 6 concerning language and logical reasoning).

Harris's (1969) view also appears to be reinforced by research in information processing which suggests that clients have their own networks of information stored according to "special rules for retrieving such information" (Anderson, 1974, p. 42). Anderson therefore maintains that such organizational structure provides support for a "client-interpretation," or, one might say, client-centered, approach to therapy (as opposed to an analytical or didactic interpretation by the therapist). According to Anderson, for example, any topic introduced by the therapist might conceivably represent a source of potential information. However, he says, "to what degree such information can effectively be worked with by the client" seems to depend "upon its prior grounding in stored rules" (p. 42) in the client's network of stored information. In other words, he explains, the therapist's "construction of events, perceptions, images, thoughts, memories, feelings, and the like," may be a source of potential information "no matter how far removed it may be" (p. 43) from the client's own network. However, by selectively dealing with information in this way, he maintains, the therapist may "run the risk of simply bypassing the client's, or network's, capacity for personal growth by ignoring the principles inherent in experimental studies of information processing" (p. 43) (which, as previously noted, also parallels the *temporal* organization of stored information revealed by the neurological studies of Penfield and Roberts (1959).

THE ROLE OF THE "OTHER"
IN THE REPROCESSING OF INFORMATION

Within a client-interpretation or client-centered approach to therapy, the need for another human being to facilitate reprocessing of information is supported by Penfield and Roberts (1959). Citing George Herbert Mead, for example, they observe that the "self" is "realized in relation to others" (p. 204). Or as Goldberg (1992) puts it, "The self requires dialogues with other selves in order to reveal its own intentionality to itself." In this sense, Goldberg maintains, creating new self-possibilities requires "engagement with other selves in order to actualize the potentialities in each." This is so, he says, because reality exists for the self "only by virtue of the way it relates with other selves," thus making communication "an extremely powerful vehicle" (p. 122).

Wexler (1974) offers a similar explanation for why clients often require a therapist to help them reprocess information:

> Although the elaboration and reorganization of information so as to create change constitutes the ideal, rarely do clients seem to be able to do this for themselves. That is why they come to therapy. Indeed, clients' problems may not be what they think their problems to be, but rather the way in which they think about their problems. Clients' problems may fundamentally be deficiencies in the way they process information; their processing style is such that they are not able to process and organize information so as to create change and reorganization with respect to their concerns. (pp. 66-67)

Biological support for this view comes from Edelman (1992), who explains that the unique patterns of nervous system response, across different human beings, depend upon the individual history of a particular neural system. Moreover, he says, "it is only *through interactions with the world* that appropriate response patterns are selected." This uniqueness and variation of response, caused by differences in human experience (and genetics) across individuals, Edelman further maintains, occurs both "between different nervous systems and within a single system across time" (p. 226). This need for another human being to aid in this "selection" process may further illuminate Jourard's (1971) observation that "No man can come to know himself except as an outcome of disclosing himself to another person" (p. 6). In this sense, therefore, Penfield's pioneering neurological work may support the humanistic contention that "other people" are required for the "fulfillment and enhancement of the organism's self-fulfillment" (Barton, 1974, p. 170).

In describing this "selection" and reprocessing process, Harris (1969) maintains that personal recollections are evoked by the stimuli of day-to-day social experience "in much the same way that they were evoked artificially by Penfield's probe" (p. 7). In this dialogical respect, therefore, Harre and Gillett (1994) maintain that Penfield's work may have developed the "processing structure" underpinning the discursive skills evident in perception, action, and problem solving—a processing structure they describe as containing:

> ... Some kind of "record of past experience" that can be used to make available the recall of autobiographical episodes. As a result of these properties of the brain, a person is provided with a narrative resource that is built out of their own individual history, much as the arrangement of the iron particles on a magnetic tape may hold the "record" of a conversation. The structure of this "record" and the skills that enable the subject to make use of it are a function of the discourse but the brain is the substrate for the requisite mental activity. (p. 83)

Without the help of another human being, however, facilitating or activating this "record," according to Penfield and Roberts (1959), is difficult, if not impossible. As they explain:

> No man can involuntary reactivate the record. Perhaps, if he could, he might become hopelessly confused. Man's voluntary recollection must be achieved through other mechanisms. And yet, the recorded patterns are useful to him, even after the passage of many years. They can still be appropriately selected by some scanning process and activated with amazing promptness for the purposes of comparative interpretation. (p. 55)

THE PSYCHOTHERAPEUTIC IMPLICATIONS OF PENFIELD'S WORK

With respect to psychotherapy and consistent with the view of Harre and Gillett (1994) that the reconstruction of this record occurs as a function of human discourse, the thesis of this book suggests that the "scanning process" required to activate the "record" (analogous to

Penfield's electrical probe) may be the facilitation of client verbal-ization and self-disclosure promoted by nonverbal therapist behav-iors—chief of which being dominant eye contact (about which more will be said in the final chapter of this book). In other words, as Harre and Gillett (1994) put it, "When we want to unlock particular capacities that are realized in the brain, we need to return the person to something similar to the discursive contexts in which the relevant meanings and significations were developed" (p. 94). This replay of past memories may thus allow the client to access information inter-fering with inter- as well as intraindividual communication, thereby facilitating the reprocessing, revision, or updating of meanings in a manner consistent with the client's reality or *real self.* This, how-ever, as Wexler (1974) points out, is not "a brief, one-shot affair." Rather, he says, this process is characterized by "groping, search-ing, repetition, continued refining of what is meant, the bringing in of additional information, and the exclusion of other information." In other words, he adds, it is a process of elaborating new informa-tion and "reorganizing it by finding new meaning in it" (p. 67).

To further illustrate the possible relevance of Penfield's neurolog-ical work to psychotherapy, such knowledge might conceivably help provide a rationale for why therapists generally advocate moving at a rate the "client can tolerate" (Combs, Richards, and Richards, 1976, p. 287), not rushing or forcing the rate of therapy (Rogers, 1951), and "timing" or "pacing" client disclosure in psychoanalysis (Bordin, 1974, p. 11). Given this neurological knowledge, for exam-ple, the natural rate of therapy and client disclosure might therefore depend upon psychobiological factors such as the kind of informa-tion contained in the client's neuron pathways, the organization of these memories or experiences stored in such networks, and the amount and content of the disclosure previously elicited during therapy. This psychobiological organization might also underlie such therapeutic observations as that of Carl Whitaker (1989), who contends that unless what transpires in therapy can be "fitted into the patient's standard life experience, operational theory, or psycho-logical programming of thought, nothing will be different"—no change will occur that is "useful therapeutically" (p. 188).

Penfield's neurological experiments might also help provide a psychobiological explanation for what psychoanalysts have termed "repressed" or "unconscious" information. For example, based on Harris's (1969) and Harre and Gillett's (1994) reasoning, the so-called "unconscious" might possibly consist, in part, of past experiences stored in neuron pathways blocked by other memories stored ahead of them, as if on tape. By "playing the tape," or facilitating client disclosure, therefore, the therapist may thus be helping the client gain access to thoughts and feelings from his or her previously blocked neuron pathways. Or as Anderson (1974) puts it: "The so-called unconscious thus may not exist in repressed memories or stored information, but only in misapplications of attentive capacity or stored and abstracted rules for retrieving such information" (p. 42). In other words, according to Wexler (1974), there may be no need to invoke "subceived" (p. 64) concepts. In his view, "unconscious" phenomena may be due more to the fact that, at that point in therapy, "information cannot be handled and organized, or it can be handled and organized only partially" (p. 64).

The acknowledgment of parallels between developmental modes of personality organization and certain aspects of memory storage, in psychoanalysis, is further noted by Bordin (1974). In his estimation, these "developmental assumptions" underlie, what he terms: "the layering scheme of personality organization whereby certain experiences and modes of responding are lodged behind others, which must be released before the next layer 'approaches the surface' and comes within reach of awareness" (p. 11). This psychotherapeutic view further seems to parallel that of Rice (1974), who maintains that the client's memory of an experience is more complete than his or her construction of it (suggesting two separate processes to be operating in such instances). As a client talks about an experience, Rice notes, "his account will be a mixture of levels, including both his construction of the experience and also some material much closer to the original experience that is not encompassed by the construction." This extra material, she says, may not be inconsistent with the construction but may have been "left outside the original scheme, displaced by other materials that were more salient" at the time "the original experience took place" (p. 300). In this respect, however, she adds that it is important for the "client," rather than the "therapist," to arrive at "new constructions" (p. 301). (This possible additional constructivistic speech process is discussed in greater detail in Chapter 6 concerning language and logical reasoning.)

Similarly, the concept of "resistance" in traditional psychoanalytic theory, or the apparent reluctance of information in the "unconscious" to be brought to the client's consciousness, might be viewed more as a failure by the therapist to properly tune in to the client's network of stored information (possibly a matter of not facilitating sufficient disclosure from the client to allow for the spontaneous release, reprocessing, or unblocking of the more deeply stored inaccessible and troublesome information). As Omer (1994) observes: "All too often what we smugly call 'resistance' or 'lack of motivation' reflects no more than our rigid adherence to doctrinarian therapeutic goals and enshrined models of psychological health, with little consideration for the patient's pains and preferences" (p. 70). In other words, as Rossi (1993) states from a psychobiological perspective, so-called resistance may therefore be viewed more as "a problem in accessing state-bound information and transducing it into a form in which it can be utilized for problem-solving" (p. 114).

To redress this possible "accessing" blockage, Lewin (1965) suggests that therapists should focus more on their own nonverbal behavior. Otherwise, he says, "certain resistances" will develop without the therapist knowing their source. While he searches for the cause in the client's past, Lewin (1965) states, "the answer may lie, neglected, within the confines of the doctor's office" (p. 394). Supporting this view as well, Dreikurs (1967) observes that what appears as resistance may simply constitute "a discrepancy between the goals of the therapist and those of the patient" (p. 65). In other words, such clients may not necessarily be "resisting" treatment, Efran, Lukens, and Lukens (1990) contend, they may simply be "pursuing their own goals as they construe them" (p. 188) (or as their information processing capacity will allow). In this sense, therefore, as Wexler (1974) suggests, the client's goals may be more neurologically than psychologically based.

Moreover, when a client is not engaged in a productive mode of "experiencing" and seems defensive, Wexler (1974) says, "it is a difficult task to listen carefully for significant facets of information evoked to respond to." It is far easier, he notes, "to conjure up and create significant experience for the client than it is to engage in this difficult task and work with the information in process in the client." In other words, he maintains, it is generally much easier to "tell people our reactions to them than it is to understand them" (pp. 112-113). Therefore, when such "resistance" occurs, Garfield (1992) observes, "we have too frequently blamed the client" when therapy has not progressed as we would have liked. However, he adds, despite the fact that some clients may seem "difficult or recalcitrant," and the possibility of helping them in therapy may seem "extremely limited," the professional is still nevertheless "responsible for what takes place" (p. 181). And what may be "taking place" in such instances, as evidence from neurology and information processing suggests, could be a failure by the therapist to properly tune in to the client's information network to help release, reprocess, and/or update information interfering with intra- as well as interpersonal communication. In this regard, painful though it is, says Carl Whitaker (1989), "all failures in psychotherapy are failures of the therapist. The patient never fails. The patient only loses by the therapist's failure" (p. 193).

Finally, indirect support for this view may also derive from the apparent implications of this model for understanding certain psychological disorders. Severe cases such as "multiple personality," for example, according to Rossi (1993), could be due to a disorder of the information storage and retrieval system itself. In quoting J. Lienhart, PhD, a researcher in this area who reportedly personally experienced this disorder, Rossi (1993) suggests how such personality splitting might occur:

> Just as hypnosis requires intense concentration rather than "sleep," the multiple has learned to concentrate totally on certain memories from the past. The underlying problem appears to be one of retrieval from an infinite number of memory sets. It is within the retrieval process that the perceptual distortions occur. This creates a chaotic confusion because the individual memory units are not encapsulated within the proper "sets" in an orderly fashion. Thus, a memory cue from one period of life is stored with the wrong "memory set." Consequently, certain stimulus cues may trigger one of the behavior response sets but within the wrong context or sequence. The process is crudely similar to the

distortions, condensations and symbolic connections which occur during the dream state. Knowledge which is accessible in one state is not available during the altered state as it is integrated poorly and distributed more randomly within the range of recall of the dominant personality.

Another interesting feature demonstrated by multiples that is not well understood by researchers is the emotional detachment from the appropriate "intellectual" set. It would appear that some affective experiences are stored independently from their intellectual counterparts. As a result of this, an emotional unit from one set may attach itself to a constellation of cues which make up a totally different set. (p. 64)

Shapiro (1995) similarly points out the relevance of information processing in psychotherapy as applied to a "posttraumatic stress" context: "Disturbing events can be stored in the brain in an isolated memory network. This prevents learning from taking place. The old material just keeps getting triggered over and over again. In another part of your brain, in a separate network, is most of the information you need to resolve it. It's just prevented from linking up to the old stuff" (p. 124).

"BLOCKS" TO INFORMATION PROCESSING AND INTERPERSONAL COMMUNICATION

While the psychoanalytic school may attribute nonconscious blocks within clients to a specific area of the mind termed the "unconscious," nonconscious phenomena are viewed by humanistic proponents (Jourard, 1971; Price, 1978, p. 201; Rogers, 1961) as dysfunctional *communication* rather than as products of a subconscious mind. Jourard (1971), for example, observes that in therapy, the client often "remembers things which surprise him" (p. 138). Rogers (1961) similarly states:

In the "neurotic" individual, parts of himself which have been termed unconscious, or repressed, or denied awareness, have become blocked off so that they no longer communicate themselves to the conscious or managing part of himself. As long as this is true, there are distortions in the way he communicates himself to others, and so he suffers both within himself and in his interpersonal relations. The task of psychotherapy is to help the person achieve, through a special relationship with a therapist, good communication within himself. Once this is achieved, he can communicate more freely and more effectively with others. We may say then that psychotherapy is good communication within and between men. (p. 330)

Yalom (1975) similarly observes that Karen Horney also emphasized the individual's need for self-knowledge and self-realization through improving self-communication. And in doing so, Yalom observes, the task of the therapist is to "remove obstacles in the path" of "autonomous processes" (p. 54).

That such autonomous processes may further be biologically based is suggested by Butler (1974), who maintains that the generation of new experiences "by way of one's own responses" is "inherently reinforcing" (p. 183). In expressing themselves, Butler says, clients reveal "satisfaction" or "pleasure," which he believes to be evidence that such disclosure "fulfills a biological need" (p. 180). Likewise, citing the study of Fishbein and Laird (1979) which suggests that the major benefit of self-disclosure in psychotherapy is to help clients "feel good about themselves" (p. 155), Derlega et al. (1991) seem to support this inherent tendency toward self-satisfaction through self-disclosure. Butler (1974) agrees by maintaining that studies in sensory deprivation tend to support this biological predisposition or inherent need. In his words, "That this need for experience is such that extreme sensory deprivation results in anomalous neural and behavioral development is now well established (see Riesen, 1966)." On the motivational side, he adds, "it has been shown that animals, when deprived of stimulation (transactional experience), will both work to get it and acquire new responses in the process" (p. 179).

Conversely, without environmental demands for their use, Riesen (1975) maintains, "some neurological organizations are lost, their structural substrates diminished, and the brain chemistry is altered." But when certain sensory requirements are imposed, he says, "exaggerated neural growth patterns and restructuring of function beyond the ordinary occur" (p. 2). He therefore concludes that stimulation contributes to shaping the rapidly growing nervous system "anatomically and physiologically under the overall guidance of a genetic code" (p. 277). The apparent biological advantage of this phenomenon and its inherent or "adient motivation" (p. 183), Butler (1974) maintains, is that the use of sensory neurons results in the development of "larger size, more complex structure, and increased physiological reactivity" (p. 179). Citing Riesen (1966), Butler further contends that such stimulation is necessary for optimal growth and development of neural systems. For this reason, he says, primates will "work and acquire new responses" (p. 180) in order to activate this occurrence. (Support for this view also comes from the environmental enrichment work of Hebb [1949, 1959] about which more will be said in the Chapters 6 and 7.)

Relating this form of psychobiological growth to therapeutic change, Rossi (1993) similarly maintains that the heightening of brain activity by what is "novel and fascinating to clients" is, in his estimation, an important though generally "unappreciated precondition" for "all forms of creatively-oriented psychotherapy and mind-body experiences" (p. 31). This is apparently so, according to biologist Kornhuber (1988), because the "inborn order of the brain" is "differentiated, tested, and validated by interaction with the environment"(p. 249). The physiological process by which such brain growth occurs, Ornstein (1993) further contends, involves more the growth of the pattern of connections between neurons or cells, called "synapses" (p. 184), than it does the production of new neurons. Consequently, Ornstein and Swencionis (1990) state, "The commonplace experience of skills improving with practice is more than a psychological phenomenon, it is reflected in changes in brain structure as well" (p. 4). In other words, while the human brain may not grow new cells beyond a certain age, according to Ornstein and Swencionis, the connections between them "may be as important" (p. 4). To produce such growth or to actualize the brain's physiological potential, Dubois (1990) maintains, its functions must be used. If not, he says, they may remain "unexpressed" and can further "deteriorate, after they are developed" (p. 141). (The relevance of this phenomenon to psychotherapy may therefore lie in its parallel with the concept of *therapeutic growth* traditionally regarded by humanists as occurring through the process of self-actualization.)

Paralleling this psychobiological view of growth from a cognitive science perspective is Toukmanian's (1992) application of an information processing perspective to psychotherapy, specifically schemata (the cognitive structures which she defines as containing past experiences and meanings constituting the content of client disclosure). From this theoretical vantage point, she says, "an individual's attained level of perceptual development vis-à-vis a given domain may be thought of as a skill that is acquired and refined with experience." She elaborates:

> It involves learning to use and "time share" mental operations for the purpose of elaborating and differentiating the relevant structures and expanding the network of existing associations among them. In other words, it is suggested that, while schemata play an important role in determining the kind of information that can be anticipated and accepted into the individual's perceptual system, it is the extent of the existing schematic *links* and *associations* that ultimately determines the range of alternative perspectives that a person is capable of generating when interacting with the environment. In this sense, the precise course of people's perceptual development in a given domain of experience is seen to be a cumulative product of what they have actually *learned to do* with the information involved in the transactions with the environment, that is, the particular kinds of mental operations and networking strategies that they have learned to use for the construal of events entailed in particular domains of experience. (p. 83)

The significance of Toukmanian's work to psychotherapeutic theory building lies in the fact that her information processing research may support the existence of "autonomous processes" within the client, resulting from self-disclosure and activated by the therapeutic encounter. In other words, based on the above studies, it may seem logical to suggest that a proposed nonverbal procedure for facilitating client discourse and self-disclosure might possibly be similar to Rogers's (1961) facilitation of "growth" by activating an "actualizing tendency" (Rogers, 1977, p. 249) or releasing autonomous, spontaneous processes within the client. Such processes may further be similar to what some have termed: "a striving for adequacy" (Combs, Richards, and Richards, 1976, p. 132), "a creative becoming" (Allport, 1955), "patients automatically search for understanding" (Yalom, 1975, p. 93), or Victor Frankl's (1963) "search for meaning" in logotherapy.

If clients in therapy *do* move automatically toward an enhanced state of personal functioning, Wexler (1974) nevertheless observes that "simply invoking a motive to realize one's potentials as an explanation for this change" does not reveal much about the nature of the processes involved. In his estimation, a more operational definition of this apparent inherent phenomenon, more in keeping with the traditional client-centered emphasis on "experiencing," might result if it were instead "explicitly based on a well-defined theoretical model for the experiencing process" (p. 52). To be more specific, Wexler (1974) maintains that this "striking characteristic" (i.e., the drive toward self-actualization) of a client's behavior is expressed in "his continued attempt to organize and articulate as clearly as possible the meaning of information" to which he is "attempting to give order and form" (pp. 99-100). (In this regard, Chapter 6 on language addresses in greater detail this apparent inherent motivation of clients toward articulating a better understanding of their world.)

This inherent drive toward meaning or "understanding" may further produce cognitive enrichment within clients—achieved, Wexler (1974) states, with the help of a therapist through "experiencing" or facilitating self-disclosure within the client. In this regard, he observes that in client-centered therapy, for example, the therapist principally deals with "self-produced arousal," that is, arousal the client generates within him- or herself. When clients' modes of experiencing are optimal, Wexler further explains, they contribute to their arousal in two ways: (1) heightened processing activity is itself "a source of arousal," and (2) the facets of meaning generated and integrated "produce a change in the structure" of their field and, in turn, "a change in arousal" (p. 86). This process of experiencing Wexler claims to be "self-perpetuating," involving an ongoing and continuous activity of "differentiating and integrating meaning to achieve a change and reorganization" (pp. 72-73) of the client's information field.

Activation of this "experiencing process" in psychotherapy, as well as the postulation of resulting autonomous change processes within the client, was further implied in the following description of psychotherapy proffered by Perls, Hefferline, and Goodman (1977):

> Our view of the therapist is that he is similar to what the chemist calls a catalyst, an ingredient which precipitates a reaction which might not otherwise occur. It does not prescribe the form of the reaction, which depends upon the intrinsic reactive properties of the materials present, nor does it enter as part into whatever compound it helps to form. What it does is to start a process, and there are some processes which, when once started, are self-maintaining or autocatalytic. This we hold to be the case in therapy. (p. 17)

However, as mentioned previously, the state of knowledge in psychotherapy concerning what specific therapist actions or behaviors possibly "precipitate" these "autocatalytic" processes leading to self-insight, as Strupp (1973) points out, is typically "not very well articulated to the kinds of changes of learning to be effected." Rather, he says, "it seems that the therapist sets in motion a complex process whose consequences are predictable only in a very broad sense" (p. 100). Strong and Matross (1973) provide a similar molar view of psychotherapy as arising out of the "interaction of psychological forces inside the client which the therapist affects" (Strong, 1978, p. 104). The task of the future, Strupp (1973) therefore concludes, "is to achieve greater specificity concerning the effects of particular kinds of interventions" (p. 100).

Toward achieving greater operationalism or specificity, Wexler (1974) suggests the variables to which the therapist should attend within an information processing/psychobiological model:

> Seeing the therapist's response as serving to refocus the attention and subsequent processing of the client raises the question of what the therapist should use as his guide for making his selection in what to respond to and what to ignore. The traditional client-centered answer would be that the therapist should respond to feelings. . . . The therapist should listen carefully for and select those facets of information that seem to refer to central

aspects of the client's functioning and that either seem to have an unfinished flavor for the client or seem to present processing difficulties for him. (p. 99)

In Wexler's estimation, to simply say that the client is experiencing his feelings ignores the fact that affect is being generated by the client within the context of creating "a cognitive organization for a particular subset of information in his life." Feelings, Wexler says, are not things devoid of substantive information but are "generated in the process of organizing such information" (p. 54) (and are ostensibly relived or released in psychotherapy during the reprocessing of past experiences and meanings resulting in the revision and reconstruction of the self).

In any event, such a description of the therapeutic process would appear to be consistent with the approach proposed herein. That is, therapist nonverbal behaviors might be considered "catalysts" facilitating or "precipitating" "autocatalytic" change processes within the client, resulting from self-disclosure, thereby releasing or unblocking deeply stored or nonconscious information. Such a procedure might also be similar to what Rice (1974) terms "the evocative function of the therapist." This function, she states, is one of "reevoking in the client the client's own reaction to a key situation" so that he or she can successfully "reprocess" or form "more accurate constructions" (p. 298) of past experiences. In her opinion, such a procedure results in a greater assimilation of information that during storage may have become "isolated" (p. 299). Replay of this experience with the help of a therapist, she says, results in such isolated or nonconscious material becoming "integrated with the rest" (p. 299). (How the client may achieve these "more accurate constructions" is discussed in greater detail in Chapter 6.)

To recap thus far, because of its emphasis on empirical research rather than hypothetical constructs, the above work of Penfield and Roberts (1959), Harre and Gillett (1994), Harris (1969), Anderson (1974), Wexler (1974), Butler (1974), and Rice (1974) might provide an empirical basis "for anchoring" in the "basic biological nature of the organism" (Wexler, 1974, p. 50), the apparent preexisting potential within the client for self-change. Harris (1969) appears to concur by observing that Penfield's experiments "demonstrate" that the memory function, which is often referred to in psychological terms, "is biological also" (p. 11). That this sort of psychobiological perspective may become more pervasive in the field further appears to be supported by Strupp and Bergin (1973). They feel, for example, that the time "for discerning a new gestalt in the multifarious concepts and bits of evidence" may not be far off. Intuitively, they state, "we feel that the future of research will build on and produce a closer integration between experimental and clinical approaches" (p. 801).

As for the relative scarcity of research and hypothesizing in this area thus far, however, Strupp and Bergin (1973) observe:

> We are impressed with the impoverished character of the major theories in this area. Running the gamut from psychoanalysis to behaviorism, we fail to see fertile theories emerging. While the global theorizing that has dominated the field of personality has become largely defunct, more appropriate mini-theories centered on specific clusters of data have not emerged. We view the need for new theories as a vital one. Crucial concepts such as "repression," "defence," "cognitive mediation," "conditional response," and "experiencing" all need major overhauling or replacement. We view this as a prime task for advancing the field. (p. 804)

With this reported theoretical "impoverishment" in mind, the nonverbal behavioral approach described herein might be viewed as one such attempt at scientific theory building through universal "nonspecific" variables in psychotherapy (supported by empirical research in the broader area of behavior influence and grounded in my clinical practice). In other words, building upon knowledge derived from allied areas of human behavior, relevant to psychotherapy, in order to "recouple the theory with the data," may help clarify some of the current confusion in the field and lend credence to Wexler's (1974) assertion that human nature need not be viewed as "complex." It is only our interaction with a highly complex and varied environment, he says, that makes us "appear complex." The processing system "that acts on information received from that environment," he adds, although "elegantly geared to adaptive and flexible functioning in the varied environment," may nevertheless "be relatively simple" (p. 94).

It is in this sense, therefore, that an eclectic and integrative perspective may help eliminate some of the mystery shrouding psychotherapy. To be more specific, if it is true that "the process of therapy is designed not to change patients but to help patients change themselves" (Strupp, 1978, p. 4), then a nonverbal behavioral approach to psychotherapy might offer operational skills with which to, stated in humanistic terms, "facilitate each person in his self-directed process of becoming" (Rogers and Skinner, 1956, p. 1064). In the past, as Combs, Richards, and Richards (1976) note, some therapists have focused their attention on analyzing the dynamics of the client's behavior or personality. The rationale behind such an approach was that if the client could view or be shown his *perceived self* more clearly, change might occur. However, they point out, "unfortunately, this process rarely works" (p. 195). Or, as psychotherapeutic researcher Orlinsky (1994) concludes from his review of the literature in this area, "interventions typically discouraged by the psychoanalytic model, such as therapist self-disclosure and the giving of advice, have not been shown to be effective" (p. 119).

This may be so, Combs, Richards, and Richards (1976) suggest, because "the phenomenal self is a product of a person's experience" (p. 195) and not a product of "will" (Anderson, 1974, pp. 45-46). As such, it therefore appears that change in the phenomenal self can "only occur as a consequence of some new experience" (Combs, Richards, and Richards, 1976, pp. 194-195). Or as Friedman (1992) puts it, "We become ourselves through each particular action; we choose ourselves in each act of becoming." Our human resources, he adds, "are inseparably bound up with the direction we take as persons in response to what calls us out in the concrete situation" (p. 5). This opinion also seems to be supported by researchers in the field, Strupp (1973), for example, who contends that "the patient needs an experience, not an explanation" (p. 101).

Similarly, Watzlawick's (1978) view with respect to the psychotherapeutic implications of hemispheric brain theory seems to support this experiential perspective. In his estimation, if the language or process of psychotherapy involves the more symbolic language of the brain's right hemisphere, then in his words:

> ... *It also reveals the inappropriateness of a procedure which essentially consists in translating this analogic language into the digital language of explanation, argument, analysis, confrontation, interpretation, and so forth, and which, through this translation, repeats the mistake which made the sufferer seek help in the first place—instead of learning the patient's right-hemispheric language and utilizing it as the royal road to therapeutic change.* (p. 47)

That this exploratory and experiential view of psychotherapy further appears consistent with psychobiological theory, is implied by Schwartz (1978) when he states: "A person learns through experience because the brain learns through experience. Thoughts and feelings, memories and wishes, skills and plans, involve the restructuring of the brain and its regulation of bodily organs." Boldly stated, he says, "psychotherapy is ultimately a psychobiological process" (p. 68).

Supporting this psychobiological perspective is the work of Eric Kandel of Columbia University, who, for the past three decades, has investigated "how experience changes the nervous system, or the cellular and molecular mechanisms of learning and memory" (Livermore, 1992, p. 46). Reporting on Kandel's work, Livermore further reiterates that exposure to novel tasks and stimuli "generates the development of new circuits and synapses" (p. 43). Thereafter, she maintains, further stimulation strengthens these pathways and enhances their interconnections. She explains:

> Whether it is a new sensation or a fresh idea, every outside stimulus is first converted into electrical signals as it enters the cranium. These electrical signals trundle down pathways, splitting off into multiple directions for processing. Where the lack of prior experience has left no established route, the signal will forge a new one, linking neuron to neuron as it travels along. The resulting chain is called a brain circuit, and the next time the same stimulus enters the brain, it speeds efficiently along its old route, now grooved into an expressway. Hundreds of millions of brain circuits are created by millions of experiences. (p. 44)

Moreover, how these findings from biology, and from the broader area of behavior influence, may relate to "growth" in the more specific psychotherapeutic experiential context is explained by Wexler (1974):

> . . . Unlike a rat, which may explore a maze for change in stimulation, man need not be dependent on the external environment for change, but can create it for himself via his own processing of information. Through his ability to create meaning, man has the potential to be his own source for creating reorganization and change in experience by distinguishing and synthesizing new facets of meaning in the diverse and complex information in his life. (p. 66)

When clients engage in such "experiencing," Wexler says, they tend to ascribe meaning to their experience in what he terms, "highly vivid forms such as metaphor and imagery" (about which more will be said in Chapter 6 concerning language). Because these language mechanisms are rich in terms of the information they evoke, Wexler notes, they are, in his estimation, "an extremely potent vehicle for providing an enriched substrate of new information for further processing" (p. 75).

In this sense, Wexler (1974) maintains, "the effect of a good empathic response on the client is always further differentiation and integration of new facets of meaning." An accurate response, he says, therefore "serves to provide an organized substrate from which the client can go on and distinguish and synthesize new facets of meaning that emerge from the organization" (p. 100). In other words, instead of viewing such experiential exploration as passive, information processing involves what Wexler (1974) terms "active and constructive" (p. 80) processes (which are discussed in greater detail in Chapter 6 concerning language). Thus, what happens to clients directly, as Combs, Richards, and Richards (1976) observe, is "much more vivid and clear than the words we speak" (pp. 194-195) to them.

In this respect, however, the insight resulting from this experiential process, which appears to be sudden and meaningful to the client, Combs, Richards, and Richards (1976) observe, occurs only at the end of a "long sequence of prior differentiations" (p. 211).

Supporting this experiential view is the research of Staples and Sloane (1970), who found that the more the client speaks in therapy, as compared to the therapist, the greater the therapeutic change. In addition, the authors report that the longer the duration of the client's speech, the greater the therapeutic improvement. Supporting this view, Vinogradov and Yalom (1990) report similar findings by Peres (1947); Truax and Carkhuff (1965); and Lieberman, Yalom, and Miles (1973) indicating that as a general rule, patients who are ultimately successful in group therapy "make more self-disclosing statements" (p. 194). This result was also confirmed in a study by Richards et al. (1990) in which they examined the interpersonal style of clients who exhibited clinically significant improvement, or deterioration, following sixteen weeks of group psychotherapy. Commenting on the results of this study, Lambert (1992) observes that a stable pattern emerged for patients, regardless of who in the group they were speaking to or who was speaking to them. Those who improved were "self-reflective," he says, while those who deteriorated "tended to avoid self-reflection, were warded off and closed up" (p. 121).

Conversely, Butcher and Koss (1978) note that the study of Malan (1976) found a negative correlation between the number of *therapist* interpretations and positive outcome. This finding, they contend, "suggests that the more the therapists attempted to interpret or clarify problems by giving the patient information related to his or her problem, the less successful the treatment" (p. 743). Likewise supporting this finding is the study by Jones, Cumming, and Horowitz (1988) which studied client attitude and behaviors in addition to therapist actions and techniques. Commenting upon the results of this particular study, Lambert (1992) again observes that clients who were initially more seriously disturbed seemed to respond better to supportive interventions, i.e., "avoidance of threatening interpretations, directing the dialogue, and support of defenses (rather than analysis of defenses)" (p. 120).   •

These results would also seem to support the view of some therapists, Bordin (1974), for example, that psychotherapy should be "directed at conditions against which the usual efforts at teaching and socializing have failed" (p. 158). Or as Combs, Richards, and Richards (1976) put it, the problem of changing goals and values is not one of "seeking their control." Rather, they say, it is a problem of "seeking experience which makes possible the selection of new perceptions or the modification and extension of old ones" (p. 291). The same principle might also apply with respect to the reported inhibitive effect resulting from excessive therapist disclosure. As Grosch and Olsen (1994) state:

> Occasionally the feeling of superiority is manifested by the therapist communicating an excessive amount of information about himself or herself. This can be destructive to treatment. Such a therapist is often unconsciously implying "Be like me." Even though patients often experience temporary relief from their symptoms by imitating a role model, they rarely achieve the kind of enduring benefit that results from discovering and following their own path. Transference improvement, often based on pleasing the therapist, is usually temporary, since it does not coincide with real character change or growth. (pp. 56-57)

If so, then it might also follow that a nonverbal behavioral approach to facilitating therapeutic change through fostering client disclosure (as opposed to didactic analysis and interpretation of the client's concerns by the therapist) might possibly provide operational skills with which to help realize what previously have been molar or global humanistic objectives (i.e., promoting "growth" and/or "self-actualization"). In other words, these operating skills such as eye contact (through which Griffin [1978] and Ellsworth and Ross [1975] report an increase in self-disclosure), together with the other facilitative nonverbal behaviors outlined in Chapter 7, may, as my clinical experience suggests, turn out to be the more immediate stimuli intervening between therapist attitudes and client change within the therapeutic relationship. That is, as Watzlawick (1978) explains: "If instead of engaging in the time-honored but futile exercise of exploring anamnestically 'why' a human system came to behave the way it behaves, we decide to investigate 'how' it behaves 'here and now' and what the consequences of this behavior are, we shall find that the actual problem is what the system has so far tried to do in order to solve its supposed problem . . ." (p. 158).

SUMMARY AND CONCLUSION

In summary, the self, self-growth, or self-actualization have been generally referred to as the "what" of psychotherapy. The psychological self is further believed to be structured by meanings (derived from past experience) informing and/or motivating its activity and creating its moral individuality when relating to others. In this sense, therefore, idiosyncratic psychological identities or personalities may be said to exist within individual human beings. In this respect, as well, alienation from self and others may be viewed as the root of psychopathology, termed *neuroses* or *incongruence,* whose remediation and/or prevention may therefore involve a change, reprocessing, or updating of the self.

With the discipline of information processing came the possibility of scientifically exploring the processes of change, occurring within the client, in relation to this self. To achieve a reprocessing of self*,* depth of client self-exploration has been suggested by humanists as a fourth major ingredient of therapeutic encounters (in addition to the other three Rogerian attitudes). This intensive experiential exploration, which appears to be a common or universal factor cutting across the major psychotherapies, in turn, places responsibility upon the client's active participation in his or her "cure." As a result, asymmetry is created within the therapeutic relationship—not only in terms of power, but with respect to the degree of self-disclosure elicited by its participants.

It is from this perspective, therefore, that psychotherapy within this volume is viewed from a client-centered, or client self-disclosure context whose biological grounding derives from the neurological work of Wilder Penfield and his followers (which indicates that memories and their associated feelings are stored in temporal succession in the brain). This neurological storage organization may further account for the psychotherapeutic observation of "blocking" within clients. In this regard, for example, deeply stored mem-ories may not be readily accessible for reprocessing at that particular point in the client's life. Consistent with the psychotherapeutic observation referred to as "pacing," or moving at a rate the client can tolerate, self-disclosure may therefore operate as Penfield's electrical probe or "scanning process." That is, it may function to unblock neural pathways by releasing stored information, possibly blocking other memories stored ahead of them as if on tape, thus preventing their accessibility for reprocessing. This temporal storage factor may also account for what psychoanalysts term "resistance" or forces operating behind discourse preventing the "unconscious" from coming into consciousness.

As for the "how" of psychotherapy, there is evidence from "nonverbal" psychotherapy sessions cited in the literature (similar to my clinical practice) suggesting client self-disclosure to be facilitated mainly through therapist nonverbal behavior. Indirect empirical support for this phenomenon also derives from comparative process studies which indicate therapist verbal behavior to differ across therapies while, at the same time, comparative outcome studies report no differential efficacy of treatment. These findings may therefore suggest that therapists should attend to, or direct, their working focus toward facilitating client disclosure, nonverbally, as opposed to analyzing the "content" (Phillips, 1990, p. 117) of that disclosure (which is primarily the client's responsibility). This interactional process may in turn spontaneously activate autonomous neurological and psychological change processes within the client (to be discussed in greater detail in Chapter 6).

In conclusion, the heuristic rationale underlying the observed therapeutic "growth" seemingly generated through this intensive experiential exploration in psychotherapy is provided by Gendlin (1974): "Experience is basically process, it is liv*ing,* and not just this or that content. Contents are not basic, they are made from process, they are aspects of living, and they change if liv*ing* changes" (p. 238).

Chapter 6

The Talking Cure:
Language as a Remedy for,
and Source of,
Neuroses and Incongruence

. . . There can be no complete science, and certainly no science of human beings, until consciousness is explained in biological terms. Given our view of higher-order consciousness, this also means an account that explains the bases of how we attain personhood or selfhood. By selfhood I mean not just the individuality that emerges from genetics or immunology, but the personal individuality that emerges from developmental and social interactions.

—Gerald Edelman, 1992

. . . To a great extent our functioning as artisans or craftsmen of our own experience, including its mapping into behavior, eludes us, so blinded are we by the "giveness" or the "reality" of that with which we deal.

—Wayne Anderson, 1974

The psychological, that which happens within the soul of each, is only the secret accompaniment to the dialogue. . . . The coming into the light of the hidden human image is inseparable from the dialogue itself—a dialogue of mutual contact, trust, and shared humanity.

—Maurice Friedman, 1992

Our culture beats on us constantly, and we see this most clearly in the occasional wild child, the wolf boy, who has been lost in the woods. The human without culture is not a viable creature. Our nervous systems need culture as much as they need chemicals. Without language and culture, we are like headless monsters.

—Oliver Sacks, 1995

With language he will bridge the enormous gulf between person and person, universe without and world within, perception and concept, reality and imagination. . . . And language will set him free.

—Joel Davis, 1994

Can talking cure? According to Ferrara (1994), it is not only the therapists who believe so. The many thousands of people in the United States, alone, who seek therapeutic discourse and are willing to pay for it, she states, are "eloquent testimony to the efficacy of the talking treatment" (p. 168). Moreover, that researchers in psychotherapy need to focus greater attention on speech and speech production is suggested by Stanley Strong's recent address to the field (Strong, Yoder, and Corcoran, 1995) upon receipt of the 1993 Leona Tyler Award from the American Psychological Association:

> Words are tools for accomplishing social tasks. Speech is less symbolic and representational than it is active and presentational (Austin, 1962). It has force and consequence on events. Using these tools in endless negotiations, people generate a world of agreements, expectations, allowances, and disallowances—a moral world. (p. 379)

Speech, or language production, appears significant to therapeutic process because, in a manner paralleling the therapist as both instrument *and* provider of psychotherapy, capable of both fostering *and* inhibiting therapeutic growth, there is evidence to suggest that language may also serve both as a remedy for, and source of, neuroses and incongruence. This dual feature of language may further be due both to the temporal manner in which the brain stores and processes information—as well as the constructivistic nature of speech production itself. As Russell (1994) observes, "language constructs as it describes" (p. 173). That is, during interpersonal discourse, meanings, forming the basis of the self, are created spontaneously or without preconception. For example, when deeply engrossed in talking, Zimring (1974) explains, human beings are not usually conscious of fully formed ideas or concepts. However, he adds, if you are interrupted and have to wait to speak, then a formed idea occurs. Thus, he says, "an idea (in the sense of a formed concept or entity) is not necessary for you to make a complicated point, although it may be necessary for you to retain all aspects of it" (p. 124).

Commenting upon the significance of this spontaneous experiential process, from an intraindividual perspective, Dennett (1991) asks: What good would talking to yourself do if you already knew "what you intended to say?" He elaborates:

But once we see the possibility of partial understanding, imperfect rationality, problematic intercommunication of parts, we can see how the powerful forces that a language unleashes in a brain can be exploited in various forms of bootstrapping, some of them beneficial, and some of them malignant.
Here is an example:
You are magnificent!
Here is another:
You are pathetic! (p. 301)

This chapter therefore explores the process by which such "imperfect rationality" may occur, resulting in problematic intraindividual communication, a topic seemingly relevant to self-revision in psychotherapy.

With respect to the remedial function language may serve in such self-concept formation and/or revision, Ferrara (1994) enunciates a fundamental premise of psychotherapy—that "perceptions can be mediated through the filter of words and that talking to another about those perceptions can bring about an enhancement in mental health" (p. 84). She points out, however, that narrative scholars have yet to define "the core that all narratives share" (p. 57). Similarly, Haley (1963) maintains that the idea that clients undergo major changes as a result of conversations is generally accepted. However, Haley, too, notes that while it seems reasonable to talk to patients with psychiatric symptoms, he nevertheless admits that there is "not yet general agreement on what to talk about" (p. 3).

Nor, more specifically, is it apparently clear how the act of talking itself, within human discourse, actually changes clients. In this respect, however, as the thesis of this book suggests, the content of the therapeutic conversation may be less relevant to the therapist as facilitator, or to therapeutic methodology, than the process of the client disclosing it to him- or herself, thereby reprocessing past experiences and meanings and revising the self. As Sexton and Whiston (1994) observe, citing the conclusions of Gergen and Kaye (1992), the "transformational dialogue" in therapy may therefore turn out to be "the agent of change" (p. 67). If so, how does language accomplish this feat both linguistically and neurologically?

LINGUISTICS AND PSYCHOTHERAPY

More than sixty years ago, Ferrara (1994) states, Edward Sapir advanced the notion that linguistics could provide valuable insights for psychological studies because of its "objective nature" (p. 49). Nevertheless, as Davis (1994) observes, the relevance of this field of knowledge to psychotherapy may be limited by the fact that "the search for the meaning of *meaning* has been all but abandoned by contemporary linguistics." For better or for worse, Davis states, "modern semantics is not much concerned with following this particular road in the forest called language." Semanticists, he says, "look at *meaning* in much the same way physicists consider concepts like *height* and *width*. . . . These concepts have existence only in their application" (pp. 81-82).

This omission or neglect of meaning may further be due to the fact that, as Dennett (1991) notes, one of the "skeletons in the closet of contemporary linguistics" is that it has focused its attention more on *hearing* and has largely ignored *speaking* which, in his estimation, is the "most important half" of the communication process (or the half wherein meaning is supposedly generated). As Dennett observes, although there are many detailed theories and models of language "perception" and of the "comprehension" of heard utterances (i.e., the paths from phonology to syntax, semantics, and pragmatics), no one, not "Noam Chomsky nor any of his rivals or followers" has had "anything very substantial (right or wrong) to say about systems of language *production*" (p. 231).

Thus, while sociolinguists study language in use, or discourse as it is "shaped and reshaped" (Ferrara, 1994, p. vii) within the social interaction of daily life, such studies apparently do so by analyzing the syntactic interaction and influence words have upon themselves, once they are constructed, as opposed to addressing their psychobiological origins and how they contribute to meaning and intentionality. Complicating this situation, as Ferrara (1994) notes, is the fact that language is "paradoxically, both the method of diagnosis and the medium of treatment in this cultural practice" (p. 4) called psychotherapy. Expanding upon this dual function of language within discourse, Harre and Gillett (1994) state:

> It is the medium of many discursive activities, particularly those we classify as cognitive. But it also serves as a basic model or analogue for analysis of episodes in which the actions are performed nonlinguistically, say, by postures and gestures, facial expressions, and so on, that is, by the use of other systems of signs. It is a main thesis of discursive psychology that episodes in which psychological phenomena are brought into being by the use of nonlinguistic signs should be analyzed as if they were through and through linguistic. (p. 99)

SEEKING THE BIOLOGICAL BASES
OF LANGUAGE AND MEANING

Further compounding this problem for psychotherapy, Kimura (1993) similarly reiterates from a neurological perspective that, like linguistics, "very little of the literature on the neuropsychology of speech actually deals with the behavior of *speaking*." Much of it, she maintains, relates to the "semantic and syntactic frameworks within which speech is presumed to be organized" (pp. 2-4). Furthermore, she says, "Investigation into the cortical systems involved in speaking has largely been a matter of describing disorders in individual cases of brain damage" (p. 42). Consequently, due to the apparent limitations in neurological and linguistic knowledge concerning this aspect of human communication, psychotherapy may have to turn to other sources such as psychobiology, discursive psychology, and the study of consciousness, itself, in an attempt to bridge the "gap" between *phenomenology* and behavior.

This may be necessary, as others have pointed out, because it appears to be the speaking process of the client (and not its end-product in the form of words or content) or, by the same token, the listening process of the therapist, which requires closer scrutiny in psychotherapy. As Nichols (1995) observes, "Effective listening—empathic listening—promotes growth in the listener, the one listened to, and the relationship between them" (p. 249). Expanding upon this therapeutic process, Gross (1972) states:

> The depth of Freud's understanding of people is reflected in the novel idea that a prolonged encounter between two people, where one is primarily a speaker and the other primarily a listener, could be useful. There has been much effort on the part of clinicians and researchers directed at understanding such asymmetrical encounters that use natural language as a vehicle for information exchange. Some of the discontinuity between the clinical and research literature is, in part, unavoidable, but the interchange between the two could be enhanced if both would focus on the listening skills of interviewers. (p. 281)

The prospect of psychotherapy research exploring this particular speaking/listening aspect of the therapeutic relationship, especially within a procedure characterized by its founder as "the talking cure," seems timely (Strong, Yoder, and Corcoran, 1995), if not somewhat overdue at this juncture in the field. This is especially so given the recent psychobiological evidence regarding the benefits, as well as hazards, of various kinds of human discourse. As Lynch (1985) states:

> . . . When a person speaks, he or she is inviting others to come inside his or her world, into his or her reality—that is, into his or her body and ultimately into his or her mind's heart. Opening one's mouth to speak signals an attempt to share something inside oneself with someone else. *Real speaking* is communication in the most profound sense: it is an act of communion.

In that sense, speaking is an immensely intimate act—a most intimate form of sharing. (p. 243)

From his psychobiological perspective, Lynch (1985) goes on to explain that a "remarkable series" of physiological changes occur during human speech, including "ones in intrapleural pressure, heart rate, peripheral resistance, blood pressure, cardiac output, and tissue-oxygen content" (p. 173). Of the research which yielded this knowledge, Lynch reports other fortuitous findings as well:

> While we initiated these studies to further the understanding of the mechanisms involved in the blood-pressure communication response, we discovered that human dialogue is far more subtle and complex than we had ever dreamed possible, and we gained not only knowledge, but a new image of the human body. The entire body, even down to the microscopic levels of circulation and exchange of blood gases in individual tissues, is involved in human dialogue. Since the cardiovascular system nourishes every cell in the human body, every one of those cells is at least potentially influenced by human dialogue. Thus, however little perceptible by naked eye or listening ear, the entire human body is activated when one speaks—just as when we flick a switch in a dark house at night, every window lights up. (p. 173)

Thus, Lynch (1985) concludes that gradually, a new equation in the regulation of the human cardiovascular system began to emerge from his work—an equation, he maintains, which "factored the importance of dialogue as central to the regulation of the human body" (p. 181).

Others, as well, such as Efran, Lukens, and Lukens (1990), appear to recognize the apparent power inherent in human discourse in their following account of the psychological influence language exerts upon the self. Language, they maintain, "changes everything"; without language, "there is only 'now'—life unfolding moment by moment without self-consciousness or meaning." But with the advent of language, they say, "an observing 'self' is created and experience is evaluated" (pp. 33-34). Or, as Omer (1994) observes in a quote from D. Spence (1983): "Part of my sense of self depends on my being able to go backward and forward in time and weave a story about who I am, how I got that way, and where I am going, a story that is continuously nourishing and self-sustaining." Take that away from me, he says, and "I am significantly less." In the final analysis, living only for the moment, he adds, "I am not a person at all" (p. 46).

Furthermore, "weaving that story" in psychotherapy seems to be facilitated by the active listening of an empathic therapist. As Nichols (1995) observes, listening strengthens a relationship by cementing the connection with another person while fortifying that other's "sense of self" (p. 10). In the presence of a receptive listener, he says, we are able to "clarify what we think and discover what we feel" (p. 10) (possibly through accessing deeply stored information while simultaneously activating other autonomous processes to be discussed later in this chapter). In the process, Nichols maintains, by giving an account of our experience to someone who listens, we are better able to listen to ourselves—the self thus being "coauthored in dialogue" (p. 10). He elaborates:

> The self is how we personify what we are, as shaped by our experience of being responded to by others. Character is formed in relationships, and the quality of self depends on the nature of that response, the quality of listening we receive. (p. 25)

In this respect, therefore, as Harre and Gillett (1994) explain, the sense of self "is an experience." Their thesis (or that of discursive psychology) holds that experiencing oneself as having "a location in a manifold of places" and in relation to others is, in their estimation, "a necessary condition" (p. 111) for being able to use and to understand language. Dennett (1991) further describes what an individual's world of self-consciousness might be like, without language, in a 1908 quotation by Helen Keller describing the deaf and mute world she inhabited prior to her own language acquisition:

> Before my teacher came to me, I did not know that I am. I lived in a world that was a no-world, I cannot hope to describe adequately that unconscious, yet conscious time of nothingness. . . . Since I had no power of thought, I did not compare one mental state with another. (p. 227)

Moreover, comparing "one mental state with another" is apparently a primary biological function of the brain which Edelman (1992) describes as follows:

Please keep in mind the generalization that as a selective system, the brain (especially the cerebral cortex) is a correlator. It correlates temporal inputs during its own development, and it correlates the properties of signals and scenes in its adult functioning to give rise to consciousness. . . . Consciousness arises from a special set of relationships between perception, concept formation, and memory. These psychological functions depend on categorization mechanisms in the brain. In addition, memory is influenced by evolutionarily established value systems and by homeostatic control systems characteristic of each species. (p. 149)

In other words, as Edelman suggests, the brain, acting as a "correlator" of concepts and experiences, gives birth to consciousness. And since we think in terms of words or symbols, consciousness might in this sense be termed a process of self-reflection through language (a phenomenon which may further have inspired the philosopher Descartes to assert his famous quote, "I think, therefore *I* am" [Italics added], i.e., my self exists). Edelman (1992) elaborates:

Higher-order consciousness arises with the evolutionary onset of semantic capabilities, and it flowers with the accession of language and symbolic reference. . . . The speech areas mediating categorization and memory for language interact with already evolved conceptual areas of the brain. Their proper function in a speech community connects phonology to semantics, using interactions with the conceptual areas of the brain to guide learning. This gives rise to syntax when these same conceptual centers categorize the ordering events occurring during speech acts. As syntax begins to be built and a sufficiently large lexicon is learned, the conceptual centers of the brain treat the symbols and their references and the imagery they evoke as an "independent" world to be further categorized. A conceptual explosion and ontological revolution—a world, not just an environment—are made possible by the interaction between conceptual and language centers.

By these means, concepts of self and of a past and future emerge. Higher-order consciousness depends on building a self through affective intersubjective exchanges. (pp. 149-150)

(By contrast, the *dream* state, Kornhuber [1988, p. 250] observes, is an example of what happens to consciousness and the self when the mind operates without mediation by these "conceptual centers" of the brain.)

Throughout this process of self-creation, as Davis (1994) explains, language plays a role in the "level of sophistication" of consciousness. That is because, he observes, "language provides one more level of *distancing*, if you will, of the person from the object." In other words, he says, it distances something we call self "from objects 'out there'" (pp. 214-215). This *linguistic* view of higher-order consciousness, according to Edelman (1992), may further shed light on how meaning is generated. In this regard, once a self is developed through social and linguistic interactions during consciousness, he states, "a world is developed that requires naming and intending." This world, he adds, includes inner events that are recalled, and imagined events, as well as external events that are perceptually experienced. In this way, Edelman says, "Tragedy becomes possible—the loss of the self by death or mental disorder, the remembrance of unassuageable pain." Thus, he contends, "a high drama of creation and endless imagination emerges" (p. 136). However, ironically, he notes, the self is "the last thing to be understood by its possessor, even after the possession of a theory of consciousness" (p. 136).

The creation of this self therefore appears to be influenced by the fact that, as Rossi (1993) observes, "Consciousness (and mind in general) thrives on information." Mind, he says, *"is nature's supreme design for receiving, generating, and transducing information"* (p. 273). As for the particular relevance of mind to psychotherapy, Orlinsky and Russell (1994) note that modern therapies are often viewed as "applications" or "sciences of the mind" (p. 192) . Underlying these "sciences of the mind," as Harre and Gillett (1994) observe, is the fact that human beings live in two worlds:

> One world is essentially discursive in character; that is, it is a world of signs and symbols subject to normative constraints. It comes into being through intentional action. That is the world that we claim is the proper subject of psychology as a science. The relationship of a person to that world is to be understood through the idea of skillful action. A human being can live in

the world of symbols and intentional normative activity only through the skills they have acquired, and therefore become and continue to be a person. There are two main kinds of skills that are often brought into play together and in complementary ways. There are manual skills, those we use to manipulate material stuff, and there are discursive skills, those we use in our symbolic interactions. (p. 99)

Given this dual function of mind-body, it may therefore seem reasonable to suggest that successful therapists may be nonconsciously utilizing and activating processes in both spheres of human activity. That is, they may be employing interactional and/or nonverbal processes (between therapist and client) to facilitate discursive processes (by the client), resulting in psychobiological and cognitive processes (within the client), acting as primary agents of self-change. This sort of duality, or the fact that a phenomenological mind and material brain can be "embraced within the same conceptual framework," further appears to be supported by the psychobiological work of Rossi (1993). In quoting Karl Pribram, for example, Rossi describes their interrelationships and specific emphases:

I do not mean to convey here that there is no distinction between a behavioristic and an existential-phenomenalistic approach to mind. Elsewhere, I detail this distinction in terms of a search for causes by behaviorists and a search for informational structure reasonably (meaningfully) composed by phenomenologists (Pribram, 1979). What I want to emphasize here is that both approaches lead to conceptualizations that cannot be classified readily as either mental or material. Behaviorists in their search for causes, rely on drives, incentives, reinforcers, and other "force"-like concepts that deliberately have a Newtonian ring. Existentialists in their quest for understanding mental experience come up with structure much as do anthropologists and linguists when they are tackling other complex organizations. And structural concepts are akin to those of modern physics where particles arise from the interactions and relationships among processes. (p. 273)

In other words, similar to the figure-ground phenomenon previously described (or to the story of the blind men studying the elephant), behaviorists, humanists, and psychoanalysts may view human nature from different legitimate, but narrow, perspectives. Consolidating knowledge and observations from their respective schools through the eclectic and integration movement may therefore provide the more comprehensive holistic view required to "put the person back together"—an objective toward which discursive psychology appears to aim as discussed in the following section.

COGNITIVE AND PSYCHOBIOLOGICAL CHANGE THROUGH LANGUAGE AND DISCOURSE

While the greater part of this book thus far has explored nonverbal interactional processes between client and therapist, the remainder of this chapter addresses discursive processes, by the client, hypothesized to result in psychobiological and cognitive change, within the client, acting as the primary agent of therapeutic self-change. Toukmanian (1992) appears to support this view, the main thrust of her work reportedly having been fueled by the conviction that psychotherapy process research should be guided by what she characterizes as "an explicit conceptualization of client cognitive-affective functioning" to serve as a framework for the integration and utilization of "relevant theory and research in the cognitive sciences" (p. 103).

Toukmanian (1992) further observes that an equally important impetus for her work has been the belief that, if an understanding of how clients change is to be achieved, "process and outcome evaluations of psychotherapy should be based on sound assessment methods and procedures that adequately represent the theoretical constructs being studied" (p. 103). Consistent with this objective, the behavioral, biological, and cognitive expressions of therapist attitudes presented herein—expressions which may themselves prove to be the more immediate interactional catalysts promoting cognitive and psychobiological change processes within the client—should be more conducive to empirical study than the hypothetical therapist constructs, "attitudes," or the client's "unconscious."

Paralleling Toukmanian's information processing orientation, but from a discursive perspective, Harre and Gillett (1994) similarly maintain that discursive psychology aims to "reinsert the agent into the story, the one who initiates the action, the one who, in some way, is significant in giving meaning to what he or she does and who they are." Concerning this *agency of the client,* whose introspective process of self-reflection may be termed consciousness within the mind, Harre and Gillett observe that it is not sufficient to acknowledge "a certain agnosticism about the inner causes of behavior." Rather, they state, "We must find a way of understanding a person as an individual focus of discourse and as having a productive role in their own conscious activity" (p. 117).

In attempting to further this understanding of the client's "conscious activity," the exploration of mind and its possible relationship to brain or somatic processes begs the following question by Rossi (1993) in his quote from K. Bowers:

> Now, in mind, with its capacity for symbolizing in linguistic and extra-linguistic forms, can also be regarded as a means for coding processing and transmitting information both intra- and inter-personality. If information processing and transmission is common to both psyche and soma, the mind-body problem might be reformulated as follows: How is information, received and processed at a *semantic* level, transduced into information that can be received and processed at a *somatic* level, and vice versa? (p. 27) (Italics added)

And how, one might also add, is this process facilitative or inhibitive of therapeutic growth? Answers to these questions, it appears, may ultimately depend upon an understanding of how language influences and structures the mind and brain, the topic of the next few sections.

LANGUAGE AS A BRIDGE BETWEEN MIND AND BRAIN

The interaction of mind and brain, until recently, had traditionally been considered the purview of philosophy. This situation may further have existed by default, according to Rossi (1993), since psychologists and biologists who possess knowledge in these areas "usually do not interact" (p. 234). (This circumstance may also have prevailed because biology and psychology are relatively young disciplines as compared to philosophy—considered the precursor and unifier of the modern sciences.) In any event, as Dennett (1991) notes, it has always seemed that our access to "what is happening inside our own brains" has been limited. Nevertheless, he contends, we may not have to know exactly "how the backstage machinery of our brains does its magic" (p. 312) in order to develop a scientific theory of how it functions. In other words, with the help of cognitive science and knowledge of the 'effects of asymmetrical discourse between client and therapist, a higher-order theory may emerge accounting for, and clarifying, observations of therapeutic phenomena involved in the interaction between mind and brain in much the same way that scientific field theories are formulated in the physical sciences.

What may have delayed progress in this area of psychotherapeutic theory building, as well as in the language production area of linguistics, however, may be the prevailing, seemingly redundant, approach to the study of mind-brain processes by traditional psychotherapy which, as Harre and Gillett (1994) point out, may not be necessary. In their words:

> The problem with cognitive psychology as so conceived is the assumption of the existence of mental states and processes, "behind" the mental states and processes of our discursive activities. . . . How do they come to seem to be needed? The answer lies in the dual interpretations that can be made of cognitive models of mental activity. They can either be taken as formal representations of the "grammars" of discursive activities we record and study, or they can be taken as schematic representations of the brain and neural processes necessary to the implementation of our intentions and rules of procedure. (p. 60)

In a manner similar to the limiting effect which the humanistic intrapsychic paradigm of therapist functioning appears to have had upon the field, the apparent redundancy of inferring client mental states or "unconscious motivations" behind discursive activity, in psychoanalysis, may also have impeded psychotherapeutic theory building by diverting attention away from observable phenomena. It is in this respect, therefore, that through integrating psychobiological, cognitive, philosophical, and linguistic knowledge derived from the study of mind, invoking the "unconscious" may be unnecessary and counterproductive. (In this regard, it seems ironic that mind, considered primarily psychological territory, nevertheless appears to have received greater emphasis from philosophy, and from the exploration of consciousness itself, than from psychology per se. As a result, an understanding of client cognitive and psychobiological processes, as previously noted, may ultimately depend upon an integration of knowledge from these allied fields.)

As for the current state of knowledge in the cognitive domain termed "consciousness," Dennett (1991) offers the following overview:

> This is a glorious time to be involved in research on the mind. The air is thick with new discoveries, new models, surprising experimental results—and roughly equal measures of oversold "proofs" and premature dismissals. At this time, the frontier of research on the mind is so wide open that there is almost no settled wisdom about what the right questions and methods are. With so many underdefended fragments of theory and speculation, it is a good idea to postpone our demand for proof and look instead for more or less independent but also inconclusive grounds that tend to converge in support of a single hypothesis. We should try to keep our enthusiasm in check, however. Sometimes what seems to be enough smoke to guarantee a robust fire is actually just a cloud of dust from a passing bandwagon. (p. 257)

Confusion (or "experimentation") in this area notwithstanding, the acknowledgment by biologists of the existence of consciousness and mind, as a legitimate area for scientific study, nevertheless might be regarded as progress in itself. For example, Edelman (1992) offers the following biological view:

> . . . As William James . . . pointed out, mind is a process, not a stuff. Modern scientific study indicates that extraordinary pro-

cesses can arise from matter; indeed, matter itself may be regarded as arising from processes of energy exchange. In modern science, matter has been reconceived in terms of processes; mind has not been reconceived as a special form of matter. . . . mind is a special kind of process depending on special arrangements of matter. . . . (pp. 6-7)

And that of Kornhuber (1988) as well:

Regarding the nature of the soul or the mind (Kornhuber, 1978c; Popper and Eccles, 1977; Sperry, 1983), as opposed to the body or brain, there is still confusion in the literature. The intuitive view that the mind has some autonomy or independence is correct, even in certain cases of lesions in the brain. However, an assumption of complete independence of the mind is incompatible with our law of the conservation of energy. The essence of mind is a process of order or information, and perception, thought, learning, etc., are changes in this order. It is not just modern jargon to speak of order or information in the brain: the amount of information flow in a system (not to be equated with the *value* of that information) may be measured quantitatively (Shannon and Weaver, 1949). Recently it has been found that by multivariate measurement of order in the brain's electrical activity it is possible to distinguish schizophrenic patients from normal controls: there is less order in the cerebral activity of schizophrenics (Dickmann, Reinke, Grazinger, Westphal, and Kornhuber, 1985). (p. 241)

While the apparent "redundancy" of inferring cognitive motivational states behind discursive processes, as well as the linguistic deficit in the study of language production, may have impeded the study of mind, knowledge of the change processes involved in psychotherapy may also have been limited in the past by a lack of knowledge of the brain itself. As Ornstein and Swencionis (1990) observe, "The more we know about how the brain functions to control the health of the body, the more we should be able to both optimize that health and to free the brain to be more creative and understand more of the world around us." This, they say, is what is meant by "the healing brain" which is involved in "maintaining the health of the body at all levels." Thus, they conclude, the more we learn about "the relationship between the brain and the body, the more connections relevant to health we discover" (p. 4).

THE GENESIS
OF DISCURSIVE PSYCHOLOGY

The limitations of the various human disciplines cited thus far may therefore have been the stimulus for the birth of discursive psychology (Harre and Gillett, 1994), paralleling the rise of the eclectic and integrative movement (Lazarus, 1967) in psychotherapy. This discursive approach to the study of cognition involves the integration of knowledge of mind and brain—a psychobiological view or model which, as noted in the introduction, may be more conducive to bridging the "gap" between behavior and phenomenology in psychotherapy than traditional psychotherapeutic theory alone. Enunciating the main premise underlying the discursive perspective on the study of cognition, Harre and Gillett (1994) state:

> . . . Discursive phenomena, for example, acts of remembering, are not manifestations of hidden subjective, psychological phenomena. Sometimes they have subjective counterparts; sometimes they do not. There is no necessary shadow world of mental activity behind discourse in which one is working things out in private. This viewpoint amounts to a fundamental denial of the Cartesian view of human beings, not least because it denies that the workings of the mind are inaccessible. The workings of each other's minds are available to us in what we jointly create conversationally, and if our private mental activity is also symbolic, using essentially the same system, then we can make it available or not, as the situation seems to require. (p. 27)

Their central neural network model, Harre and Gillett (1994) further maintain, provides a scientific view of brain structures and processes, as well as "a formal model of the grammar (or structure and function of discourses) created by the use of those brain structures" (p. 96). This model, Harre and Gillett contend, is an example of a "double analogy" cognitive model which links two fundamental aspects of psychobiological functioning and allows them to be scientifically accessed for research in mind/brain science. For this reason, this model may eliminate confusion in psychotherapy by helping to explicate, and thus operationalize, mind/brain processes possibly contributing to both consciousness and therapeutic change.

MIND, BRAIN, AND THE GENERATION
OF CONSCIOUSNESS THROUGH LANGUAGE

The dawning of human consciousness (our earliest recollections) tends to correspond to the onset of the development of language (around the age of three). From a physiological perspective, Kosslyn and Koenig (1992) describe, by analogy, how the interaction of mind and brain may generate such consciousness:

> Consciousness is not the same thing as neural activity; phenomenological experience cannot be described in terms of ion flows, synaptic connections, and so forth. Consciousness and brain events are members of different categories, and one cannot be replaced by the other. Consciousness is like the light that is produced by a hot filament in a vacuum: The physical events that produce the light cannot be equated with the light itself. Any theory of consciousness must describe a phenomenon that cannot be replaced by a description of brain events. . . . Thus, even though a description of consciousness cannot be replaced by a description of brain activity, brain activity is a necessary prerequisite to consciousness. By analogy, changing the nature of the filament or the glass of the lightbulb will change the quality of the light. (pp. 432-434)

(In other words, extending this analogy to psychotherapy, if consciousness is dependent upon language, then a change in this client "medium" may in turn change the "quality" of client consciousness.) However, knowing what consciousness is *not* does not fully illuminate the nature of mind, or consciousness itself—an understanding of whose essence, as previously stated, may ultimately depend upon an integration of knowledge from linguistics, discursive psychology, psychobiology, philosophy, and cognitive science.

The problem remains, as Edelman (1992) asks, how does one become "conscious of being conscious?" In order to acquire this capacity, he replies, "systems of memory must be related to a conceptual representation of a true self (or social self) acting on an environment and vice versa." Thus, he says, "A conceptual model of selfhood must be built, as well as a model of the past" (p. 131). And in psychotherapy, because language is both the medium of treatment *and* of diagnosis, this "model" of consciousness must therefore be both constructed from, and understood through, language and discourse.

Structuring Mind and Brain
Through Language and Discourse

According to Harre and Gillett (1994), the human mind is constituted by the "discourses" in which it is involved, both "private and public" (p. 104). Mind comes into existence, they contend, "in displays expressive of decisions and judgements and in the performance of actions" (p. 22). The study of mind therefore provides a way to make sense of phenomena, Harre and Gillett say, that arise when different sociocultural discourses are integrated within "an identifiable human individual situated in relation to those discourses" (p. 22). Elaborating upon this view, they state:

> We will therefore identify a person as having a coherent mind or personality to the extent that individuals can be credited with adopting various positions within different discourses and fashioning for themselves, however intentionally or unintentionally, a unique complex of subjectivities (essentially private discourses) with some longitudinal integrity. In this sense, there is a psychological reality to each individual. The difference between the mind or personality as seen in this way and the traditional view is that we see it as dynamic and essentially embedded in historical, political, cultural, social, and interpersonal contexts. It is not definable in isolation. And to be a psychological being at all, one must be in possession of some minimal repertoire or cluster of skills necessary to the management of the discourses into which one may from time to time enter. (pp. 25-26)

The idea that the mind is "a social construction" is evidenced, according to Harre and Gillett (1994), by the fact that human concepts "arise from our discourse and shape the way we think" (p. 22)—a process which they maintain applies not only for concepts of the physical world but also to those of mental origin. Moreover, this model of mind (as a product or construction of the symbols and concepts available in our discourse) may partially explain how the hypothetical construct, the "unconscious," arose in psychoanalysis, i.e., to account for the revelation by clients of unpreconceived dialogue and/or the release of nonconscious information from previously blocked neuron pathways during therapeutic discourse. Rather than resulting from "devious unconscious forces" operating behind, or motivating, discursive activity, however, such revelations, according to Harre and Gillett (1994), may instead be products of the temporal storage characteristic of the brain as well as the constructivistic nature of language and dialogue.

In other words: this discursive factor (accounting for the creation of unpreconceived thoughts and revelations), combined with the possible unblocking of previously unaccessible memories through the release of information which may have been blocking neural pathways, together with the resulting growth of synaptic connections in the brain, may be, or be fueling, autonomous processes within the client (processes which may in turn promote information reprocessing, revised meanings, and self-change—resulting in improved intraindividual communication). That this approach to explicating the processes underlying therapeutic change appears consistent with the views of those who study consciousness is evidenced by the following similar observations of Dennett (1991):

. . . We persist in the habit of positing a separate process of observation (now of inner observation) intervening between the circumstances about which we can report, and the report we issue—overlooking the fact that at some point, this regress of interior observers must be stopped by a process that unites content with their verbal expression without any intermediary content-appreciator. . . . Internal communications created in this way do in fact have the effect of organizing our minds into indefinitely powerful reflective or self-monitoring systems. Such powers of reflection have often been claimed to be at the heart of consciousness, with good reason. (pp. 319-320)

Additionally, the emphasis which this view of consciousness places on verbal expression and self-reflection appears similar to the discursive perspective of Harre and Gillett (1994), who accord priority to language in defining the phenomena for a "scientific psychology." In so doing, they say, cognition can be both presented and understood through "the ordinary languages through which we think, rather than looking for abstract representations of them" (p. 27). Qualifying this stance, Harre and Gillett (1994) maintain that words per se do not "structure" cognition. Rather, they state, discourse—composed of the communicative use of signs and symbols, pictures, and words in use—is the "medium in which cognitive activity takes shape" (p. 57). Furthermore, because these "ordinary languages," or systems of communication, both comprise and construct the information stored in our brains, they may therefore provide the link between mind and brain—a link which, as suggested earlier (and as explored in greater detail in subsequent sections), may help bridge the gap in psychotherapy between behavior, meaning, and intentionality.

Computerlike Functions in the Brain

In his study of consciousness, Dennett (1991) offers an analogy that may illuminate the functions of brain involved in the formation of mind:

How could the brain be the seat of consciousness? . . . It turns out that the way to imagine this is to think of the brain as a computer of sorts. The concepts of computer science provide the crutches of imagination we need if we are to stumble across the *terra incognita* between our phenomenology as we know it by "introspection" and our brains as science reveals them to us. By thinking of our brains as information-processing systems, we can gradually dispel the fog and pick our way across the great divide, discovering how it might be that our brains produce all the phenomena. (p. 433)

Commenting upon the "brain as computer" analogy in relation to mind and brain, Rossi (1993) cautions, however, that human functioning compared in this manner "would have to be described as a sort of transcendent computer that is continually reprogramming itself as a function of ongoing life experience" (p. 157). Strong's (1995) view in this regard appears similar as implied in his statement: "The meaning of the past must be constantly reevaluated and revised in light of what is emerging in the present" (p. 378). And Wexler's (1974) observations seem consistent as well: "Differentiation and integration do not occur only in one single isolated moment in therapy," he says. They characterize "what the client is doing continuously" (p. 68).

Kornhuber's (1988) biological view also appears to take this automatic human reprogramming characteristic into account. As he explains:

> The relationship between brain and mind is analogous to that between hardware and software in a computer. Although only certain types of software are compatible with a given hardware, the software is not a function of the hardware: on the contrary, it makes the hardware work in a specific way. Whereas in species such as worms most of the software is an automatism of the network, in humans (if we leave out the "operating systems") it is the result of education, culture, self-improvement, and learning. Again, it is not just jargon to speak of "software" in the brain; it is everyday experience that to some extent we are able to change the programs operating in our brains at will (at least under proper conditions, such as being alert, free of drug addictions, etc.).
>
> Brain software use that results in the formation of habits even influences the fine structure of the hardware (e.g., synapses). There are sensitive phases in the ontogenetic development of cerebral hardware, during which the consolidation of synapses depends on stimulation, learning, and action. For instance, physiological and behavioral deficits will develop in kittens following early monocular deprivation (closure of one eye) for two or three months after birth (Wiesel and Hubel, 1963). Similarly, in the human infant there is a sensitive phase for language-related hearing in the first year: hence the importance of early diagnosis of hearing disorders by means of audi-

tory evoked brain stem potentials, and of obtaining a hearing aid if necessary. If the opportunity of the sensitive period is missed, the resulting structural deficit in the hardware may limit the software development. (pp. 241-242)

Viewing human psychological and biological functioning from this computerlike information processing perspective also appears consistent with what Rossi (1993) terms, the "profound shift that is currently taking place in our understanding of the biology of life from the study of its matter to the study of its energy dynamics to the current study of its informational structure" (p. 237).

Nevertheless, to avoid diminishing the function of the brain in its computerlike role, Kornhuber (1988) cautions that the task of the brain is not to serve as a "maximum-size memory store" but rather, to act as a behavior guide "for the welfare of the individual and those it is close to." The brain therefore has to be a rapidly working device for "cognition, planning, and decision making." Thus, while memory may be an indispensable helping function, he says, it is not the "primary function of the brain" (pp. 245-246). In other words, extending this computer analogy further, bridging the gap between mind and brain may not only involve gaining an understanding of RAM (random access memory), but also of the "hardware" of the brain working in conjunction with the "software" of the mind to perform the task of self-development and the preservation of self and allies.

While memory may not be the primary function of the brain, Edelman (1992) contends that it nonetheless performs an essential function in the maintenance of consciousness in conjunction with other processes. As he explains:

A person, like a thing, exists on a world line in four-dimensional spacetime. But because individual human beings have intentionality, memory, and consciousness, they can sample patterns at one point on that line and on the basis of their personal histories subject them to plans at other points on that world line. They can then enact these plans, altering the causal relations of objects in a definite way according to the structures of their memories. It is as if one piece of spacetime could slip and map onto another piece. The difference, of course, is that the entire transaction does not involve any unusual piece of physics, but simply the ability to categorize, memorize, and form plans according to a conceptual model. Such an historical alteration of causal chains could not occur in so rich a way in any combination of inanimate nonintentional objects, for they lack the appropriate kind of memory. (p. 169)

In short, bridging the "gap" between phenomenology and behavior in psychotherapy would involve gaining an understanding of the total software of the mind and its relationship to the hardware of the brain. Through the software, memories are expressed and then reprocessed to produce what Edelman (1992) terms, "a historical alteration of causal chains"—a process possibly similar to Hill's (1994) "mechanisms of change involved in transformational dialogue." However, without a holistic understanding of these processes, Hill cautions that psychotherapy could simply end up, as it has in the past, "with a description of what takes place in therapy rather than an explanation of how change comes about" (p. 95). And how it "comes about" may depend heavily upon the apparent power of language and discourse operating in conjunction with the correlative function of the brain.

The Generative Power of Language

With respect to the exploration of *transformational dialogue*, Harre and Gillett (1994) contend that the role of language in forming and refining thoughts may be becoming increasingly clearer "from theoretical, clinical, and experimental work in cognitive psychology (Kormiloff-Smith, 1979; Luria, 1973; Vygotsky, 1962)" (p. 82). Consistent with this view, Dennett (1991) similarly observes from his study of consciousness that language "infects and inflects our thought at every level." The words in our vocabularies, he says, are "catalysts that can precipitate fixations of content as one part of the brain tries to communicate with another." The structures of grammar, Dennett further states, "enforce a discipline in our habits of thought, shaping the ways in which we probe our own 'data bases'" (p. 301).

Dennett (1991) elaborates upon the role which language plays in the formation of mind:

Think of all the structures you have learned, in school and else-where: telling time, arithmetic, money, the bus routes, using the telephone. But of all the structures we become acquainted with in the course of our lives, certainly the most pervasive and powerful source of discipline of our minds is our native tongue. (One often sees best by looking at contrasts; Oliver Sacks, in *Seeing Voices*, 1989, vividly draws attention to the riches language brings to mind by recounting the terrible impoverishment of a deaf child's mind, if that child is denied early access to a *natural* language—Sign, or sign language). . . . Vocabulary at our disposal influences not only the way we talk to others, but the way we talk to ourselves. (p. 300)

Furthermore, from a biological standpoint, language and the mind appear to accomplish these feats through the constructivistic property and function of speech characterized by Kosslyn and Koenig (1992) as "generative." In other words, an infinite number of utterances or sentences can be produced and understood through an "ability to combine a finite set of words in new ways" (p. 212) . Or as Edelman (1992) puts it, the mind utilizes words in the formation of concepts by "recursively restimulating portions of global mappings containing previous synaptic changes," thus giving rise to "combinations of relationships and categories" (p. 110). The categorizing and generalizing power of this conceptual system, interacting "reentrantly and recursively with specialized language areas of the brain," he says, is nearly "unlimited" (p. 131).

From a linguistic perspective, the brain may achieve such "expressive variety," Jackendoff (1994) contends, by storing not whole sentences, but rather "words and their meanings, plus *patterns* [schemata] into which words can be placed" (p. 12). He further characterizes this constructivistic property as innate. What human nature gives us, he states, "are the building blocks from which the infinite variety of possible concepts can be constructed" (p. 190). The argument for this construction of experience, he adds, may further derive from the fact that the act of understanding language is not just a passive absorption of information. It also involves a great deal of nonconscious activity, he says, "organizing (or reorganizing) the input signal in accordance with the patterns of mental grammar" (p. 164). The way we experience language, he therefore concludes, is dependent upon the mental representations we non-consciously construct "in response to the physical signals striking our sense organs" (p. 163).

With respect to their nonconscious nature, Jackendoff (1994) observes that we are not normally aware of these processes of inter-pretation by which we create meaning. In other words, he states, it is impossible "to turn them off and hear spoken language as mere sounds" (p. 163). Thus, this ongoing, creative, spontaneous, constructivistic ability of language, whose dialogical content within social discourse is generally unpreconceived and dependent upon the individual's unique environmental history, as well as the discur-sive context at hand, both creates the idiosyncratic self—and serves as the mechanism to change or revise it. Self-actualization opera-tionalized in this way therefore appears consistent with Wexler's (1974) view of the phenomenon which he defines as: "the develop-ment and utilization of the capacity to process and organize informa-tion in such a way that the person is able to be his own source for creation of new experience and change through his cognitive func-tioning" (p. 90).

This creative, constructive property of language may further have been what influenced George Herbert Mead (1962) to describe the "essence of self" as dialogically cognitive. The self lies, Mead observed, "in the internalized conversation of gestures which consti-tutes thinking, or in terms of which thought or reflection proceeds" (p. 173). Furthermore, the unpredictability, in content, of this construc-tive speech process may also account for the strong humanistic conten-tion, as articulated by Friedman (1992), that no "general theory of psychogenesis and no general knowledge of persons will tell us in advance what will be their actual mixture of spontaneity and compul-sion in any particular situation" (p. 169).

Accounting for this spontaneity, Friedman describes "many-faced otherness" as the quality to which he attributes the uniqueness of each individual. The other not only has "a different mind, way of thinking or feeling, conviction or attitude," he says, but also has "a different perception of the world, a different recognition and order of meaning, a different touch from the regions of existence, a differ-ent faith, a different soil" (p. 154). And this "soil" from which the self arises, according to Sexton and Whiston (1994), is language from which meanings are generated from the individual's environ-mental experience and social history. They elaborate:

> . . . It is by virtue of how language is used in the coconstruction of explanations about self, others, and events that meaning is developed in relationships. Because the basic premise of social constructivism is that meaning is coconstructed, the role of language is crucial in this context of a social interaction. There-fore, because human systems are, by their nature, language-generating systems, they are consequently meaning-generating systems (Anderson and Goolishiam, 1992).

> There are two ways in which language is important. On the one hand, words and vocabulary are symbols that carry implicit meaning. As meaning-laden symbols, language might stimulate affective cognitive experiences. Language might create an idiosyncratic brand of knowledge because these sym-bols are based on a distinctive set of social assumptions and beliefs (Maturana and Varela, 1987). As a symbolic medium, language is also used to develop narrative explanations about one's life, one's culture, and one's relationships that are the reference point for understanding and generating meaning (Gergen, 1985). (p. 64)

While language in the form of words and thoughts may generate meaning, Harre and Gillett (1994) nevertheless contend that thoughts are not objects in the mind, but the "activity and essence of mind." Thoughts, they state, reside in the uses we make of public and private systems of signs. To be able to think, therefore, Harre and Gillett maintain, is to be a "skilled user of these sign systems" (p. 49) or to be capable of managing them properly. Illustrating how a skillful user likely achieves this proper psychological operation, they state:

> When a person thinks, he or she does not merely undergo a set of internal processes that perform calculations on data but searches for meanings by trying different moves between constructions of the world. This activity enables someone to find ways of making the most sense of their current situation

(real or hypothetical) in the light of everything else they have experienced (and interpreted in the light of their constructs). When a person acts, they do not execute certain operations as a result of this or that inner force. Human actors adopt constructions and use them to organize their activities in the light of the meanings they find in things. (p. 136)

These "constructions," Harre and Gillett further maintain, allow one to anticipate events in ways that "recapture the useful features of similarly construed events in the past." This abstraction process, they contend, determines which similarities and differences will enter into the content of a construct, thereby offering "a set of reproducible strategies that may or may not prove their worth in practice." In other words, Harre and Gillett (1994) state, having made the assimilations required to construct events in a certain way, a person is provided with "a strategy for adaptive action." Thus, they say, "the person as scientist is in the business of finding and refining useful ways of predicting and psychologically adapting to the challenges of life situations" (p. 134).

In this regard, Rossi (1990) describes the probable physiological hardware underlying the somatic connection between these phenomenological "constructs" and behavior:

Most researchers believe that psychological experience and behavior are somehow encoded within the neural networks of the brain. What is really new is the idea that under the impact of stress (any form of emotional or novel experience), many informational substances are released throughout the body. Many of these substances can reach the neural networks of the brain to encode our life experiences in a state-dependent manner; that is, what we remember, learn, and experience is dependent on the different psychological states encoded in the brain by informational substances. The same informational substances that encode psychological experience simultaneously regulate the biology of cellular metabolism right down to the molecular-genetic level. These informational substances are the new bridge between mind and body. Any life experience that upsets the stress-prone homeostatic processes that regulate health and illness therefore can be encoded throughout the mind-body on many levels by these informational substances; sensation and perception, mood and behavior, psychological complexes and psychosomatic problems are linked by this common network of informational transducting on the molecular level. From this psychobiological perspective, the goal of all forms of psychotherapy, from hypnosis and psychoanalysis to the cognitive, behavioral, and body therapies, may be recognized as different approaches to facilitating the many pathways of mind-body information flow (Erickson and Rossi, 1989; Rossi, 1980; Rossi and Ryan, 1986). (p. 357)

In addition, shaping this physiological hardware, and possibly enabling the very existence of psychotherapy itself, is the role which the environment plays in this equation. As neurologist Damasio (1994) observes:

Much of the brain's circuitry, at any given moment of adult life, is individual and unique, truly reflective of that particular organism's history and circumstances. . . . Each human organism operates in collectives of like beings; the mind and the behavior of individuals belonging to such collectives and operating in specific cultural and physical environments are not shaped merely by the activity-driven circuitries mentioned above, and even less are they shaped by genes alone. To understand in a satisfactory manner the brain that fabricates human mind and human behavior, it is necessary to take into account its social and cultural context. (p. 260)

As a result of the influence of this "social and cultural context," as expressed through language, the proper domain of psychology per se, as previously noted, therefore appears to be more directly related to the brain's software composed of the cognitive (thoughts) and linguistic (words) functions influencing the person as "scientist" as well as the "scientific data" or meanings (in the form of information and experiences stored as memories in the brain). These topics therefore comprise the next section of this book.

THOUGHT AND THE FORMATION OF MIND

According to Harre and Gillett (1994), thoughts are comprised of the concepts which compose them, i.e., the "words that make up the verbal expression of the thought, or the components of the picture, real or imagined" (p. 40), with which we think. Thoughts, they say, "have objects of which a person can give account; they encompass our reasons for behaving thus and so; they aim at truth and propriety" (p. 51). In expressing thoughts, Harre and Gillett observe that symbols or signs mediate semantic responses to presentations. In other words, rather than being controlled by unconscious forces during these responses, individuals instead "aim to be true to a practice located in a discourse in which they participate" (p. 121).

In describing the resulting effect of this dialogical constructive process which aims at "truth and propriety," Harre and Gillett (1994) contend that an individual's semantic response is "a signification," and in making it, the person takes an active role in structuring his or her domain of activity. In other words, they say, individuals actively structure their field of action "according to the symbols available to them in certain discourse" (p. 121). In this respect, "rules" governing the use of signs, according to Harre and Gillett, "permeate and structure the intentional or mental lives of human beings." These rules, they state, are "discernible and explicable when we locate them in language games and forms of life where the people who follow them live their lives." Furthermore, they say, without an appreciation of the workings of the relevant rule-governed tracts of human activity (about which more will be said in a later section of this chapter concerning logical reasoning), "the meanings that inform the behavior of the human being" (p. 20) cannot be understood.

As for the schematic and/or conceptual nature of the signs or symbols themselves, they have been variously termed "memes" (Dawkins, 1978, p. 206) or "lexemes" (Davis, 1994, p. 83). These terms refer to units of stored information which, according to Dawkins (1978), can spread from brain to brain on a psychological level in a manner analogous to genes on a biological level. Dawkins elaborates:

> Examples of memes are tunes, ideas, catch-phrases, clothes fashions, ways of making pots or of building arches. Just as genes propagate themselves in the gene pool by leaping from

body to body via sperm or egg, so memes propagate themselves in the meme pool by leaping from brain to brain via a
process which, in a broad sense, can be called imitation. If a
scientist hears, or reads about, a new idea, he passes it on to his
colleagues and students. He mentions it in his articles and his
lectures. If the idea catches on, it can be said to propagate
itself, spreading from brain to brain. (p. 206)

In this manner, Dennett (1991) maintains, "thousands of memes,
mostly borne by language, but also by wordless 'images' and other
data structures, take up residence in an individual brain, shaping its
tendencies and thereby turning it into mind" (p. 254).

In this model of mind, the schematic structure, which Toukmanian
(1992) purports to influence "meanings, values, and intentions,"
might further be analogous to, or composed of, memes. Expanding
upon the relevance of such informational structures to psychotherapy,
Toukmanian states, ". . . The more complex the schematic structures
with respect to an event, the broader will be the range of a person's
explorations and consequently the higher the probability of noticing
more of the available information." What individuals attend to and
select from in a given context and at any given moment, she therefore
maintains, depends "on their schematic readiness, or on the network
of structures that is available to them" (p. 81). The concept of the
schematic structure may further be similar to that of sets described
by Gutsch (1990) as "personal patterns of thinking and/or behaving
that provide people with a readiness to respond in a given way"
(p. 153). (In explaining how this phenomenon might relate to psychotherapy in predisposing therapist action, for example, Beitman
[1992] describes countertransference as "interpersonal schemas"
structuring the beliefs and values of therapists, which may result in
distorted thinking, and/or behavior, and thus prejudge or "interfere
with their carrying out effective treatment" [p. 214].)

Finally, consistent with what some believe to be the thrust of
future counseling research (toward the explication of "choice, will,
and volition" which Strong, Yoder, and Corcoran [1995, p. 383]
view as fundamental to human agency and its enhancement), this
section on mind and thought concludes with Kornhuber's (1988)
biologically based observation that although language is indispensable to communication, it does not provide its main behavioral

impulsion. In his estimation, the language system "interprets rather than causes behavior" (Gazzaniga, 1980, p. 249). By implication, therefore, the instigation of conscious behavior might thus be viewed as a function of the self fueled by meanings, generated through language, directing the hardware of the brain to coordinate the execution of somatic and behavioral functions. As Smedslund (1995) observes:

> This is why it appears plausible that people get angry because they, or persons they care for, are insulted, that they become afraid because they believe there is danger, that they believe a certain act will lead to the goal because it did so in the past, that they focus on negative aspects when they are in a bad mood, and so on. These relationships cannot be otherwise, given the way we talk. (p. 200)

Concluding this section and summarizing these synergistic mind-body processes from a biological perspective, Kornhuber (1988) states:

> . . . Cognition and thinking are carried out by the brain by means of parallel analogue computation; by pattern recognition and identification of objects by self-organizing systems using inborn detection, constancy mechanisms, and other hardware, "operating systems," and learned rules; by the creation of new thoughts through fantasy; and finally, with evaluation by means of feedback and volitional goals. . . . The inborn order of the brain is thus differentiated, tested, and validated by interaction with the environment. (p. 249)

MIND AND THE PHENOMENON OF THERAPEUTIC GROWTH

Within the theoretical substrate of memes, schematic structures, and "operating systems," therapeutic growth might therefore be viewed as: self-development through psychological environmental enrichment (discourse stimulating the reprocessing of information) induced by the generation and orchestration of symbols and concepts within the client's mind. (Or, as one of my recent clients replied when asked by a friend why he was involved in therapy: "I'm seeing a psychologist to reprogram myself"—a statement which, although it provoked laughter from both individuals at that time, may nevertheless not have been far from the truth.) In other words, as Wexler (1974) puts it, "Cognitive processes act on and transform information." Thus, information (in the form of words and thoughts), he says, is "the raw data or input for the process of experiencing" which may derive from "stimulus sources external to the person or from stimulus sources internal to him" (pp. 59-60). Moreover, these linguistic symbols, as products of self-disclosure in therapeutic discourse, appear to be spontaneously generated and simultaneously employed by the client to revise the self and expand the mind. As the mind expands through language or software development, it in turn creates greater capacity for growth in the hardware or synapses, which increases the growth potential of the software, and so on.

In addition to the growth achieved through the schematic software changes of self-revision, such development may also be influenced by the act, itself, of talking to another human being. In this respect, there is evidence to suggest that the environmental enrichment provided by human discourse may effect synaptic development as well. Observations in therapy such as those by Efran, Lukens, and Lukens (1990) further seem to support this hypothesis. As they state, "the fact that we are talking is sometimes more important than what is said"—a process, they maintain, which is "intuitively" appreciated. In this regard, Efran, Lukens, and Lukens note that clients in individual and group psychotherapy settings often report "being nourished simply by being there—linked in conversation—despite the fact that they didn't gain any particularly new or noteworthy insights" (p. 66).

The plausibility of neurological growth resulting from discourse also appears consistent with the psychobiological behavioral development theory proposed by Gandelman (1992). He points out, for example, that development being altered "as a consequence of the young organism's interaction with its environment" is a phenomenon that has received a great deal of attention. This he claims to be conceptually straightforward: "Behavioral reactivity to certain kinds of stimulation alters brain function, which in turn alters brain development. An altered brain leads inevitably to altered behavior" (p. 167).

Furthermore, Gandelman maintains, environmental enrichment may have therapeutic applications since this phenomenon has been shown "to attenuate behavioral deficits caused by damage to certain regions of the brain" (p. 190). How the brain may achieve this neurological "cure" is suggested by Damasio (1994):

> . . . Since different experiences cause synaptic strengths to vary within and across many neural systems, experience shapes the design of the circuits. Moreover, in some systems more than in others, synaptic strengths can change throughout the life span, to reflect different organism experiences, and as a result, the design of brain circuits continues to change. The circuits are not only receptive to the results of first experience, but repeatedly pliable and modifiable by continued experience.
>
> Some circuits are remodeled over and over throughout the life span, according to the changes an organism undergoes. Other circuits remain mostly stable and form the backbone of the notions we have constructed about the world within, and about the world outside. (p. 112)

Further expanding upon this phenomenon of environmental stimulation, Gandelman (1992) states:

> The rationale behind this experimental strategy is that the augmented stimulation provided by the enriched environment enhances brain activity, which eventually manifests in physiological and behavioral change. Therefore differences should be apparent between the brains and behavior of subjects from enriched and impoverished environments. That the brain responds to "exercise" is not at all a new concept. . . . According to Renner and Rosenweig (1987), the Italian scientist Malacarne (1744-1816) demonstrated with birds that enriched experience enhances brain growth.
>
> Modern study of environmental enrichment was given impetus by Hebb (1949), who proposed that enriched experiences occurring early in life lead to alterations of the brain, which in turn improve an animal's problem-solving ability. This proposal led to a number of researchers, including Hebb's own students, to test the effects of environmental enrichment.

Although more than four decades have elapsed since the publication of Hebb's book, interest in environmental enrichment continues. This enduring attention is probably due in large measure to the marked changes in the brain that have been reported to result from exposure to what appears to be a rather innocuous manipulation. (p. 183)

The form of brain growth which occurs in response to environmental enrichment appears to vary with the age of the organism, however—a developmental process described by Kornhuber (1988) as follows:

Whereas nerve cells proliferate in the brain of the human fetus only up to week 22 and migrate only up to week 27, there are then about four years of cell differentiation and myelogenesis, as well as the chance to alter synaptic functions over the entire lifetime. During all these years, software use obviously contributes to the maintenance of cerebral hardware function. A conclusion from rehabilitation research with brain-lesioned and geriatric patients is that while half the recipe for maintaining health and freedom is proper food and rest, the other half is exercise and active learning. (p. 242)

Among the psychological operations to be exercised "over the entire lifetime," according to Kornhuber (1988), is learning by "looking at things from different points of view, including those of other people." In his estimation, it is not just that we need feedback from the environment to test our programs, "we must also search for reality and accept it" (p. 249). And, as previously noted, this sort of looking at things from different points of view, gaining feedback from the environment, and searching for reality appears to occur automatically within the client, through experiential exploration in psychotherapy which, in turn, simultaneously revises the self and alters the mind.

This alteration of mind, as Rossi (1993) points out, may thus effect physiological change through the body's immune system as well. As he states:

. . . The well-documented research cited by Ader (1983) and Locke et al. (1984) concerning the influence of psychosocial factors, mood, and belief systems on illness, disease, and healing clearly indicates that the mind is continually modulating the immune system. What success mind-body therapy currently achieves in modulating immune functions is via the nonspecific approaches that work to a certain degree (even spectacularly well in some cases), even though we usually do not know what the therapeutic mechanisms of action are. We can drive a car quite well without knowing how the engine operates, but when there is a breakdown, the more detailed our knowledge of engine mechanisms, the better we will be able to fix it. The present state of our psychotherapeutic knowledge of these mind-body mechanisms is somewhat akin to the average driver who knows there is an engine somewhere that does something when we turn on a key and push the gas pedal. (pp. 225-226)

In other words, according to Rossi (1993), citing the work of I. Black, "environmental events may alter gene readout by altering nerve impulse activity." In turn, he states, "alteration of gene readout changes neural and behavioral function." This, Black maintains, is not a "modest" claim. In his estimation, "Experience alters the function of neurons at the most fundamental level, the genome" (Rossi, 1993, p. 165).

Again, however, this hardware notwithstanding, the question remains as to how these biological processes are activated by psychotherapy—and how they translate into therapeutic growth—the mechanisms for which, as previously noted, may be imbedded within language and discourse itself.

THERAPEUTIC GROWTH
VERSUS MENTAL "ILLNESS"

Rather than being categorized as abnormal or catastrophic, therefore, viewed from an information perspective, psychological symptoms and problems, according to Rossi (1993, p. 271), can be positive signs signalling the need for "creative change." In this sense, viewing psychotherapeutic change processes from constructivistic language and information processing perspectives may help dispel the stigma attached to mental "illness." In other words, neurosis and incongruence might therefore be regarded as an opportunity for personal growth thus making the term "treatment," as Wexler and Rice (1974) put it, "something of a misnomer." This is so, they believe, because therapeutic intervention within this model involves less the "correction and removal" of psychopathology than it does the "facilitation and enhancement" (p. 314) of growth.

Rossi (1993) expands upon this point in a quote from Jungian analyst, Albert Kreinheder:

> Our wound is the place where the Self finds entry into us. The calamity that strikes may be the election, the call to individuation. . . . When neurosis or a sickness comes to one, it does not mean that he is an inferior person with a defective character. In a way, it is a positive sign showing potentials for growth, as if within there is a greater personality pressing to the surface. . . . As conditions change, there are new psychic contents to integrate. Once a window is opened to the archetypal world, there is no way to close it again. Either we grow with the individuation urge, or it grows against us (pp. 269-270).

This view of neurosis also appears similar to the humanistic perspective put forth by Friedman (1992). As he notes, "If we begin by honoring each person's unique relation to reality, then to say of a person that he or she is 'sick' does not imply that this person is outside reality, but only that he or she needs help in being brought into the dialogue . . ." (p. 120).

Paralleling this view, and quoting one of the seasoned psychotherapists in his study of master practitioners in the field, Goldberg (1992) reports:

> *After thirty years of practice, I now see the positive side of psychopathology. I now see the meaning and value of disturbed behavior. Before I would shame the patient because of his neurosis. The first few years of practice I thought everyone had to be like me. This wears you down after a while.* You find out that people have to be who they are. It is a fallacious message, I believe, that you know how another person should live. (p. 99)

In fact, Goldberg (1992) reports that with time and experience, most of the master therapists in his study had "greatly changed" their views on neurosis. In his words:

> They are less grandiose about their skills. They regard them-
> selves less *the crucial* agent of change and more as a useful
> facilitative agent. Changes in one's view of neurosis and
> human nature are strongly affected by one's understanding of
> human suffering. The need to change their views about human
> behavior came from their gradual recognition that their clinical
> training had been directed by misguided clinical theories. . . .
> These practitioners, both males and females, currently have a
> greater respect for and a firmer faith in their patients' healing
> capacities than in the past. . . . Because they themselves have
> lived more fully, they are now less captive of the authority of
> abstract theory—which is actually the distillation of other
> practitioners' experiences, presented as universal occurrence.
> (p. 49)

In other words, these master therapists may have come to the realization that a symptom can be converted into a "signal" (Rossi, 1993, p. 271) for therapeutic change—change which can be facilitated and actualized through "dialogue" with a receptive and understanding human being (i.e., the "scanning process" referred to earlier by Penfield and Roberts, 1959). Or, as Lynch (1985) maintains, other human beings are necessary, in the process of self-actualization, to remind us that we feel and to teach us how and what we "feel" (p. 270).

LANGUAGE AND DISCOURSE AS A REMEDY
FOR NEUROSES AND INCONGRUENCE

In addition to teaching us what we "feel," this need for other human beings might also apply to facilitating an understanding what and how we *think*. In this regard, the dyadic thought-guided experiential process of therapeutic growth, activated through discourse, is achievable, according to Harre and Gillett (1994), because human beings can "pool" (p. 43) their thoughts and, through infinite generativity, can achieve change that would be impossible individually. The target of such therapeutic change might further be that aspect of the self which Beitman (1992) refers to as the "core interpersonal schema" (p. 207) or the map by which clients interpret and construct their reality (a concept possibly similar to the *belief systems* of rational emotive therapy or the *lifestyle* of Adlerian therapy). In facilitating therapeutic change, the successful therapist might in this sense be said to activate a process of self-disclosure within the client which unblocks information and aids in reprocessing it by automatically reorganizing intrapersonal schemas composed of meanings structuring the self.

Throughout this self-revision process, the "social-verbal context" (Hayes, 1990) is targeted for change as opposed to individual thoughts or feelings (thus respecting the client's unique or idiosyncratic reality). Hayes provides the rationale for doing so by pointing out that the destructive relation between thoughts and feelings and overt behavior is produced by contexts of "literality, reason giving, and emotional control." Thus, he says, "we focus on changing the context itself, not the thought or feelings," which then permits the client to feel a feeling "as a feeling without having to have it structure overt action of any kind" (p. 142). This process by which client change is activated through targeting "social-verbal contexts" may further be illuminated by the discursive approach of Toukmanian (1992). She maintains, for example, that change facilitated at the level of clients' internal mental operations occurs through "a variety of linguistic and paralinguistic acts" comprised of "features or characteristics specific to the type of information being processed (e.g., sensory, imagistic, affective, conceptual)" (p. 101).

These "linguistic and paralinguistic acts" might also be viewed as applications or expressions of thought, whose relationship to language and discourse is summarized by Harre and Gillett (1994):

> Thoughts are *intentional*, in the sense that they are about things or are directed to ends that arise in human activity. They are, at heart, communicable; other signs (concepts) are learned as we deal with things around us in the presence and with the help of others. As we do this, we latch on to the skills of referring to them and isolating their common features that are made available by the other people who train us to use them. Thoughts

play a part in the *explanation of behavior* because they account for the links anyone makes between their present and past experiences, and these links (or the words and signs [concepts] that capture them) shape their activity in present experiences. Thoughts have a *link to truth* because to be successful one must master the trick of thinking of the world as it really is (using terms and expressions in their validated ways), not just as one might wish it to be. *Language* and thought are tied to one another because talk about thought is a way of talking about discursive activity. (pp. 48-49)

Moreover, "thinking of the world as it really is" would seem to involve a search for meaning, facilitated, as Harre and Gillett (1994) maintain, through certain kinds of discourse which "make available movement and negotiation in relation to the meanings that inform one's behavior." These tend to be found, they state, "in contexts in which the intersection of discourse and dialogue between patterns of signification is itself a validated type of activity." In other words, they say, "If individuals are affirmed and exposed in nonthreatening ways to the alternatives presented by different constructions, then one would expect them to develop and be comfortable with the skills of discourse (p. 127). And, since the "affirmation of individuals" and the "nonthreatening context" appear similar to the objectives of the therapeutic relationship, a parallel between such discourse, and that of the therapeutic encounter, might thus be drawn.

Presenting a similar psychotherapeutic example, Garfield (1990) observes that if the client is motivated and the therapist is perceived by the client as an "interested, competent, and nonjudgmental person, the likelihood of a positive outcome is increased" (p. 240). With respect to the nonjudgmental character of such interaction (corresponding to the Rogerian construct "unconditional positive regard"), Wexler (1974) explains that the therapist, functioning "as a surrogate information processor," simply attempts to "organize as accurately as possible the meaning of the information in process in the client, whatever the nature of its content." Judgement, evaluation, approval, or disapproval, he says, just do not happen to be "involved in the task" (p. 110). In other words, the absence of therapist *inhibitive* judgments (countertransference) ostensibly predisposes clients toward more readily reprocessing information through self-disclosure—the growth or extent of which, Harre and Gillett (1994) therefore maintain, "crucially depends on the quality and nature of the experiences and encounters that form the history of one's own subjectivity" (p. 174).

As for the content of therapeutic disclosure facilitated in this nonjudgmental manner, it appears to be predictable to both client and therapist only in its broad outline and not in terms of the specific actions clients exhibit or the specific words they choose to express themselves. This characteristic would further appear consistent with a key tenet of humanistic psychology as expressed by Friedman (1992):

> The human image does not mean some fully formed, conscious model of what one should become—certainly not anything simply imposed upon us by the culture or any mere conformity with society through identification with its goals. The paradox of the human image is that it is at once unique and universal, but universal only through the unique. For each one of us, the human image is made up of many images and half-formed images, and is itself constantly changing and evolving. In contrast to any static ideal whatsoever, it always has to do with the unique response to the concrete moment, a response that cannot be foreseen and cannot be repeated, objectified, or imitated.
>
> The human image is our becoming in the truest sense of the word, that is, our becoming as a person and as a human being. (p. 132)

Extrapolating from Friedman's observations: without "a conscious model of what one should become," the therapist's analysis and understanding of the information reprocessed by the client (the *what* of psychotherapy) would therefore appear secondary to the understanding achieved in therapy by the client—who is the expert on his or her self—the therapist possessing primarily expertise concerning the interactional processes (the *how* of psychotherapy) promoting that client's understanding and revision of the self. In this sense, consistent with humanistic theory, the client's individuality and intentionality are not sacrificed by promoting self-disclosure through facilitative therapist behavior, mainly because the center of evaluation and disclosure (content and direction of the dialogue) essentially remains within the client as opposed to the therapist. As Wexler (1974) explains, if the therapist is fully engaged in the task of attending to the client and responding empathically, then "ideally the only information in process in him would be that which might be in process in the client; there would be nothing else." What is unique about this approach, he notes, is that the client-centered therapist "does not introduce information that from an external frame of reference might be seen as significant; instead, he works in the client's frame of reference with the information that the client thinks is significant" (pp. 111-112).

This approach therefore results in the client maintaining the primary responsibility for redefining or revising his or her self which, as previously noted, tends to resist change and which may therefore be why another human being is required to facilitate its revision. To achieve its revision, Harre and Gillett (1994) contend that a person has to be open to the possibility of abandoning the self-conceptualizations that structure action and identity if he or she is to "reformulate and reform his activity." This is a process which involves self-risk, they maintain, because it contains an unknown. Or, as Harre and Gillett observe, it requires not only a change in behavior but "a recasting of oneself" (p. 128)—the end result of which is unpredictable in its specifics by either client or therapist. This element of self-risk may also contribute to the relative stability of the self-concept, since risk generally predisposes individuals to resist change. In any event, change of self-concept is possible and is the therapeutic result most widely acknowledged in the therapeutic literature. Or, from a discursive perspective as stated by Harre and Gillett (1994), the significations which structure and give meaning and identity to the self "are all revisable" (p. 126).

In this regard, when clients enter into different discursive contexts, they encounter different ways of conceptualizing and reacting to particular events. Thus, Harre and Gillett (1994) say, such individuals must then position themselves in relation to these possibly conflicting ways of construing events and choose alternative means of conceptualizing them. This process of revising "significations" which structure the self, which in turn determine the direction of "adaptation," have often been attributed to the individual's character. However, Harre and Gillett point out, "one's character is part of the commitment one makes" (p. 126). (In other words, consistent with humanistic and existential philosophy, human beings define themselves by their choices.) In this sense, Harre and Gillett observe, the "commitment" some individuals make to the self-revision process often involves participation in dialogue during which discursive possibilities for change, available to the individual, "must be affirmed, owned, and used in some practice" (p. 127). Expanding upon this revision process, Harre and Gillett (1994) state:

> To be free of constricting situations and the intrinsically limited meanings that create them, the significations giving rise to them have to be resisted by the subject/agent. Given that a person is always trying to make sense of their life and the situations around them, they cannot just abandon their established discursive positionings and put nothing in their place. Alternative meanings have to arise and be validated in some way. For some individuals, this validation may be more or less independent of any values evident within shared interpersonal contexts but for others the existence of shared context for the new evaluations is crucial. (p. 127)

And this "shared context" is apparently crucial, as Ferrara (1994) notes, because language is interactive. Discourse is more complex, she says, than "the simple concatenation of monologues into conversation." People create meaning for each other, she maintains, with reality being jointly constructed "as bits and pieces of one's own and other's talk are interwoven" (p. 6). Furthermore, this notion that the past is "reconstructed" rather than solely "recovered," Ferrara (1994) notes, comes from Freud (1917;1957), who observed that active listening can "make a tale gain momentum and depth" and thus "expand it toward plural contexts" (p. 61). If so, as the next section suggests, why posit the "unconscious"?

CONSTRUCTIVISTIC LANGUAGE PROCESSES, OR THE "UNCONSCIOUS"?

The unpredictability of verbal content during therapeutic discourse appears to be *the* observed client behavior about which humanists and psychoanalysts disagree. Concerning this discursive phenomenon, Dennett (1991) notes that we have "scant access to the processes by which words 'occur to us' to say, even in cases where we speak deliberately, rehearsing our speech acts silently before uttering them." He elaborates:

> Candidates for something to say just spring up from we know not where. Either we find ourselves already saying them, or we find ourselves already checking them out, sometimes discarding them, but even these occasional intermediate steps give us no further hints about how we do them. We just find ourselves accepting or discarding this word or that. If we have reasons for our judgements, they are seldom contemplated before the act, but only retrospectively obvious. . . . So we really have no privileged insight into the processes that occur in us to get us from thought to speech. (p. 304)

In this respect, this lack of specialized "insight" into what we want to say in the jointly constructed discourse of psychotherapy may conceivably have been one factor influencing Freud's formulation of the "unconscious," i.e., to account for the disclosure of unpreconceived dialogue by the client in therapy. However, as noted earlier, there may be no need to posit subconscious forces motivating, or operating behind, human discourse. This spontaneous linguistic phenomenon may instead be a product of the inventive constructivistic property of language and discourse itself, combined with the correlative function of the brain, which structure the mind and generate consciousness. Through this creative discursive ability, Dennett (1991) says, we are constantly rebuilding ourselves, discovering new things we want to say "as a result of reflecting" on what we have just found ourselves "wanting to say, and so forth" (p. 310). Or as Zimring (1974) puts it, these experiential acts "become the stimulus for the next response and hence remain available for further processing" (p. 133).

Dennett (1991) elaborates upon this constructivistic character of language and dialogue in a quote from Stephen Straight:

> The truly "creative" aspect of language resides not in its "infinite generative capacity" but in cycles of production and comprehension mediated by a mind capable of reflecting upon the

multiple meanings attachable to an utterance, meanings that need not have been present in the thought that gave rise to the utterance but which become available through self-comprehension (or deep interpretation of another's utterance) and can lead to a new thought to be expressed and re-interpreted, and so on indefinitely (H. Stephen Straight [1976], p. 540). (p. 297)

Furthermore, this spontaneous ability of the mind to generate or construct meanings through language, as Dennett (1991) maintains, may have motivated E.M. Foster's incisive question, "How do I know what I think until I see what I say?" (p. 245).

With respect to psychotherapy, clients may "see what they say," or engage in the exploratory self-disclosure, as a prelude to reprocessing information and reformulating or choosing alternate premises in the reconstruction of their reality. As Dennett (1991) puts it, "We often do discover what we think (and hence what we mean) by reflecting on what we find ourselves saying—and not correcting" (p. 245). Rather than being controlled by "unconscious" forces, however, such unpreconceived thoughts, as previously noted, may instead be the result of accessing deeply stored information whose neuron pathways may have been blocked by other information stored ahead of it, as if on tape, thus impeding accessibility for reprocessing. Or they may be products of the constructivistic nature of language, itself, operating in conjunction with the correlative function of the brain to revise and/or update this older information.

At least this is what an integrative review of research from disparate fields of human study seems to suggest and what some proponents of the humanistic perspective imply in their following similar descriptions of the "unconscious" proffered by Gendlin (1974) and Friedman (1992). Of this phenomenon, for example, Gendlin states:

> The unconscious is not a vague realm. The unconscious is the body. It is that vast amount more that we are, but have not formed in concepts. . . . The unconscious isn't really unconscious, for it can be felt. However, one feels only one step at a time. If one allows that felt sense to open up and to be lived forward in words, images, or acts, then there is change and shift. . . . The steps one goes through in this way are a process. (p. 242)

And that of Friedman (1992) based on the philosophy of Martin Buber:

> Martin Buber has suggested that the unconscious really may be the ground of personal wholeness before its elaboration into the physical and the psychic. . . . The unconscious, by this reading, is our being itself in its wholeness. Out of it the physical and psychical evolve again and again and at every moment. Therefore, the exploration of psychology is not of the unconscious itself but rather of the phenomena that have been dissociated from it. The radical mistake that Freud made was to think that he could posit a region of the mind as unconscious and at the same time deal with it as if its "contents" were simply repressed conscious material that could be brought back, without essential change, into the conscious. (pp. 110-111)

This humanistic view of the "unconscious" appears to parallel the discursive perspective of Harre and Gillett (1994) as well:

> ' . . . The notion of the unconscious is best understood in relation to what can be affirmed and validated within discourse. There are meanings justifiably assignable to what a person is doing that are either poorly mastered or incommensurate with the values arising from that person's discursive self-location as a conscious agent. These meanings have a validated use but it is not available to that very person, for reasons we might come to understand by appreciating the rest of his or her self-construction. The person whose actions evince these significations will therefore neither be in control of nor fully responsible for the things they are doing because they cannot adequately locate their content. (p. 142)

In other words, rather than bringing the unconscious back into consciousness, successful psychotherapy may instead involve therapeutic growth—a spontaneous, coconstructive development and revision of meanings and the self—a process which, although unpredictable in its specific discursive content, may nevertheless be less so with respect to mechanisms or processes of change. Moreover, it is at its most basic level, the interpersonal dyad, that this change process or coconstruction of reality becomes most evident. As Ferrara (1994) observes, to be fully human is to know joint construction of reality. For most people, she says, this reality is constructed through discourse because talk is central to everyday life. (Or, more specifically, communication may be central to everyday life—a process involving both verbal and nonverbal interaction.) As Ferrara states, "interweaving bits and pieces of your own and other's talk is the primary mode of creating a sense of your own place in the world" (p. 168). (This seemingly infinite constructive potential of language through discourse may further be why humanists believe that the true essence of human nature can never be fully discovered because, as Shaffer [1978] explains, "human nature is always in the process of redefining itself" [p. 22]. That is, the self is always in the process of growing, revising, or updating itself, automatically, especially within the asymmetric discourse of psychotherapy.)

During this revision of self, Ferrara (1994) explains that a piece of information that is particularly troublesome to the client will generally "resurface," over and over, until the client has satisfactorily dealt with it. She further observes that if a therapist misses a "crucial sign" from a client, the fact that it is crucial, she says, generally ensures that it will "arise again in the dialogue" (p. 53) (perhaps in the client's attempt to better reprocess and assimilate it in a more meaningful way). Repeated narratives may also occur because, at the time of the initial disclosure, insufficient additional information blocking its neuron pathway might have been disclosed to release it and effect successful reprocessing. Or the information may have been improperly disclosed, through inappropriate pacing or other inhibitive therapist procedures (discussed in Chapter 7), to successfully unblock intrapersonal communication and allow the repeated narrative to be updated and the self-concept revised.

Describing this process, Wexler (1974) observes that if the therapist's response "hits," the client will "go on to elaborate new facets of meaning that emerge." If not, he says, the client will probably "correct, refine, or ignore what the therapist says" (p. 111). Or, in the extreme case, the client might be inhibited from disclosing further information and the therapeutic process effectively curtailed. Such inhibition of the therapeutic process can occur, Rossi (1993) explains, because memory does not operate exactly like a tape recorder through which the client simply plays back what he or she has learned. Rossi points out that memory is "always a constructive process whereby we actually synthesize a new subjective experience every time we recall a past event" (p. 91) (ostensibly while automatically integrating new information, and building upon the old, through the correlative, information reprocessing capacity of the brain and/or the constructivistic ability of language or speech production). Rossi elaborates:

> . . . The natural mind, by contrast, tends to repeat the same story with variations, seemingly seeking to constantly update and reframe "reality" in keeping with the new information and views it is spontaneously generating. . . . When the mind naturally reviews memories from slightly different perspectives, for example, it is spontaneously engaged in constructing alternative realities. This spontaneous construction of alternate realities has survival value in a constantly changing environment. People who do not recognize, welcome, and integrate these spontaneous changes are condemned to living an uncreative existence in an outmoded past. (p. 91)

LANGUAGE AND THE RECONSTRUCTION OF PERSONAL REALITY

Throughout this self-revision process, language therefore appears to play a crucial role in the reconstruction of personal reality. Davis (1994) suggests why it may be so influential in this regard. Each language is like "a collection of living beings," he says, a "linguistic ecology," as it were. And although not everyone accepts the same set of "linguistic values," he notes, the various dialects of a particular language "continue to grow and evolve and cross-fertilize" (p. 14). This living quality of language is further exemplified in psychotherapy by the fact that, as Ferrara (1994) observes, therapeutic narratives arise "spontaneously" and are "evoked and facilitated by the situation and its norms, rather than being elicited, as in speech events like the interview" (p. 52). In this regard, Rice (1974) describes her similar observations of these dialogical constructive processes:

. . . Little mention has been made about the way in which the client uses these new data to reorganize schemes. Often this seems to happen spontaneously, without an explicit focus on the reorganization process. The client simply finds himself reacting differently in a variety of situations. Other clients seem to want to discuss the meaning of the new experience and try out verbally new ways of viewing situations and exploring their implications. It is not clear whether the latter is really a necessary step to responding differently, or whether it is simply the client's need to understand what has happened spontaneously. In either case, the crucial point is that once the old organization has been disrupted by the new data, the reorganization almost always leads to schemes superior to the old ones [i.e., "Knowledge grows from that which precedes it"]. (p. 302)

Paralleling this unpreconceived property of language, Rossi (1993) describes a similar spontaneous coconstruction of personal reality observed in successful psychotherapy. This therapeutic process, he says, "can only be defined as autocatalytic and creative if there is a genuine aspect of surprise, a certain degree of involuntariness (outside the person's typical sense of directing or controlling their thoughts, feelings, or behavior) and unpredictability about the experience." Otherwise, he maintains, "it is merely another form of traditional 'talking therapy' with the therapist playing the role of 'expert' directing or programming the patient just like they do in the movies with a rather outmoded ideology of authority and stimulus-response psychology" (p. 130).

From what may therefore be viewed as a client-centered perspective, Rossi (1993) observes that it is understandable how "habitual and mindless application of suggestions for relaxation and comfort," at the beginning of the therapy, may actually distort the client's own "natural mind-body signals." Anxiety, stress, tension, and symptoms at the beginning of therapy, he says, are natural readiness signals to do important psychotherapeutic work. This readiness energy, Rossi contends, needs to be properly accessed and utilized—"not frittered away with spurious placating and reassurances by the therapist" (p. 99). He further contrasts this broader perspective, of capitalizing upon the client's emotional momentum, with the novice therapeutic approach he utilized earlier in his career. In the following passage, he outlines the consequences of ignoring the client's experiential integrity (or forgetting that it is the client who needs an experience, not the therapist) and describes the alternate therapeutic procedure he should have employed:

> She looks at me with puzzlement and expectation for an answer. For many years I would respond to this bait and offer the poor helpless patient a brilliant answer, a wonderful psychodynamic reconstruction of the patient's experience that would in one stroke clarify a pathetic life of neuroticism and confusion. Of course, I was thereby robbing patients of their own potentially creative moments (Rossi, 1972/1985). (p. 98)

What clients need, Rossi goes on to explain, is to maintain the "locus of control" within themselves. In other words, he says, this particular client needed to be "empowered to receive, monitor, and facilitate her own therapeutic process in a more adequate manner than any outside therapist could possibly do" (p. 98). From a psychobiological perspective, Rossi therefore maintains, the fundamental task of each client is to "learn how to access and utilize his or her own unique inner repertory of psychobiological resources that can ultimately modulate biochemical processes within the cell" (p. 216). And the task of the therapist, he contends, is to help the client access these resources which, as the thesis of this book suggests, is accomplished through both therapist interactional and client discursive processes.

Furthermore, because of the synergistic relationship between mind and brain, the successful activation of these resources through client discourse may ultimately depend upon the brain's corresponding hardware. As Harre and Gillett (1994) point out, it is plausible to suppose that brain networks are structured according to the way "presented patterns of information" figure in discursive contexts. In other words, they say, representations of experience are organized in the brain "according to the structure and content of the discourses in which the subject is [was] embedded" (p. 94). This view is supported by the neurological work pioneered by Penfield and Roberts (1959), wherein memories have been evoked, in temporal succession, by electrically probing the brain, as well as by studies in information processing. Consequently, it may seem reasonable to suggest that successful reprocessing of information and revision of the self might involve, among other things, properly tuning in to the client's neural networks—a function which "pacing" and client-centered, as opposed to therapist-directed, therapy appear to serve.

This successful reprocessing of information and revision of the self further seem to occur on two levels, or what Ferrara (1994) terms "surface and deep structure." As she explains:

> It bears emphasizing that the making of associations between disparate elements, the work of interconnecting, drawing together isolated bits and pieces to "create sense," is what trained therapists are practiced in. When presented with multiple tellings, the therapist's role in interpreting narrative is to listen to stories on at least two levels, one called "content" and the other called by them "process." In explaining these two levels, one therapist said these two levels are somewhat analogous, in linguistic terms, to surface and deep structure. What matters primarily, he explained, is the underlying meaning, the "subtext" rather than the events. (pp. 53-54)

However, what may specifically "matter" more in successful psychotherapy may not necessarily involve the *therapist* fulfilling the responsibility of "making associations between disparate elements," but enabling clients to do that interconnecting work themselves.

In order to successfully accomplish this interconnecting work, Martin (1992) suggests in his cognitive-mediation approach that when a therapist responds, the client must perceive that response and understand it within the context of information possessed in "episodic, experiential memories of the previous therapy session and memories of a variety of specific situations" in which he or she has reacted with the "kind of panic, fear, and anger" experienced in the past. Over time, Martin goes on to explain, this dynamic, ongoing process of interpersonal interaction and intrapersonal cognition, in therapy, can affect the content and organization of the client's cognitive/experiential structures and memories. This in turn creates what he terms, "a more adequate cognitive basis for novel and refined client behaviors in everyday life contexts that are more congruent with the personal therapeutic goals of the client" (pp. 112-113).

Within this ongoing experience of "intrapersonal cognition," Rennie and Toukmanian (1992) point to forms or levels of processes which clients may activate to coconstruct and revise meanings through therapeutic discourse:

> It can be argued that a therapeutic event is not monadic and is instead an occasion for two main forms of activity. The first form is reflexive. . . . The client is aware of the event, deliberates on its significance, and decides what to do about it, if anything, and when and how. The second form of activity is more nonreflexive. The event in therapy may be thought of as being experienced as a "step"—a shift in the direction of experiencing things differently. . . . The process of the development of elaborated schematic networks is now in place. . . . From that point onward, the client encounters the self and the world within the framework of the new step, assimilates new information to it, and furthers the evolution of the new construction. This evolution may occur in the context of the client's relationship with the self, the therapist, and/or the world. (p. 245)

This coconstruction of "elaborated schematic networks" during the course of therapeutic discourse, according to Martin (1992), is the symbolic representation, in the minds of clients, of "newly acquired problem-solving structures" or "empowered self-schemata." Once they become part of clients' long-term memory and knowledge/theoretical structures, he maintains, these structures can be activated when clients perceive problem stimuli in their everyday life experiences, thus providing them "with a cognitive basis for competent action that resolves or copes with these everyday situations" (p. 130). The result of such client action, he says, is the further elaboration of the client's expanding cognitive competence—a competence, he observes, "that was initiated in the social construction and processing of information during counseling" (p. 130). Consequently, he adds, these cognitive structural changes and "integrated information" (p. 114) render clients better able to operate in a cognitively more competent manner.

In addition to these primary cognitive changes occurring within the client through this kind of information processing activity effected by language and discourse, Wexler (1974) describes other enduring changes that may accrue. As he points out, there are likely to be long-term effects on the way the client processes information in the future. Because it satisfies a basic need for new experience and change, he says, "engaging in an optimal mode of experiencing will be intrinsically reinforcing for the client" (p. 78). The client, he adds, is then likely to engage in this mode more frequently and, by doing so, "learns that he can be his own source for creating new experience and change via his own cognitive functioning" (p. 78).

REPROCESSING INFORMATION THROUGH ASYMMETRIC RELATIONSHIPS

The process by which this creative experience and self-revision likely occurs has been variously termed reprocessing, or reframing, a concept prominent in the work of Milton Erickson. According to Rossi (1993), Erickson accessed and utilized clients' own unique repertory of life experiences "to help them create new mental frameworks and identities that engaged their aroused emotions and personality structures" (p. 268). In quoting Erickson, Rossi (1993) explains how he (Erickson) facilitated this process:

> Therapy results from an *inner resynthesis* of the patient's behavior achieved by the patient himself. It is true that direct suggestion [hypnosis] can effect an alteration in the patient's behavior and result in a symptomatic cure, at least temporarily. However, such a "cure" is simply a response to suggestion and does not entail that reassociation and reorganization of ideas, understandings and memories so essential for actual cure. *It is this experience of reassociating and reorganizing his own experiential life that eventuates in a cure,* not the manifestation of responsive behavior which can, at best, satisfy only the observer. (pp. 88-89)

And, as previously noted, this "reassociation and reorganization of ideas," forming the basis of self-revision, is hypothesized to occur automatically as a product of the client's self-disclosure within therapeutic discourse. As clients utilize these discursive skills (or as therapists facilitate these discursive processes within the client), Harre and Gillett (1994) maintain that clients expand their consciousness or "extend the range of matters to which they can attend and of which they are aware" (p. 175). Elaborating upon this process, they state:

> The greater the ability to build an organized system of antic-ipations and order them according to what the actor values, the greater is that actor's ability to act with assurance. If a person elaborates for him- or herself a system of interrelated con-structs that have a wide range of useful applications in different experiential situations, then that person will be well adapted to the world. Each individual has a unique reordering of such constructs and they vary in their modifiability in the light of new experience and in the ways in which they are applied to objects, including that very active subject. This cognitive constellation defines the individual and allows us to understand and relate to that individual as a self-defining agent. (p. 137)

That this process of facilitating the client's "cognitive constella-tion," or self-growth, is enhanced more so in psychotherapy than in ordinary discourse is further likely due to the asymmetrical nature of the therapeutic relationship which maximizes disclosure by the cli-ent (as opposed to the therapist), thus promoting access to deeper levels of stored information while activating constructivistic lan-guage processes. This more concentrated form of self-disclosure in psychotherapy, as compared to normal dialogue, may further ac-count, in part, for the research finding noted by Maling and Howard (1994) that "psychotherapy accomplishes in 15 sessions what spon-taneous remission takes two years to do" (p. 249). This asymmetri-cal characteristic of the therapeutic relationship may in turn be a function of empathy through which, as Friedman (1992) observes, therapists tend to lose sight of themselves and their "side of the relationship" (p. 50) in order to enhance or magnify treatment effects within the client. And this occurs, as Ferrara (1994) notes, because the conversational requirement justifying a relatively unin-terrupted turn in dialogue is "loosened" in therapeutic discourse. In other words, she says, "It is expected that clients will talk at length and the sole criterion is that their talk have relevance to them" (p. 55).

However, as Wexler (1974) notes, there are parameters to this process. Just as the attentional and processing capacities of the client are limited, he says, so too are those of the therapist. For example, to function on a moment-to-moment basis in an optimally empathic manner, he states, "necessitates that all the therapist's attention and processing capacities be allocated to understanding the meaning of the information in process in the client, and to organizing a response that accurately captures this meaning" (p. 110). (However, as the evidence presented herein suggests, the selective attention characteristic of human concentration may limit the therapist's focusing ability mainly to the *interactional* process of facilitating client self-disclosure—the understanding of that disclosure being secondary to the therapist but primary to the client.)

In other words, evidence seems to suggest that in successful psychotherapy, clients may be helped to "talk at length" by facilitative interactional behaviors nonconsciously employed by the therapist to promote asymmetry within the relationship. In this sense, therefore, asymmetry may foster effectiveness of information reprocessing (a result less likely to be achieved in normal interpersonal relationships that generally lack asymmetry and, thus, the more concentrated ability to access deeper levels of stored information). Additionally, as others in information processing have noted, clients' identification of which stored events are significant in this revision process can be predicted from the therapeutic discourse. That is, experiences that promote dialogue conducive to deep, elaborative, and conclusion-oriented information processing tend to be selected by clients as important. And, as the thesis of this book suggests, helping clients experience these deeper forms of information reprocessing may be achieved through "non-interfering" (Maslow, 1976, p. 91) therapist behavior designed to maximize client disclosure thereby unblocking neuron pathways, activating con-structivistic language processes and correlational brain functions, revising meanings, and facilitating intrapersonal communication and self-growth.

THERAPEUTIC OUTCOME: FACILITATING SELF-GROWTH

In my experience, when these deeper levels of stored information have been successfully accessed and "reprogrammed" through client self-disclosure (within discourse facilitated by appropriate non-interfering therapist nonverbal behavior), this psychotherapeutic approach generally results in an experience, for both therapist and client, similar to that described by Friedman (1992) in a quote from Carl Rogers: "When there is this complete unity, singleness, fullness of experiencing in the relationship, then it acquires the 'out-of-this-world' quality which therapists have remarked upon, a sort of trance-like feeling in the relationship from which both the client and I emerge at the end of the hour, as if from a deep well or tunnel" (p. 38). And this "deep well" quality, this book contends, may result, in part, from the therapist working within the client's frame of reference to reprocess information from deeper levels of memory storage during their encounter.

Successful reprogramming or reprocessing of information during such "trance-like" sessions has further been compared by Rossi (1993) to accessing a "rest phase of an ultradian rhythm," a naturally occurring biological phenomenon in humans which he reports to be physically recognizable. (Similar responses have been observed by myself after extended periods of client disclosure during which they often lose track of the time.) As Rossi observes, "The patient will appear to be in a quiet moment of reflectiveness or inner reverie: the body becomes immobile; reflexes such as eye blinking may be slowed or absent; the eyes may manifest a 'far away' look. . . . Heart beat and respiration are slowed, and so forth" (p. 203). When clients emerge from this state, or when a successful reprocessing and assimilation phase has been completed, they are usually more relaxed, tension and anxiety have decreased, and they may then be more open to the therapist's input (possibly evidence that improved intrapersonal communication has resulted in improved interpersonal communication).

THE ASYMMETRICAL TALKING "CURE"

Eventually, when sufficient information has been reprocessed in this manner over the course of therapy, the client's symptoms decrease or disappear. At this point, as stated above, clients are generally more receptive to the experience of others and less absorbed in themselves. Or, as Friedman (1992) puts it in a quote from Carl Rogers, "If the client could really experience fully the therapist's side of the situation, the therapy would be about over" (p. 43). In other words, by the end of therapy, Friedman (1992) states, "The self of the client recognizes and appreciates the uniqueness of the self of the therapist, and by extrapolation, the self of others" (p. 90).

In contrast, clients in crisis generally talk extensively about themselves, as if attempting to reduce anxiety (a universal verbal phenomenon discussed in greater detail later in this chapter). In addition, they are usually oblivious to therapist input as evidenced by the nonverbal, client-centered experiences of Maslow, Garfield, and Lazarus, cited in Chapter 5, similar to my own clinical practice (likely a function of the client's need to reprocess information with a minimum of interference from the therapist). Wexler (1974) describes this verbal phenomenon as follows:

> It is a frequent occurrence that in elaborating to another why one is anxious, there is a reduction in the anxiety. By way of explanation we tend to say one has ventilated his anxiety or gained insight into it. Such terms, however, do not really serve to explain adequately how anxiety can be reduced through such elaboration. In elaborating possible causes for the anxiety, one is generating structures that serve to give order to disordered information. There is a reduction in anxiety when one "understands" its cause, not because the understanding one has is "true," but because the cause elaborated is plausible and functionally serves to provide order in an otherwise disordered field. (pp. 75-76)

In this sense, as Goldberg (1992) observes, excessive talking on the part of clients in crisis may occur because "all behavior emanates from a health striving—the intention of making sense of one's being in the world" (p. 129). This may further be why humanists believe that the client "needs an experience, not an explanation," since the creation of this experience seemingly requires that the client set the agenda with respect to the content of his or her self-disclosure. Meanwhile, the therapist functions primarily as a facilitator of that disclosure—the resulting interconnection of information and past experiences occurring automatically and primarily within the client. In other words, whether the therapist is privy to the details of this interconnecting work appears secondary to the client's reprocessing of this information, and his or her apparent resulting spontaneous understanding of it, through the universal correlative function of the brain.

As Ferrara (1994) observes, during this process, clients will ideally develop sufficient self-awareness to do the connecting work themselves. The therapist having "modeled" this type of behavior, she states, clients eventually learn to be their "own therapist" (p. 71). However, as noted earlier, and as suggested by the nonverbal, client-centered sessions previously described by Maslow, Garfield, and Lazarus, this connecting work appears to be an ongoing universal human phenomenon occurring automatically within clients (in the guise of bringing the "unconscious" to consciousness in psychoanalysis, for example) through unblocking stored information and/or activating constructivistic language abilities. Describing the autocatalytic nature of this phenomenon, Wexler (1974) states, "When the client's experiencing is rich and at a 'peak', the therapist will often have to do little." In fact, he says, "the therapist can even be inaccurate in his responses and miss what the client is saying and the quality of the client's processing will typically not suffer." In such a situation, he observes, "the client will keep on his track and continue in his rich mode of experiencing" (p. 108).

This "rich mode of experiencing" may further occur through the correlative functions of both human hardware and software processes. In other words, in addition to the biological correlative function of the brain, clients, as "incipient scientists" (Neimeyer, 1990, p. 160), appear to have an inherent nonconscious cognitive capacity for *inductive and deductive reasoning* as well and, under appropriate environmental conditions within asymmetric human discourse, can likely thereby automatically revise false or unrealistic intrapersonal premises by themselves. The nonconscious nature of such information processing is described by Kornhuber (1988):

> Most information flow in the brain is, by the way, unconscious [or automatic] (for review, see Kornhuber, 1983a). The soul is not "richer" than the body: on the contrary, most of the processing in our central nervous system is not perceived. The unconscious (which was discovered and elucidated long before Freud) is the most ordinary process in the central nervous

system. We just look at the results, but we are able to direct the focus of attention. (p. 246)

Moreover, rational ability has not been a quality which therapists have readily attributed to clients (possibly due to this nonconscious characteristic of human information processing as well as clients' inability to resolve personal concerns by themselves). As Omer (1994) notes, "Among the many slurs that we cast on patients, disparaging their intellectual 'defenses' is among the most ubiquitous." However, he adds, the capacity for critical thinking and abstract conceptualization "is a major achievement, and we should beware of shrugging it off" (p. 96). Furthermore, these reasoning abilities appear to be activated even without the therapist's direct modeling example as evidenced by my twenty-five year clinical practice (similar to the client-centered sessions of Maslow, Garfield, and Lazarus cited earlier wherein therapist verbal behavior was minimal). In this respect, Rossi (1993) observes, during self-disclosure, the client's mind "simply receives the new idea and subjects it to validation and integration with previous patterns of understanding" (p. 102).

AUTONOMOUS PROCESSES: THE "HARDWARE" UNDERLYING THE "SOFTWARE"

As for the probable physiology underlying these therapeutic client cognitive reasoning processes, Rossi (1993) states that "recent research in the neurobiology of learning (Rosenweig and Bennett, 1994) suggests that new proteins are synthesized in appropriate brain cells during learning" which, he believes, "could function as the biological basis of new behavior and phenomenological experience" (p. 102). This biological evidence thus leads Rossi (1990) to the following conclusion:

If we take the implications of recent psychobiological research to their logical conclusion, we may have a pragmatic resolution to the centuries-old Cartesian dualism of mind and body. The common denominator between mind and body is *information.* Life is a cybernetic process of information transduction. From our psychotherapeutic perspective, *mind can be defined as a process of self-reflective information transduction. Transduc-tion* refers to the transformation or flow of information be-tween the different modalities of experience such as words, metaphors, imagery, emotions, sensations, behavior, symptoms, and so on. (p. 356)

With respect to the specific brain structures responsible for these constructive processes, Rossi (1993) points out that cells in the hypothalamus "transduce information encoded in the form of the electrical impulses carried by the nerves of the higher cortex of the brain into messenger molecules of the body." This, he says, is the essence of "brain-body communication." He goes on to explain that this type of neuroendocrinal information transduction changes neu-ral information of the brain into the pituitary endocrinal information of the body—the pituitary gland being considered the "master gland regulating most of the endocrines (hormones or primary messenger molecules) of the body" (p. 140). Further expanding upon these bio-logical processes, Rossi (1993) states:

This understanding of how these neurons in the hypothalamus transduce neural information of mind into hormonal messenger molecules of the body is called *neurosecretion*; it is the central concept of modern *neuroendocrinology*. The existence of such *neuroendocrinal information transducers* is the basic reason for conceptualizing the new field of psychobiology as a branch of information theory. It is the key insight that unites biology and psychology within the single framework of information theory in a manner that makes mind-body communication and healing an empirical science rather than a pious hope. (p. 145)

This view is also supported by Carl Whitaker (1989), who contends that psychotherapy involves more than "affective exchange" and may further "change the *physiology* of the body and even the *struc-ture* of the body" (p. 73). This hardware notwithstanding, however, the software is still nevertheless that with which psychotherapists are primarily concerned, on a practical level, and the next topic of discussion.

LANGUAGE AS A SOURCE OF NEUROSES
AND INCONGRUENCE

If, on one hand, talking *can* cure, how does it also contribute to neurosis and incongruence? The detrimental effects of language may be analogous to faulty or unsuitable software in a computer, change of which may be required to enable the hardware to redirect or reprocess stored information in a more appropriate manner. Consistent with this analogy, when a computer malfunctions, the search for the source of the problem is generally directed in two areas: the hardware or the software. A similar search, Harre and Gillett (1994) maintain, should be involved in the diagnosis of human dysfunction. When a particular behavior becomes impaired, they note, specialists in each field (neurological and psychological) investigate one of two areas: neuroscience looks for damage to brain mechanisms while discursive psychology (or psychotherapy) examines "the areas of discourse and adaptation to discursive contexts that have been affected." Although these two areas of investigation have different foci, Harre and Gillett state, they should nevertheless both be involved in the study of a "complex biological organism whose nature reflects both physical capacity and discursive engagement" (p. 96).

Should organic or hardware malfunction be ruled out, the software (of which language, and therefore psychotherapy, might be considered a function) becomes the next target (as well as the medium) for diagnosis. Further suggesting where this diagnostic software search might be directed, Hayes (1990) states:

> Work in the area of "stimulus equivalence" (by, for example, Devany, Hayes, and Nelson, 1986) reveals that human beings (but not nonhumans) readily form networks of bi-directional relations among stimuli, and that stimulus functions can transfer among these stimulus networks (Wulfert and Hayes, in press). I take this to mean that through the verbal organization of events, clients may be responding in a current situation to experiences that bear only the most remote connection to the present context. To put it directly, I view human language as the source of most psychopathology.

My goal, then, is to confront directly the edifice of human language. . . . The goal is the loosening up of literal meaning so that a client can think a thought *as a thought*, not as an act that organizes the stimulus environment. Rather than try either to change or ignore thoughts and feelings, I attempt to recontextualize the relation between thought or feelings and overt action. (p. 141)

That this "recontextualization" of stored information by the client may be what reduces anxiety and neurosis is further suggested by Wexler (1974):

Anxiety. . . should not be looked at as a distinct affect outside the context in which it arises. Rather, anxiety is the subjective experience arising from an inability to organize significant information in the field. If in such a situation the client says something to the effect that he "feels anxious," this should be regarded as an integrating structure that ascribes a meaning to the state of disordered information that occupies his field and any arousal that may accompany it. As an integrating meaning structure, however, it will usually not serve to reorganize the field, but rather will often serve as a starting point for differentiating the components of the anxiety (i.e., the information that the client is unable to organize). (p. 75)

Furthermore, there is evidence to suggest that a prolonged disorganization of the client's information field might be one factor influencing chronic stress and anxiety, in turn leading to hardware or organic dysfunction. One of the most surprising and alarming findings of clinical neuroscience in recent years, Rossi (1993) states, is that "chronic stress can lead to the death of neurons in the hippocampus of the brain that are associated with learning and memory formation" (p. 79). Rossi further contends that this type of "psychobiological double bind" in which shock and stress encode traumatic events and, at the same time, impair effective coping behavior, leads to what he terms "the genesis of many types of mind-body dysfunction that are typically called 'psychosomatic problems'" (p. 57).

Moreover, as the forgoing discussion suggests, such problems may be a function of the symbiotic relationship between mind and brain, a relationship which can apparently become disorganized or incongruent, not only by breakdown of intraindividual communication but, as Lynch (1985) observes, also by dysfunctional interindividual communication. In his words:

> The belief that mind and body live together in some sort of self-contained dual existence, apart from everything and everyone else, has obscured the fact that human beings also live in and are biologically linked to their natural environment as well as to other human beings. Thus, a major source of stress arises from a breakdown in dialogue and a blindness to the links between human communication and bodily function: that is, when one is emotionally isolated.
>
> . . . This emotional isolation is complex: One can be cut off from one's own emotions and, thus, literally cannot relate to oneself. Unable to relate even to oneself, then one is unable truly to relate to others. Even if one attempts to break the emotional barrier and communicate to others, they themselves may be unwilling to respond. (p.13)

It is at this point, Rossi (1993) states, that clients usually report being "stuck" or "blocked," and experience feelings which may be difficult to express (or, stated in humanistic terms, they have become alienated from their feelings and are in a state of incongruence). Rossi observes that such clients can be "obsessively intellectualized and rigid" in that they may know something conceptually and may be able to discuss it, but may not be able to feel it or translate it into appropriate changes in their behavior. People have symptoms and problems, he says, "when their experience is stuck or state-bound in one modality or another so they cannot use the natural genius or other aspects of their nature" (p. 93).

Clients may further acquire this state of incongruence, Rogers (1961) maintains, by experiencing "conditions of worth" or "conditional positive regard" from others in their environment thereby developing, conditioning, or shaping an unrealistic or dysfunctional self-concept. Stated in behavioral terms, Nye (1975) suggests that what determines how human beings (or in this case, incongruent clients) react to their own internal stimuli depends upon how others may have interpreted these stimuli for them in the past. He points out that this can occur through being reinforced with attention and approval for identifying these stimuli "in ways consistent with others' interpretations" (p. 68). In this sense, therefore, external interpretations of their experiences may cause clients to syllogistically generalize from faulty premises and form conclusions which may be inconsistent with their real selves, or with reality in general. These false conclusions may in turn create troublesome meanings and/or schemata which result in intrapersonal conflict. Then, because meanings tend to provide behavioral impulsion, such false meanings could in turn motivate dysfunctional behavior resulting in interpersonal conflict.

Paralleling this view is Toukmanian's (1992) perceptual-processing approach to psychotherapy which she describes as follows:

> . . . The perceptual-processing approach maintains that difficulties experienced by clients are, by and large, the function of their inability to "take in" and process the elements of their experience more fully and in ways that would help them generate different and potentially more functional perspectives. This inability is seen to stem from perceptual dysfunctions that are associated mainly with the processing of events (both internal and external) in an automated fashion. As this processing strategy impedes the enactment of qualitatively different mental operations, it hinders schematic development and results in rather simple and undiscriminating construals that have limited generalizability and functional value. Being based on the developmentally stunted networks of schemata, such construals have neither the breadth nor the flexibility with which to accommodate the exigencies of varying life circumstances. As such, they lead to experiences that are vague, discomforting, devoid of personal meaning, and hence unsatisfactory for the individual. (pp. 88-89)

In other words, as Wexler (1974) puts it, as a result of the client's inability to generate an adequate organization which gives order to the information he or she may be attempting to process at the moment, further processing is "either hindered or stopped" (p. 100). In such cases, he says, the client "lacks an organized substrate from which he can go on to further differentiate and integrate meaning." When this occurs, Wexler says, anxious clients will generally "keep trying to search for exact words to generate that organized substrate" (p. 100). However, as the next section suggests, this process has limitations.

NEURAL LIMITATIONS
UNDERLYING REASONING

From a biological perspective, Kosslyn and Koenig (1992) offer the following explanation of the hardware limitation that might influence the above perceptual or software dysfunction hypothesized to result in neuroses and incongruence. (This apparent neural limitation may further account, in part, for why a second empathic human being is required to facilitate an amelioration of such dysfunctional intrapersonal communication.) As Kosslyn and Koenig explain:

> Neural networks are very good at storing associations, but not very good at the kind of serial processing that underlies much of reasoning. In this sort of system, the results of previous decisions would be easy to store and to access later when appropriate. If so, then one reason why some older people may become wise is that they have stored the results of many previous decisions, and are able to generalize properly to similar cases when they arise subsequently. (p. 442)

This apparent biological limitation in "the kind of serial processing which underlies reasoning" may also account for why clients become psychologically "stuck" and cannot use their own "natural genius" (Rossi, 1993, p. 93). It may also account for why a higher percentage of younger adults seem to seek counseling, i.e., their network of stored "previous decisions" from which to "generalize" may be less developed than those of older adults. In any event, because of their difficulty in resolving personal concerns by themselves, such clients typically solicit the surrogate psychological services of a therapist (or what Carl Whitaker [1989] colorfully terms, a "psychological prostitute" [p. 163]). During such cases, Rossi (1993) states, the psychotherapeutic objective "is to facilitate the normally creative processes of everyday-life" in order to help clients "recognize and receive their natural patterns of mind-body communication and healing" (p. 96).

When this process of mind-body communication is "blocked" or incomplete, so that the person remains stuck in a vicious cycle of "unending fatigue, depression, symptoms, or emotional crises," Rossi (1993) states, it can be stigmatized as emotional hysteria or "mental illness" (p. 96). He goes on to explain that when clients are immobilized by such debilitating symptoms, they generally expect that the therapist will "cure the symptom or provide the answer to the problem." However, he says, the successful therapist does neither. Instead, Rossi states, "the therapist offers the patient an open field of exploration, an opportunity to play with many possible approaches to accessing the state-bound sources of the problem and exposing it to the patient's uniquely personal repertory of inner resources for problem solving" (p. 96). This may in turn predispose the client to automatically bring faulty premises to the fore so they can be reprocessed syllogistically (and/or through the correlative function of the brain), thereby simultaneously promoting the revision of troublesome conclusions and creating and/or revising self-meanings.

Illustrating this phenomenon of inadequate differentiation and syllogistic construction of meaning is the following verbal transaction proffered by Wexler (1974): "Let us suppose that after the client had [has] said 'I feel very much alone—like nobody cares for me,' he said 'It's a real bad feeling.' This statement would be an integration of meaning, as it represents a superordinate structure abstracting a common meaning in the two previous statements" (p. 73). Furthermore, it may be at similar times in therapy when the psychoanalytic therapist would hypothesize the client to have delved into the "unconscious" since it is not unusual, in such cases, for clients to comment upon their disclosures something such as: "I've never thought of it that way before" or, "That's the first time I've ever disclosed this to anyone." Indeed, through the constructivistic ability of language and discourse, it may be the first time this client has ever formulated this thought and articulated it to him- or herself as well since such meanings, as previously noted, appear to be spontaneously constructed by the client's own reasoning abilities, and/or the correlative function of the brain, based upon his or her idiosyncratic history of experiences (stored temporally as memories in the brain), as well as the discursive environment contributing to these coconstructed meanings. And, as previously suggested, these processes appear to be automatically activated through the kind of facilitative asymmetrical experiential exploration described above.

That this proposal is not exactly new is noted by Goldberg (1992) in his description of the personal construct theory of George Kelly (1955). In Goldberg's words:

> Kelly indicates that the dichotomizing of experience is not necessarily a product of the individual's conflictual relation to the world or to oppositional instincts within his psyche. According to Kelly, duality is an essential attribute of thinking itself. An individual creates his own way of perceiving the world by formulating his experiences in terms of *constructs* that have varying degrees of predictive efficiency. The cardinal principle that guides the use of one construct rather than another is *the need to make sense of one's being-in-the-world* organizing all our other needs and motives.
>
> These constructs are, of course, not passive speculative beliefs. They are implicit strategies for taking action so as to live most *meaningfully.* . . . Each of us craves a sense of meaning for our existence [cf. Logotherapy and Victor Frankl's *Man's Search for Meaning*]. The recurring theme of human existence is the self's striving for personal identity, significance, and unification. (pp. 113-114)

These "thinking" or logical reasoning processes have further been widely explored in philosophy (termed the *unifier* of other disciplines). As Goldberg (1992) explains:

> Western philosophy is the endeavor that conveys knowledge about the nature of the world based upon the requirements of logical and rational thinking. *Logical thinking* is reasoning that follows from its premises. *Rationality* is based on the idea that we can best predict the course of events by first observing prior events, seizing upon certain patterns and similarities contained in each of these events in contrast to all other events, and as a result classifying these purveyed events into distinct categories. Therefore, the unifying theme in western philosophy derives from the premise that we can master our existence by interpreting the laws of nature by logical and rational thinking. (p. 73)

It is in this respect, therefore, that the reprocessing, reframing, or reconnecting activity of clients described herein may be viewed as a function of the universal constructivistic property of language and discourse operating in conjunction with these universal logical reasoning abilities and/or biological correlative functions of the brain.

BRIDGING THE "GAP"
WITHOUT THE "BLACK BOX"

It is at this point in psychotherapeutic theory where the concept of the client's "black box" would traditionally have been invoked. As Beitman (1992) puts it: "Change is 'caused' by somehow providing both insight and outsight through paying attention to the inner schema and the outer matched aspects of reality." "Somehow," with the client's cooperation, he says, "the new information alters the old and change takes place. . . . But to answer the question about how exposure of a distorted schema to new relevant information changes the schema is to go beyond current knowledge" (p. 220). However, this is where the integrative eclectic approach described herein, with the assistance of those whose research and observations are cited in this volume, may be salient. That is, when exploratory self-disclosure or "working-through" is successfully completed, the unblocking of information and the activation of the client's own inductive and deductive reasoning abilities (autocatalytic processes) appear to occur spontaneously—abilities upon which Neimeyer (1990) expands:

> Human beings are essentially interpretive, always in the process of attributing meaning to their ongoing experience. In a construct theory view, individuals are like incipient scientists who attempt to devise hypotheses (or constructs) that render the events of their lives understandable, and to some degree, predictable. Thus, unlike theorists who view human behavior as determined by past traumas or present reinforcement contingencies, construct theorists consider people's behavior as ways of testing their beliefs about the future, given the limits imposed by their current understandings. When individuals become stuck in the process of elaborating their personal theories, so that important events in their lives appear chaotic, contradictory, or meaningless, they sometimes seek profes-

sional assistance from a psychotherapist. . . . Thus the essence of therapy is the psychological reconstruction of life. . . . Construct theorists view reality as largely a personal or social invention and disorder as the development of a construct system that is no longer useful for anticipating events and channelling one's behavior toward them. (pp. 160-161)

Recapping thus far, then, if clients are like "incipient scientists," using their own correlative, inductive and deductive reasoning processes, this may be why, as Efran, Lukens, and Lukens (1990) note, human beings generally listen "only to what they expect to hear—what fits with current philosophical premises." After all, Efran, Lukens, and Lukens note, "we are 'attached' to our assumptions just as surely as we are to other aspects of our action patterns" (p. 171). In fact, this strong attachment to our assumptions may in part be biologically based due to memories being stored in temporal succession, blocking other memories stored ahead of them, as if on tape. Given such organization, therefore, significant information may not be readily available to clients at that particular juncture in their lives. This information may further be necessary to reformulate relevant premises required to deductively and/or inductively reconstruct troublesome conclusions (viz., if A=B and B=C, then A=C) necessary to properly revise self-meanings and foster functional intra- and interpersonal communication. This may therefore be why asymmetrical dialogue and pacing are required to release or unblock information within the client's neural networks—information capable of being reasonably or syllogistically accommodated by the client at that point in therapy.

In this sense, therefore, whether the therapist is privy to the details of the client's self-revision (the information involved in the client's reconstructive reasoning processes) appears secondary to the client's own apparent spontaneous awareness of it during self-disclosure. As Jackendoff (1994) explains from a linguistic perspective, suppose we think of our stored knowledge as the contents of a "filing cabinet in the brain." The information in the filing cabinet is not stored in a form "readable by outside observers." Why should it be? he adds, "It's not there for the benefit of outside observers, it's there for the use of the rest of the brain" (p. 45). Thus, this apparent universal temporal information-storage factor argues in favor of respecting the client's direction (Gendlin, 1974, p. 212), unique reality, or idiosyncratic information processing capacity—a uniqueness, which Covey (1990) notes to be characteristic of all human beings, clients and therapists alike:

> Each of us tends to think we see things as they are, that we are "objective." But this is not the case. We see the world not as "it is" but as "we are"—or as we are conditioned to see it. When we open our mouths to describe what we see, we in effect describe ourselves, our perceptions, our paradigms.
>
> . . . The more aware we are of our basic paradigms, maps or assumptions, and the extent to which we have been influenced by our experience, the more we can take responsibility for those paradigms, examine them, test them against reality, listen to others and be open to their perceptions, thereby getting a larger picture and a far more objective view. (pp. 28-29)

If so, this may further be why empathy, asymmetry, and a nonjudgmental attitude are emphasized in psychotherapy; that is, stated in psychoanalytic terms, to prevent inhibitive countertransference which may occur when the client's reality is judged by standards established within the therapist's *foreign* reality. All of which appears necessary, as the next section suggests, because of the tendency of the self to resist change due to the neural and cognitive limitations cited above.

"TRAPPED" WITHIN THE SELF

As the foregoing discussion suggests, in the absence of interpersonal discourse, a constricted image of individual human reality therefore emerges, or what Wexler and Rice (1974) refer to as, "Man alienated both from himself and from other persons" (p. 316). Further illustrating this form of *alienation*, Sacks (1995) observes, "I don't know whether what you call 'red' is the same as what I call 'red,' and perhaps I can never know." There is a privacy that can "never be breached," he says, "never be shared" (p. 33)—a view similar to that of Damasio (1994, p. 97). Harre and Gillett (1994) expand upon this universal human estrangement:

> Thus it is hard to say what I could mean by claiming that my thoughts are true, and my utterances meaningful, if I am

trapped within them and at their mercy (and they are hidden inside me). The problem runs very deep because others cannot get outside their veils of perception either. This entails that none of us knows what the world is really like, nor what others think, nor whether anything we think is actually true, nor what anyone else means by the words they use, nor indeed what I mean by the words I use. Clearly, we have to find some way to make sense of the fact that we can aim to think true thoughts and express them in a common system of signs. (p. 43)

And that "way" has traditionally been termed facilitating self-realization or self-actualization—a process seemingly occurring through the correlational function of the brain and logical reasoning within human discourse which, in its more concentrated or asymmetrical form, has been termed psychotherapy. Supporting this view, neurologist Ornstein (1993) observes that while it may not be possible to find a specific location for the self in the brain, the functions related to what we call the self, he says, "seem to depend on decisions made in the frontal lobes" (p. 65). In his words:

The self-system in the frontal lobes influences us to seek out different information, to remember differently. In tragic cases, damage to the frontal lobes results in the inability to know on a long-term basis who one is. . . . The frontal lobes participate in planning, decision making, and purposeful behavior. (p. 65)

The therapist further appears to promote this "planning, decision making, and purposeful behavior" through facilitating *experiential exploration* achieved by empathically stepping out of his or her own frame of reference and into the client's. This therapeutic intervention may become necessary, as Nichols (1995) puts it, because clients can often become "stuck" in their own "point of view." The "problem," he adds, is "linear thinking" (p. 45) (or selective attention?). To facilitate *divergent* thinking within others, Nichols (1995) therefore advocates "active listening." The person who listens well, he says, "acknowledges and affirms" the other by sustaining the "self-affirmation known as self-respect." For without being listened to, he adds, "we are shut up in the solitude of our own hearts" (p. 15). In other words, the surrogate psychological procedure of psychotherapy often becomes necessary due to what Epstein (1995) terms, the human "inability to observe ourselves properly." Problems occur, echoes Epstein, because we are generally caught in our own perspective, "unable to appreciate the many perspectives of those around us." Furthermore, he adds, we are usually "unaware of how insistently this way of perceiving drives us" (p. 44). Or, as Nichols (1995) puts it, "The past is alive in memory—and it runs our lives more than we know" (p. 79).

Thus, when this "linear perspective" becomes too far removed from reality or from the goals and objectives of the real self, another empathic human being or therapist may be required to facilitate the kind of experiential information reprocessing and self-revision described above. It is in this respect, therefore, that psychotherapy's underlying essence may be contained in the statement by Harre and Gillett (1994) quoted earlier: "When we want to unlock particular capacities that are realized in the brain, we need to return the person to something similar to the discursive contexts in which the relevant meanings and significations were developed or appreciated" (p. 94). Or, neurologically speaking, to where the corresponding "firing patterns" in the brain once occurred (Damasio, 1994, p. 101). When this occurs, the client's own "genius" or reasoning abilities seem to be automatically engaged to update meanings, which tend to become more discernible, Harre and Gillett (1994) note, as "we analyze the orientation of the subject to that context and the multiplicity of significations intrinsic to it" (p. 94).

In this sense, therefore, successful adaptation in life is not only built on biological accommodation, but also "on our cultural and social history of investing certain things with meaning" (Harre and Gillett, 1994, p. 94). It is also in this sense that an empathic (or asymmetric) process of helping the client analyze the "context" of his or her experiences and memories might be viewed as a psycho-biological means of facilitating *functional conscious activity* within the client—a process described by Kornhuber (1988):

> One could perhaps say that the higher information processing with access to voluntary activity, including voluntary guidance of information processing, is the function of consciousness. Consciousness is more simply wakefulness. There are pathological states of consciousness in which the patient is awake and acting, but not fully oriented, not planning events normally

and not transmitting experience into long-term memory. Human consciousness is also related to the autonomy of making voluntary use of programs stored in the brain. In short, "consciousness" is related to active cognitive and voluntary activity. (p. 247)

Furthermore, psychotherapy's ability to facilitate this "active cognitive and voluntary activity" within the client appears to depend heavily upon the seemingly innate ability of human beings to reprogram or update themselves, automatically, in the light of new experience. This ability, as previously noted, may be a function of the synergistic relationship between mind and brain (or phenomenology and behavior), as well as the dual function of language, about which Rennie and Toukmanian (1992) comment:

Within the phenomenology of agency, it is as if the person not only is *constituted of* beliefs, values, needs, and desires but *has* them as well (see A. Rorty, 1976). Thus the person may act not only in terms of them but also upon them. In acting in terms of them, the person is determined by them; in acting upon them, the person is determining them. It can be maintained that neurosis may be seen as a state of being in which the individual is determined by beliefs and values and incapable of intervention into them (see Macmurray, 1957). (p. 238)

In this sense, consistent with Toukmanian's (1992) view, such "neuroses" may render clients incapable (on their own) of intervention into these beliefs and values (meanings which structure the self), mainly because their perceptions (which constitute the premises underlying these values and beliefs) may be faulty or inconsistent with the clients' real self and/or objectives. As such, they may be incapable of providing functional behavioral impulsion or ideation. As Toukmanian explains, our perceptions of everyday life events play a significant role in how we act and interact with our environment. This implies, she says, that "maladaptive behaviors associated with particular classes of intra- and interpersonal events are difficulties related to perceptual dysfunction; that is, such behaviors are symptomatic of an underlying perceptual system that is developmentally arrested and restricted in the kind of information that it can accept and the way in which this information is processed" (p. 83).

This "developmentally arrested" view of the neurotic person's perception appears to parallel that of Harre and Gillett (1994), who describe the accruing results of similarly constricted "construct system":

> Problems arise when an individual's construct system does not allow adequate adaptation because it fails to anticipate events or to assimilate them to other experiences in ways that allow organized action. This leads to maladaptation and distortion in one's constructs. . . . This does lead to tensions of various kinds. For each person, there is a core of constructs that defines his or her cognitive essence as a self-conceived individual, and significant departures from this in order to accommodate experience lead to guilt—a person is aware of not being who he or she sees him- or herself as being. A person might, in another case, find that events escape adequate construction and that they cannot cope so that anticipations fail and the capacity for adaptive action is lost. In this case, one will experience anxiety. (pp. 137-138)

Examples of specific life experiences and disorders which can precipitate such "anxiety," as well as explanations from an information processing perspective of how successful psychotherapy may accomplish the task of alleviating it, are available. One such example comes from the work of Horowitz (1994) on the "mourning process," in which recollections structuring the self and intrusive memories are targeted for reprocessing and change. As he explains:

> Both the memories of the relationship long before the death as well as the memories of the event surrounding the death are important for mourners to reconsider and difficult for them to review. That is one reason a mourning process takes place over many months. Only then does the person reschematize his or her view of self in relation to the deceased; this is a modification of the structure of internalized knowledge. Until then, discrete perceptual memories, for example, of deathbed or illness scenes, may occur as intrusive images. Equally significant are inhibitions of memory during mourning. A person may be

unable to remember the deceased, perhaps for months be unable to visualize the face or hear the voice. Later on, voluntary recollection in images is once again possible, because in the interim a working-through process has occurred. (p. 200)

Similarly, it has been suggested that the difficulty experienced by therapists in working with clients afflicted with severe disorders such as "borderline personality" and "schizophrenia" might be illuminated by a discursive information processing perspective. In describing individuals diagnosed as borderline, for example, Harre and Gillett (1994) observe:

When talking to such individuals, one finds that they are poor at articulating or understanding the events of their lives and the relationships among them. They tend to have a very limited discursive context within which to negotiate and elaborate their responses to life events. . . . This lack of depth and richness in the discursive content of their subjectivities translates itself into a human and relational lack in their lives in general.

The case of these unfortunate and limited subjects illustrates the fact that consciousness is the subjective springboard of agency. One cannot do that of which one cannot conceive and one cannot conceive of content for which one lacks the discourse-based skills. This is particularly true when the topic at the center of consciousness is oneself. (p. 175)

Lynch (1985) reports similar discourse-related limitations, with physiological consequences, in schizophrenic patients:

. . . Schizophrenic patients who were the most socially withdrawn tended to have the lowest blood pressure levels. With surprising frequency and consistency, investigators reported that the blood pressure of severely withdrawn schizophrenics (usually labeled "catatonic" or "hebephrenic") were the lowest observed in the hospital populations. *Catatonic and hebephrenic patients are characterized by acute social withdrawal and lack of talking and are generally regarded as the most severely disturbed schizophrenics.* (p. 185)

In contrast, Lynch (1985) characterizes his successfully treated hypertensive clients as people who had "literally and all unwittingly talked their way into such cardiovascular disease" and who, through psychotherapy, were taught "to talk their way back to health" (p. 9). With the help of computer technology, Lynch was able to monitor blood pressure levels in clients during therapy and to thus facilitate the kind of therapeutic dialogue which alleviated the hypertension. At the conclusion of therapy, one of his successful clients described his hypertensive condition in this way: "Thought I had gotten the past out of my system—but it appears what I did was push it out of my head and into the cardiovascular system" (p. 20).

Concerning this pathogenic process, Lynch (1985) notes that during treatment, his clients learned that they had been disconnected not only from an awareness of blood pressure and feelings (incongruence), but also from their "fellow men and women" (p. 20) (alienation). Of the dialogue contributing to hypertension, Lynch (1985) reports:

> Hypertensive dialogue. . . seems to be characterized not just by marked elevations in blood pressure when one speaks, but by an equally marked inability to listen when spoken to. Rather than listening, our hypertensive patients appeared to be preoccupied, thinking about what they wanted to say next, almost as if they were continuously engaged in a contest or a fight rather than in a comfortable dialogue. Instead of listening, they appeared to be defending against what others had to say. Whether in response to a therapist or mate, the pattern was similar . . .
>
> In this light, it becomes obvious that those people who communicate most intimately with patients play an important role in their cardiovascular health. If hypertensive patients not only significantly elevate their pressure when speaking, but also have difficulty listening to others or attending to their environment, then it is likely that this problem profoundly affects those who try to communicate with them. (p. 161)

However, from an information processing perspective, clients who appear to be "defending against what others have to say" may, at that point in therapy, be defending their own self-concepts based upon the limited information available to them from their long-term memories or "data banks." Thus, taking a confrontational or even analytical approach with such hypertensive clients would likely be futile and, according to Lynch (1985), could also be hazardous. So vital to human health is the "language of our hearts," he states, that "if ignored, unheard, or misunderstood—it can produce terrible physical suffering, even premature death." This language, he says, "cries out to be heard," "demands to be understood," and "must not be denied." Therapists, he adds, must therefore "learn to listen and to understand" (p.10).

It is in this sense, therefore, that a client-centered approach with hypertensives might be required, in part, since it is conducive to "listening" and pacing by the therapist—interactional processes which would appear to be fundamental to accessing deeply stored information comprising faulty premises. Accessing this information may in turn automatically engage the client's reasoning abilities to promote reformulated conclusions and revised meanings that are more in line with, or functional to, the self (a procedure which may therefore obviate the kind of confrontational or even didactic discourse which may have contributed to, or exacerbated, the hypertension in the first place). Through fostering, integrating, and/or revising meanings during the process of self-disclosure, in other words, the anxiety often associated with a disorganized information field subsides. And this occurs, Wexler (1974) says, as the client gives increased organization and structure to information by "subsuming the differentiated facets in a superordinate structure" (i.e., knowledge grows from that which precedes it). Thereafter, he states, "the accessibility of this information in long-term memory for activation in future processing is enhanced" (pp. 75-76). That is, cognitive growth, as well as the *biological and cognitive* capacity for further growth, have ostensibly occurred.

ANXIETY AS A SIGNAL FOR CHANGE

Before the inception of professional psychotherapy, as Whitaker (1989) observes, therapeutic change was "catalyzed by the experience of stress in the person whose anxiety level was high." This factor, coupled with "the presence of a giving, nurturing professional or socially available older or more tolerant individual," Whitaker states, was sufficient to eradicate symptoms. Shamans, rabbis, priests, and other individuals, today, he says, all "slip into the role of being a social therapist—all function therapeutically in this manner" (p. 154). The significance of "anxiety" in signaling the need for growth or "creative change" (Rossi, 1993, p. 271) is further underlined by the interpersonal communication studies of Siegman and Pope (1972) who report that anxiety-arousing content in client's self-disclosures produce greater verbal quantity (Harper, Weins, and Matarazzo , 1978, p. 53). In their studies, the latter researchers also analyzed clients' verbal behavior on anxious and nonanxious days, reporting that speech rate was significantly greater on high anxiety days. Consequently, Harper, Weins, and Matarazzo (1978) conclude that anxiety is perhaps the single variable most frequently related to verbal productivity in studies utilizing the amount of speech produced as an indicator of variations in psychological states.

The significance of these findings to psychotherapy lies in their apparent support of the existence of "autonomous processes" within the client, activated through this reported natural increased frequency of verbal behavior during anxious states. In this regard, the universal constructivistic language abilities and human reasoning processes (termed "autonomous" processes or "self-actualization tendencies"), activated during these increased verbal states, may therefore account for why humanists believe human nature to be "something that can be trusted." As Friedman (1992) puts it, "the motivation toward the positive or constructive already exists in the individual and will come forward if we can release what is most basic . . ." (pp. 46-47). And what is "most basic," or what separates human beings from lower animals, is their superior inductive and deductive reasoning abilities operating through the constructivistic property of language and discourse and/or the correlative function of the brain.

Supporting this view and concluding this chapter are the words of Dennett (1991):

> The philosopher Justin Leiber sums up the role of language in shaping our mental lives: Looking at ourselves from the computer viewpoint, we cannot avoid seeing that natural language is our most important "programming language." This means that a vast portion of our knowledge and activity is, for us, best communicated and understood in our natural language. . . .

One could say that natural language was our first great original artifact and, since, as we increasingly realize, languages are machines, so natural language, with our brains to run it, was our primal invention of the universal computer. One could say this except for the sneaking suspicion that language isn't something we invented but something we became, not something we constructed but something in which we created, and recreated, ourselves (Leiber, 1991, p. 8). (p. 302)

SUMMARY AND CONCLUSION

In summary, despite Freud's heuristic labelling of psychotherapy, "the talking cure," little progress has seemingly occurred in determining how this discursive act achieves therapeutic results—or what linguistic, cognitive, and neurological mechanisms may be involved in this "cure." The delay in exploration of this aspect of psychotherapy may further have been due to limitations in the study of language or speech production (wherein meaning is likely generated) by the other major areas of human inquiry with investments in this phenomenon, namely linguistics and neurology. As a result, psychotherapy has had to turn to other sources (e.g., cognitive science, discursive psychology, psychobiology, philosophy, and consciousness) for an understanding of this linguistic process in an effort to bridge the "gap" between phenomenology and behavior.

Language further appears to be crucial in this regard due to its role in human consciousness (defined as the process of self-reflection through language), as well as its function in the formation of mind (termed the process of receiving, generating, and transducing information through language). Due to the dual existence of body and mind, therapists currently are therefore likely to nonconsciously activate and/or employ processes in both spheres of human activity; that is: interactional and nonverbal processes between therapist and client likely facilitate discursive processes, by the client, resulting in cognitive and neurological processes, within th client, which act as the primary agents of self-growth or "self-actualization." Thus, a higher-order psychotherapeutic theory appears to emerge accounting for, and clarifying, observations of therapeutic phenomena involved in the interaction between mind and brain (or phenomenology and behavior) in a manner consistent with the formulation of other scientific field theories (which incorporate knowledge from diverse scientific sources).

What may have delayed progress in this area of theory building in psychotherapy (in addition to single-school adherence—or possibly because of it) is the apparent redundancy of inferring mental states and processes operating behind the mental states and processes of discursive activity, as well as the intrapsychic search for processes of change within the therapist. However, despite the apparent resulting diversion of the scientific enterprise caused by these intrapsychic preoccupations, the recognition of mind and self by the biological sciences (and by other areas of human inquiry) may have enhanced the search for a higher-order theory through integrating the knowledge these disciplines contribute in clarifying controversial psychotherapeutic observations. In fact, the forward-thinking characteristic of human consciousness, or "self-actualization tendency" may be what prompted physicist Blaise Pascal to observe: "We almost never think of the present, and when we do, it is only to see what light it throws on our plans for the future" (Damasio, 1994, p. 165). This forward-thinking tendency may further be due to the universal constructivistic nature of language and discourse, operating through the correlative function of the brain, coupled with the universal human propensity to create meaning through logic (processes seemingly accelerated through the asymmetrically discursive psychotherapeutic relationship).

These factors, combined with the interpersonal communication finding that increased anxiety results in increased verbal behavior, may account for the widely reported observation within the therapeutic community of autonomous processes operating within clients, driving the therapeutic process. In this sense, therefore, the increased verbal behavior during anxious states may provide the increase in self-disclosure required to unblock neural pathways and release information necessary for the syllogistic and/or correlational revision of faulty premises comprising meanings which may be impelling dysfunctional behavior. In other words, by the therapist acting as a "surrogate information processor" facilitating self-disclosure, universal language mechanisms, correlative brain functions, and logical reasoning abilities may be automatically activated within the client to reprocess and update premises comprising troublesome meanings motivating dysfunctional ideation and behavior. Thus, such information reprocessing may provide the client with more functional coping strategies, schemas, or constructs for adaptive living (in the guise of bringing the "unconscious" to consciousness in psychoanalysis, for example).

In conclusion, how the therapist can facilitate this information reprocessing—behaviorally, biologically, and cognitively—is the topic of Chapter 7.

Chapter 7

Facilitative Therapist Behaviors as a Modus Operandi: Integrative Eclecticism Within Transtheoretical and Common Factors Integration

. . . Having a mind means that an organism forms neural representations which can become images, be manipulated in a process called thought, and eventually influence behavior by helping predict the future, plan accordingly, and choose the next action.

—Antonio Damasio, 1994

Problems result from the way we construe our lives, play our roles, and interact with the construals of others.

—Haim Omer, 1994

What counselors do reveals assumptions that, in principle, people choose how they will act, that they do so on the bases of the meanings they ascribe to events, and that these meanings are open to elaboration and change through conversation.

—Stanley Strong, 1995

Each man has a self, and enlarges his self by his experiences. That is, he learns from experience; from the experience of others as well as his own; from their inner experiences as well as their outer. But he can learn from their inner experience only by entering it.

—J. Bronowski, 1966

Life is growth—continual, unending, open process. Man is appropriately termed constructive; he is becoming as well as being. Man is never finished in the sense of having a final identity. Each achievement in realizing his potentialities becomes a new base from which to grow and further realize himself.

—Carolyn Cochrane and Joanne Holloway, 1974

While in his groundbreaking work, *Counseling and Psychotherapy*, Carl Rogers (1942) may not have intended to portray himself as *the expert* on the client, the intrapsychic model of psychotherapy nevertheless may have essentially done so by concentrating the search for therapeutic catalysts, or processes of change, on nonobservable therapist attitudes. By the same token, Freud's postulation of "unconscious" motives controlling human nature may also have unwittingly delayed scientific progress by precluding, what Goldberg (1992) terms, "a theory of action—that is to say, a methodological system for making constructive processes happen in therapeutic sessions" (pp. 138-139). (On the other hand, by labeling psychoanalysis "the talking cure," Freud may in effect have postulated language and discourse as the means "for making constructive processes happen.")

In any event, Freud, may also have been as perplexed as present-day researchers appear to be. As Stanley Strong puts it: "How do we do scientific work in counseling psychology when we conceive of people as having choice and will and as residing in a social world that they themselves construct?" (Strong, Yoder, and Corcoran 1995, p. 382). To which he adds: "Who we are as social entities we jointly construct in concert with those [with] whom we converse."(p. 380). Moreover, as the thesis of this book suggests, based on the behavioral, biological, and cognitive evidence cited herein, the psychobiological "engine" driving this constructive "conversive" process appears to reside within the client in the form of constructivistic language and/or logical reasoning abilities which have been characterized as "autonomous," but which require activation or facilitation through asymmetrical discourse conducive to accessing deeper levels of stored information.

In this way, clients therefore become the experts on their own self-revisions by reprocessing, refraining, and/or reconstructing past experiences as information or memories stored temporally in the brain. In this sense, as Goldberg (1992) observes in a quote from Elvin Semrad, "The patient is the only textbook that we will ever need" (p. 91). In other words, whether *therapists* make the relevant analytical or syllogistic connections between these experiences from the client's past appears secondary to clients making these connections or correlations for themselves at their own pace. As stated earlier, this point has import due to the selective attention property of human concentration which would make it difficult, if not impossible, for the therapist to attend equally to the facilitation of client self-disclosure *and* gaining a complete understanding of the client's revised self. Indeed, to do so, the therapist would require knowledge of the client's environmental history equal to that of the client, which would be impossible. As Rice (1974) explains:

> The [therapist's] response should be accurate in the sense of being a real and recognizable part of the client's experience, but it need not and cannot attempt to encompass the whole experience. Although the therapist tries to grasp each new attempt of the client toward more adequate construction, he avoids any attempt of his own toward closure. The client, rather than the therapist, attempts the new constructions. . . . By helping a client to get further and further into his own experience, encouraging him to check each new synthesis against this experience, the therapist is less likely to build in his own distortions and oversimplifications [countertransference]. In fact, when evocative reflection is functioning well, and the client's experience is unfolding, many aspects of it will come as a surprise to the therapist [and often, as previously noted, to the client as well]. . . . The purpose of the therapist's response is to evoke more of the experience for the client. (pp. 301-302)

SCIENTIFIC ROADBLOCKS

Concentrating research efforts on nonobservables such as therapist intrapsychic states and the client's "unconscious" may have delayed progress in the field, thwarting research and thus leaving psychotherapy so broadly defined as to render it obscure. In fact, Rogers (1977) himself may have eventually come to this realization, essentially supporting an integrative vision, when he observed: "If we can identify the environmental influences that promote a continuing internal harmony . . . these findings could be put to preventive use" (p. 249). As for what promotes *disharmony* of the self, Rogers (1977) acknowledges that he gradually came to view incongruence (the dissociation, rift, or estrangement from the real self) as "something learned, a perverse channeling of some of the actualizing tendency into behaviors that do not actualize." In this respect, he adds, his thinking changed:

> Years ago I saw the rift between self and experience, between conscious goals and organismic directions, as something natural and necessary, albeit unfortunate. Now I believe that individuals are culturally conditioned, rewarded, reinforced, for behaviors that are in fact perversions of the natural directions of the unitary actualizing tendency. (p. 247)

That these environmental influences may be of fundamental relevance to psychotherapy is further noted by Danziger (1976). He suggests, for example, that "the psychotherapist's style of communication should be such as to stimulate those aspects of the patient's communication that are associated with therapeutic change." He admits, however, that "much research still needs to be done to identify all aspects that are relevant in this context" (p. 111). Furthermore, that psychotherapy has not yet actively pursued this area of inquiry (as evidenced by the current "nonspecific" status of nonverbal communication) seems unusual. The significance of this omission is further underlined by those who work in the field of nonverbal communication, who report that "people are typically not aware of what they do with their hands, feet, or other parts of their body when they talk with others"(Exline and Fehr, 1978, p. 121).

As for explicating therapeutic processes in the interactional and standardized terms described herein, critics of technique may find solace in Wexler's (1974) words of reassurance:

To some it may seem that our view of the therapist as a surrogate processor who organizes the meaning of the information in process in the client [or enables the client to do this reprocessing for him- or herself] is one that makes the therapist seem like some sort of response machine, devoid of human qualities. Such is not the intent. Neither has our intent been to poeticize and romanticize what the therapist does. Our intent has only been to conceptualize what it is the therapist overtly does and what are its effects. (p. 113)

In other words, the therapist behavioral interventions suggested herein should be viewed more as noninterfering "facilitation," than unfeeling "manipulation," since they do not impinge upon the client's freedom of choice concerning what to disclose. (In fact, as explained later in this chapter, this form of therapy might be viewed as less manipulative than the current externally directed systemic therapies since it respects the individual client's direction or "openness to experience" [Rogers 1961, p. 115] as opposed to that of the group or family.) In other words, as Barretta, Barretta, and Bongiovanni (1990) explain, "It is not the purpose of therapy to re-create the individual along the lines of some master design, but rather to provide the [experiential] tools necessary for that individual to re-create his or her own design replete with choice" (p. 392).

FACILITATING THE RE-CREATION
OF THE CLIENT'S "DESIGN"

Many typical therapeutic encounters, Rossi (1993) observes, begin with the client in "tension, distress, and perhaps even negative expectations about the possibility of getting help." At this beginning stage of therapy, Rossi states, most therapists have been trained to do "exactly the wrong thing"; they try to calm, reassure, and relax the client. As a result, he says, the client's high charge of emotional energy for therapeutic change is immediately lost through the therapist's "insecurity and misunderstanding of the value of what is being presented." The therapist, Rossi maintains, rarely needs to distort the client's "natural mind-body signals of the typical signs of high performance energy associated with the anticipation of problem solving" (p. 113) by telling the client to relax at the beginning of the therapy session. This view also parallels that of Carl Whitaker (1989) who contends that "as long as the symptoms or source of stress are being relieved or modified or lessened by the efforts of the therapist, it is probable that change will not take place; the patient is enjoying the relief from stress rather than demanding more of himself" (p. 196).

In such instances, therapists should be aware, Rossi (1993) further maintains, that an emotional crisis can be "a valid and valuable part of the therapeutic process of breaking through traumatic amnesias and accessing state-bound memories that are at the source of mind-body symptoms and problems" (p. 97). In other words, he says, the crisis point of therapeutic accessing need not be "shut off prematurely by the therapist who may be afraid that emotions will get out of control." It is necessary, he contends, to permit the client's emotional accessing to continue through to the "recovery of important memories and the achievement of healing and new insights" (p. 97) thereby utilizing the client's anxiety as "motivational energy for exploring and resolving her issues privately within herself" (p. 115). Paralleling this view, Goldberg (1992) suggests that therapists who view themselves as experts on the client's functioning may feel they have the prerogative to steer clients away from what they (clients) purport to want and toward what they (therapists) feel they "actually need" (p. 11). In doing so, Goldberg states, such therapists "wrestle away the 'illusion' of reality from the patient's idiosyncratic world view" and replace it with their own "objective reality" (p. 11). However, as previously stated, such directive or didactic approaches seldom succeed in the long run because they disregard the client's limited information processing capacity to accommodate a foreign reality.

Finally, in addition to capitalizing upon clients' "emotional energy" and direction as a means of facilitating exploration and resolution of issues within themselves, the successful therapist employs other *interactional* techniques and behaviors as well, which this chapter outlines (while summarizing and integrating information from previous chapters). Underlying this eclectic and integrative endeavor, as previously noted, is *information theory* which, according to Rossi (1993), may be "capable of unifying psychological, biological, and physical phenomena into a single conceptual framework that can account for mind-body healing, personality development, the evolution of human consciousness . . ." (p. 313).

TOWARD UNIFYING THE PERSON

While the seeds of rapprochement and integration (particularly between humanism and behaviorism) may have been sown during the past few years, the main proponents of these schools nevertheless appear to have been slow in responding to this challenge. For example, Rachlin (1994) describes the behavioral perspective on this problem:

> The failure of behavioral psychology to deal with the mentalistic concepts such as beliefs (which philosophers call "propositional attitudes" or "intentional states") and pains (which they call "phenomenal states" or "raw feels") has by and large left treatment of strictly mental dysfunction to non-behavioral psychology. A comprehensive behavioral analysis of such concepts does not currently exist but such analyses are possible and may be highly useful. (p. 31)

Although the work of the cognitive behaviorists in addressing the "central antecedents" (Rachlin, 1994, pp. 30-31) of behavior has been acknowledged, this approach to changing the client's belief system (essentially through teaching and/or rational emotive confrontation [Ellis, 1973]) nevertheless appears to disregard knowledge accumulating from studies in information processing and neurology. Again, the main concern arises from the possible bypassing of the client's capacity to accommodate information deemed by the therapist to be relevant. Information hypothesized to be "a central antecedent" may thus not be accessible for successful reprocessing by the client at that particular point in therapy. In other words, cognitive behavior therapy and rational emotive therapy seemingly ignore how the client's belief system comes into being in the first place (ostensibly through the constructivistic language and/or logical reasoning abilities acting upon an idiosyncratic history of experiences and memories stored temporally in the brain). In disregarding these apparent universal psychobiological factors, these therapies therefore seemingly ignore how the client achieves revision of this belief system.

The same criticism may also apply to group and family therapy. As Beck (1974) states of the group process, "It seems to be important to the group that everyone participate in the work on personal growth and in the self-disclosure process in particular." However, Beck adds, although all members are expected to participate in "some meaningful way," it is nevertheless "the group" which decides "what is appropriate" (p. 443). Similarly, Carl Whitaker (1989) points out that in family therapy, "The family, in essence, takes over the psychotherapy in a very early stage and will continue to direct it unless otherwise impeded" (pp. 117-118). As a result, such externally directed therapies do not appear to address change of belief systems and/or self-meanings in a manner which respects the individual client's information processing capacity and/or self-integrity, both seemingly dependent upon an idiosyncratic history of experiences and memories stored temporally in the brain.

Hence, while convergence of opinion may be developing around "discovering the true self" (Havens, 1994, p. 97) as the fundamental objective, or the "what" of psychotherapy, the "how" of psychotherapy still appears to be the reef upon which the many extant theories of therapy run aground. Moreover, the apparent long-standing rivalry between the humanistic and behavioral schools may have led some to regard mind and behavior as mutually exclusive entities—a view disputed by Rachlin (1994):

> If the human body evolved to better and better fit into the environment, the human mind (reasoned Darwin and his followers) must have evolved in a corresponding way; both body and mind might be understood (as Aristotle originally suggested) in terms of their functions in their environment. Twentieth-century philosophers, especially Gilbert Ryle and Ludwig Wittgenstein (1889-1951), have noted that the relationship between people's minds and the environment cannot be conceived separately from their overt behavior. The focus of the study of mind has thus shifted in our century from introspection to behavior. (p. 134)

It is in this sense, therefore, that a corresponding "shift" to focusing upon universal observable variables in the therapeutic relationship, as mentioned earlier, may help establish a clearer, empirically grounded theory of psychotherapeutic processes. Viewed from a perspective seemingly more conducive to verification through replication, one of these universal variables, client self-disclosure, for example, appears to be maximized by the appropriate employment of dominant eye contact within an asymmetrical therapeutic encounter—asymmetry, in turn, being a function of therapist empathy. As Wexler (1974) explains:

> The therapist's response serves to differentiate the meaning of a particular facet of the client's experience, but it also simultaneously serves to evoke an enriched substrate for further processing. . . . Effective empathic responding should be neither a matter of merely paraphrasing or summarizing what the client has said nor simply a matter of reflecting feelings. Rather, if it is to serve processing functions for the client, it is a matter of carefully attending to and selecting from the facets of information contained in what the client has said and what might have been evoked, and then transforming [or helping the client transform] this information into effective linguistic organizations that serve to further differentiate or integrate meaning for the client and evoke in him an enriched substrate for further processing. (pp. 107-108)

Describing the resulting asymmetric character of this continued "differentiation and integration of meaning" by the client, Derlega et al. (1991) observe that although there may be sentiments or views held by both the client and therapist, these feelings, they say, are "usually expressed only by the client to the therapist." In other words, they maintain, client and therapist must accept the particular ground rules for therapy: the client "provides the self-disclosure input and the therapist listens and comments." Thus, they say, clients are expected to maintain an open self boundary by disclosing content relevant to their personal concerns, while therapists are expected to maintain "a closed self boundary by divulging little or nothing about themselves" (p. 163). (This form of asymmetrical empathic understanding has further been termed "cognitive empathy" by Bebout [1974], who defines it as: "the ability to arrive at integrative understandings of another's perceptual field by a predominantly cognitive assimilation of the other's values, meanings, symbols, stated or implied intentions, and ideation." When successful Bebout adds, "the empathizer knows the organization of another's world or self-view" [p. 402].)

In this asymmetrical empathic form, therefore, the psychotherapeutic relationship appears "unique" (Simon, 1990). The therapist's "role definition," Simon notes, includes agreement that "one person, the patient, will openly discuss his or her personal life, while the therapist will function in a manner that will further the patient's psychotherapeutic gains" (p. 207). And in this sense, as the following discussion suggests, furthering the "patient's psychotherapeutic gains" may depend heavily upon the asymmetric property of the therapeutic encounter.

ASYMMETRY AS A UNIVERSAL PSYCHOTHERAPEUTIC CHARACTERISTIC

In this respect, asymmetry within the therapeutic relationship constitutes another universal characteristic. While such asymmetry might not seem overly difficult to achieve, psychotherapy has nevertheless been termed "the impossible profession" (Malcolm, 1981). Similarly, Mahoney (1991) maintains that therapy is a "potentially draining endeavor" (p. 287) since the therapist "must often modulate his or her emotional expressions in deference to the immediate needs of the client" (p. 366). In this sense, therefore, as Carl Whitaker (1989) states, "your discipline, not just your caring, is the essence of your usefulness" (p. 152). (In this regard, the basic training I received en route to obtaining an officer's commission in the army while an undergraduate student proved to be a valuable experience in helping provide the self-discipline required to suppress one's needs in deference to meeting the needs of the client.)

Disciplining oneself further involves active listening, a process which, as those who study nonverbal behavior report is *hard work.* The physical changes which occur during the listening process, Adler and Towne (1990) point out, indicate the kind of effort required: "the heart rate quickens, respiration increases, and body temperature rises" (pp. 253-254). These physiological changes apparently occur, because, as Grosch and Olsen (1994) observe, instead of working actively and seeing positive results of their work, psychotherapists "must suspend their own urge to act in order to listen in silence for long hours." Or as Lazarus (1993b) states in his nonverbal, client-centered experience cited earlier, he had to "force" himself to listen and "refrain from offering and observations, reflections, advice, or suggestions" (p. 406). Listening, Grosch and Olsen (1994) further state, is "a strenuous but silent activity" which means that therapists "must for extended periods of time serve as containers for their clients' unhappy feelings" (p. 8). Nichols (1995) elaborates upon the demands of this listening process:

> When it's genuine, listening demands taking an interest in the speaker and what he or she has to say.
>
> *Taking an interest* can easily be sentimentalized by equating it with sincerity or caring. Sincerity and caring are certainly fine characteristics, but listening isn't a matter of character, nor is it something that good people do automatically. To take an interest in someone else, we must suspend the interests of the self. Listening is the art by which we use empathy to reach across the space between us. (p. 62)

As for what therapists should "listen" for, or attend to, within an information processing perspective, Zimring (1974) offers the following simplifying suggestion which appears consistent with the selective attention property of human concentration: "The hypotheses that the therapist forms in the moment-to-moment interaction in therapy are not about the cause of the client's difficulty or what the client is experiencing at the moment at an unconscious level; instead, they are about the meaning to the client of the client's last statement" (p. 121). Or, as Salvador Minuchin replied at a seminar attended by myself when asked how he knows "what to do next" in therapy: "The dialogue," he answered, "tells me what to do and say next." In other words, in respecting the client's information processing capacity, the therapist primarily promotes understanding of the client's immediate disclosures necessary to automatically revise premises and/or conclusions structuring self-meanings—meanings which may be counterproductive to intra- as well as interpersonal communication. As Wexler (1974) explains, "The aim of the therapist should be to focus on a significant facet of information evoked but not adequately elaborated by the client." In so doing, he says, "the therapist plays on a moment-to- moment basis a vitally important role" in helping the client both create change in the structure of his field and "provide the necessary informational substrate for meaningful reorganization" (pp. 103-104).

As for the therapist's prospects of motivating the client to "differentiate new facets of meaning" from his or her "last statement," Lankton (1990) observes that "therapists who speak the experiential language of a client will not find the client resistant" (p. 368). Edelson (1994) further suggests a guideline by which to assess whether such successful facilitation is occurring:

> I am inclined to think I am on the right track if the patient's response to my communication tells me more than I knew before, surprises me, adds a new twist to the story, carries the story further, or involves an intense expression of feeling (such as when we begin to laugh or cry, sometimes quite unexpectedly, when something about a movie—we are not always sure what it is—touches us). I am inclined to think I am on the wrong track if the patient convincingly challenges what I say by pointing out particulars that are inconsistent with it or not encompassed by it or if the patient ignores what I say (what I say has no impact on the patient or the story he or she is telling or enacting). (p. 86)

However, knowing "when the therapist is on the right track" does not explain how the therapist's nonverbal "communication" facilitates those responses from the client that "carry the story further" (which, as the next section suggests, could be a function of another universal factor, *face-to-face interaction*).

FACILITATIVE FACE-TO-FACE INTERACTION

While the biological hardware underlying the effects of psychotherapy may be becoming increasingly understood, the question of how the therapist facilitates these effects interactively still requires clarification. Commenting upon the extent of the biological knowledge accumulated thus far, Rossi (1990) states:

From a psychobiological perspective, psychotherapy is a means of accessing and therapeutically reframing the state-dependent mind-body processes that encode problems. Emotions, stress, and trauma associated with most life experiences release informational substances (messenger molecules) from many cells throughout the body that encode memory, learning, behavior, psychological complexes, and psychosomatic problems in a state-dependent manner; these same informational substances also regulate the body's biology at the cellular and genetic levels to modulate health and illness. We can utilize new process-oriented forms of psychotherapy to access these informational substances that serve as the communication link between mind and body to facilitate optimal levels of mind-body integration. (p. 356)

Again, the psychobiological effects of successful psychotherapy notwithstanding, the question remains: how best to "access" and "therapeutically reframe" the "mind-body processes" to which Rossi refers.

From a verbal perspective, facilitative interactional techniques such as mirroring, echoing, reframing, and/or reflection are relatively well-known. Until recently, however, they had not been closely investigated to determine how they influence therapeutic change. As Rice (1974) noted over two decades ago, "Even those who make liberal use of reflection find it difficult to explain how a method that makes use of uncontingent reinforcement (unconditional positive regard) and feeds no new information into the system (reflection of the client's message), can lead to change" (p. 290). However, like empathy, these therapist verbal techniques also appear to play a significant role in facilitating client self-disclosure through promoting asymmetry within the therapeutic relationship. As Ferrara (1994) explains, "Mirroring, like backchannel cues such as 'Mmhmm,' is a most minimal response intended to insure that the previous speaker continues an extended turn with little interruption." Mirroring, she says, thus "serves to quickly return the 'turn at talk' to the prior speaker and has the added advantage that it signals attentiveness and invites continuation of a topic" (p. 123). Ferrara elaborates:

By selecting a key word or phrase for repetition, and by delivering it either in a monotone or with downward intonation, therapists indicate that they are in fact listening. The data indicate that the technique of mirroring appears to foster rapid resumption by the prior speaker and a continuation or elaboration of topic. Examination of discourse segments throughout the corpus indicates that the result of a minimal speech unit produced by the therapist is client continuation or elaboration of the previously initiated topic. (p. 123)

In other words, active, accurate empathic listening by the therapist appears to promote client disclosure through communicating "understanding" and inviting elaboration. In this way, the client may thus be motivated or allowed to maintain exploratory discourse thereby accessing deeply stored information while simultaneously and automatically activating constructivistic language and logical reasoning processes to revise meanings and promote self-change. Toukmanian (1992) further explains the possible effects of therapist "understanding" upon this therapeutic process:

It may be that a client's experience of disjunction, as a perceived instance of being misunderstood by the therapist (e.g., "she does not understand what I am talking about"), is an occasion that, at least temporarily, sets an unfavorable expectancy about the outcome of the therapeutic task (e.g., "what's the use . . . I cannot make myself understood"), thus blocking the client from further attempts at exploring his or her perceptions of a given experience on deeper or more productive levels of analysis. (pp. 100-101)

Communicating "understanding" and promoting self-disclosure from the client appear to be functions of another verbal technique, the metaphor, as well. As Ferrara (1994) explains:

. . . Metaphor distills and compresses thoughts and feelings, and allows for an economical condensation of themes. Metaphors provide a glimmer of understanding by summing up and generalizing global insights. . . . I emphasize the interactive nature of metaphor when I point out that client and therapist together create meaning and that this joint accomplishment sets the stage for other collaborative work. . . . The interpretation of metaphor is work because the reverberations are not finite, but open-ended. Even long after utterance of a metaphor, new reverberations can be felt, new connections can be seen. Both clients and therapists must be alert to this ongoing nature of meaning. (pp. 129-130)

Recapping thus far, it may be, as Goldfried, Castonguay, and Safran (1992) contend, that what appears as "a unique characteristic of a particular treatment represents a specific way of implementing a common element that underlies the practice of different therapies" (p. 600). In this sense, for example: the reflected thought; the appropriate metaphor; and the well-timed psychoanalytic interpretation, accurate and timely challenge of client's beliefs in rational emotive therapy, and reframing in family therapy, Goldfried, Castonguay, and Safran (1992) suggest, "may well correspond to the same general therapeutic principle" (p. 600). And that principle, this book maintains, may involve the communication of therapist understanding and the promotion of asymmetry and pacing through listening thereby facilitating access to deeper levels of stored information. The listening process then triggers the automatic revision of troublesome meanings comprising dysfunctional self-concepts, which in turn may be impelling dysfunctional ideation and behavior.

FACILITATIVE NONVERBAL INTERACTION IN PSYCHOTHERAPY

The relatively common facilitative verbal techniques cited above notwithstanding, the so-called gap in psychotherapy nevertheless remains and appears more closely related to how the successful therapist facilitates client disclosure nonverbally. This becomes more evident when the apparent high degree of communicative power attributed to this channel of interpersonal communication (as compared to the verbal channel) is taken into consideration. Because of its reported power, the current nonspecific status of therapist nonverbal behavior therefore suggests interactional processes to have been seriously neglected by researchers in psychotherapy, thus resulting in the nebulous state of affairs regarding therapist behavior described by Yalom (1975):

> What can the therapist do. . . : I think that the answer lies in the verb "to be". He does by being, by being there with the patient. "Presence" is the hidden agent of help in all forms of therapy. When patients look back on their therapy, they rarely remember a single interpretation of the therapist, but they always remember his presence, that he was there with them. (p. 91)

Similarly, "presence" was acknowledged by a current leading proponent of the humanistic school, James Bugental, as the "one essential ingredient of therapy" (Friedman, 1992, p. 74). From a systems perspective, Carl Whitaker (1989) echoes a similar view. The therapist is the "outsider," the "catalyst," he says, who "doesn't really take part." But "somehow," he adds, the therapist's "presence precipitates the system into changing its dynamics" (p. 141). The question of how or what the therapist's nonverbal presence contributes to therapy, therefore, appears to be the crucial factor requiring clarification. In other words, if, as Safran and Muran (1994) maintain, it is the "corrective emotional experience that modifies the patient's interpersonal schema or generalized representation of self-other interactions" (p. 212), the question of how the therapist's presence behaviorally and cognitively facilitates the client's "correction" of this past experience (or unwittingly inhibits it) remains to be clarified.

To increase this understanding, Rhodes and Greenberg (1994) suggest that psychotherapy researchers "need to break down the processes involved in establishing and maintaining an alliance; they need to study the actual exchanges that are usually buried when data from measures of alliance are averaged across the session, the individual treatment, or the entire sample." By focusing on particular in-session performances of tasks related to the alliance, they state, "we are able to begin to understand what therapists and patients need to do to make treatment more collaborative and therefore effective when they are sitting across from each other" (p. 231). While such an analysis of the therapeutic relationship may seem reasonable from a scientific viewpoint, it has nevertheless encountered opposition, particularly from the humanistic school, for reasons previously cited. However, this may be where the approach presented herein could facilitate the task of interactive communication analysis *without losing sight of the person*, i.e., while maintaining a holistic perspective and without impinging upon the client's freedom of choice or self-integrity.

COMMUNICATION AS AN AGGREGATE OR HOLISTIC PHENOMENON

Because communication is a total organismic process (Birdwhistell, 1970, p. 173), the exploration of possible facilitative therapist behaviors will necessarily involve description and control of more than one therapist nonverbal behavior in psychotherapy. Others from the allied field of interpersonal communication similarly agree that communication involves the totality of a person's behavior. As Brooks and Emmert (1976) state, "Facial and vocal cues appear to be the most important nonverbal cues for communicating feelings and emotions, although it is the totality of the person's behavior—an amalgam of all the nonverbal cues—that gives us the best idea of the feeling or emotion communicated" (p. 174). That this view appears to be long held is further evidenced by the early conclusions of Allport and Vernon (1933), who emphasize the importance of focusing upon several levels of nonverbal behavior when interpreting the significance of a particular communicative act.

While an "amalgam" of facial and vocal cues may be most salient, Watzlawick (1978) nonetheless maintains that "the eyes are probably the most important part of the totality of the face" or "the mirror of the soul" (p. 70). In addition to this variable (defined herein as dominant eye contact), Tepper and Haase (1978) suggest that other nonverbal cues besides eye contact, such as trunk lean and vocal intonation, may be involved in the communication of facilitative states. Still another of these cues, "movement" on the part of the therapist while the client is speaking, is classified by Bandler and Grinder (1979) as "interfering behavior." Their neuro-linguistic work indicates, for example, that unnecessary movement by the therapist can hinder the flow of communication by interrupting the client's train of thought or "accessing" (pp. 38-39) behavior. This neuro-linguistic view also appears consistent with Carkhuff's (1977) observation that minimizing therapist movement while "attending" (p. 37) can be a facilitative therapeutic skill.

Paralleling this view from the field of interpersonal communication, Ellsworth and Ludwig (1972) suggest that "gaze aversion" in interpersonal transactions is often motivated by a desire to "avoid distractions" (p. 388) (such as may occur through therapist movement). And this may occur, as Exline and Fehr (1978) explain, because "we may be unable to take in complex sensory stimuli while simultaneously processing cognitive material for the purpose of formulating speech" (p. 129). (This client phenomenon may further be a function of the selective attention property of human concentration described earlier in relation to therapist functioning.) As Anderson (1974) explains in quoting D. Norman, "We are unable to do more than a very limited number of complex activities at the same time." In this respect, we choose the message to which we attend, he says, by "selectively restricting our attention to those physical cues and meaningful contents that we think will be relevant." However, he notes, "We can lose the message if either the physical or the meaningful cues change or are interfered with by other distracting messages" (p. 28).

This may therefore explain why experienced psychotherapists tend to cultivate the somewhat stationary position in therapy described by Scheflen (1973):

> In a formal activity like psychotherapy (especially when the participants are strangers), the posture and orientation of the position will be held stationary, fixed, relatively immobile, even rigid. . . . It is my belief that the postural configuration of the position is held deliberately—though not consciously—. . . . an evolved dimension of communication, learned and transmitted in culture. . . . (p. 25)

In this regard the physiological finding that movement is encoded into neural activity in the retina of the eye, and therefore does not appear to require prior processing by the brain (Gregory, 1977, p. 97), may also help account for this relatively acute human sensitivity to movement.

In addition, Kosslyn and Koenig (1992) report from their neuro-psychological work that movement activates recognition mechanisms and "patterns" (p. 78) in the brain which, in psychotherapy, may also interfere with the client's information reprocessing and logical reasoning processes resulting from self-disclosure. As Kosslyn and Koenig explain, "computing motion relations appears to be qualitatively distinct from computing the organization of portions of static images." Moreover, specific regions of the brain encode motion, they say, "in a distinct *motion relations subsystem*" (p. 78). Activation of this additional function and center of the brain, by therapist movement, may therefore interrupt client information processing (thus possibly accounting for, and/or necessitating, the previously noted *selective attention* phenomenon). As a result, Kosslyn and Koenig state, "one typically pays attention to a single object, registering its appearance and sounds at the same time" (p. 217).

Additional evidence suggesting that movement on the part of the therapist may interfere with communication flow from the client, by signalling the listener's wish to exchange roles with the speaker, comes from the interpersonal communication work of Kendon (1972). He reports, for example, that much of the listener's movement is speech preparatory in nature and, as such, may communicate the listener's desire to speak, thus leading the speaker to pause—allowing speech roles to reverse. The point here, therefore, is that unnecessary movement on the part of the therapist could also unintentionally and falsely communicate a desire to speak, causing the client's self-disclosure to be interrupted and thus inhibiting access to deeper levels of stored information. Supporting Kendon's work, Dittman and Llewellyn (1968) similarly report that head nods, for example, tend to occur at certain pauses in speech where exchange of roles might be a possibility. Head nods, they conclude, may therefore help communicate to the speaker the listener's wish to interject a comment or question (again, thereby possibly interrupting the client's "accessing").

Related to movement, and an activity which may likewise be of significance to interactional processes in psychotherapy, is the simple act of blinking on the part of the therapist. As Gregory (1977) observes, blinking is often assumed to be a reflex initiated by the cornea becoming dry. However, for normal blinking, this is apparently not the case (although blinking can occur by irritation of the cornea). According to Gregory, normal blinking occurs with no external stimulus, but is initiated by signals from the brain. The frequency of blinking, he says, increases under stress and with "expectation of a difficult task" and falls below average during periods of *concentrated mental activity.* Blink rate, he therefore concludes, can "be used as an index of attention and concentration on tasks of various kinds" (p. 60). If so, then minimization of blinking might also be one nonconscious behavioral means by which effective therapists not only minimize movement, but also communicate their undivided attention to, or intensive focus upon, client self-disclosure. As such, minimizing blinking by the therapist may therefore be related to the attitudinal construct, empathy, described by Orlinsky and Howard (1978) as denoting, in part, "therapist interpersonal behavior that is attentive" (p. 308).

The next therapist behavior which evidence suggests to be facilitative in nature is *leaning,* an "attending" skill which Carkhuff (1977) describes as a way of "posturing ourselves to attend personally." As he explains, "When we are sitting, we attend most fully when we incline our bodies forward or toward the helpee" (p. 35). Supporting Carkhuff's view, from an interpersonal communication perspective, are the studies of Mehrabian (1968; 1972, p. 11), James (1932), Reece and Whitman (1962), and Trout and Rosenfeld (1980) which found that if a communicator leans forward toward an addressee, he will be seen as expressing a more positive attitude than if he leans backward and away from the addressee.

Another possibly relevant nonverbal therapist behavior, previously studied by Rice and Wagstaff (1967), is voice tone or quality. From the field of interpersonal communication, Brooks and Emmert (1976) describe a related voice function, its level or volume, which may be of significance to psychotherapy as well. They maintain, for example, that as we wish to become more "affectionate, considerate, and understanding" in our communication, we "tend to reduce our volume" (p. 32). Davis (1994) elaborates:

> In spoken language, loudness and pitch are the two most important aural properties that modify meaning. Tempo and rhythm can also play a significant role. Loudness, of course, is the auditory sensation that relates to a sound's intensity. Loudness can convey fairly broad changes in meaning, as well as more subtle changes when different words or syllables are stressed. Whispered words of love have a very low sound

intensity; when we shout angry words at someone, our voices have a high intensity. There is a big difference in meaning between a whispered "I want you" and a shouted "I want you"; between "*I* want you" and "I want *you*." (p. 87)

As for the relationship between tempo and meaning, Davis (1994) notes that "Speeding up the tempo of speech can convey urgency or excitement. A slow tempo conveys emphasis or importance" (p. 87).

The final nonverbal therapist behavior which may be facilitative in nature is eye level. Maintaining an approximate eye level to that of the client may help symbolize human "equality" in the relationship. (Conversely, a judge's stand may be elevated in a courtroom, for example, to signify his or her preeminent position with respect to law.) Similarly, eliminating intervening desks or other objects between client and therapist, and facing the client directly may help symbolize an unobstructed or "open" atmosphere for communication and self-exploration.

UNOBSTRUCTED ASYMMETRICAL COMMUNICATION AS A MODUS OPERANDI

Once therapist nonverbal behavior is brought into working focus, or achieves *forefront materialization* (as it has in my own clinical practice), the employment of the above noted behaviors appear to elicit predictable client behaviors or responses of the type characterized by Rogers (1961) as "openness to experience" (p. 115). Chief of these therapist behaviors involves contacting the client's dominant eye while the client is talking and maintaining sustained eye contact, without blinking, while the client dialogues and engages eye contact. When the client is silent and looking at the therapist, on the other hand, the therapist may either elicit additional client self-disclosure verbally, through commenting upon, or reflecting, the client's immediate disclosures while sustaining dominant eye contact, or break eye contact for the duration of the silence to avoid embarrassment.

Within an asymmetric encounter, this seemingly major therapist behavior, combined with minimizing therapist movement during client discourse, appears to facilitate maximum client disclosure and self-exploration, suggesting it to be, to borrow a phrase, "the royal road" to accessing deeper levels of stored information—or the more effective "gateway to the mind." In contrast, in my clinical experience, contacting the nondominant eye of the client does not appear to produce the same degree of therapeutic efficacy (possibly due to the neurological and functional differences cited earlier between dominant and nondominant eyes). In this respect, if memories are stored in temporal succession in the brain, as if on "tape," then contacting the dominant eye of the client (whose visual cells, as Kosslyn and Koenig [1992] point out, appear to be connected to information storage and pattern activation or correlational centers in the brain) might be analogous to pressing the "play" button on that tape recorder (akin to the "scanning process" referred to by Penfield and Roberts [1959]).

When sufficient client self-disclosure has occurred through this procedure (often after only a few sessions and sometimes after only one extended encounter), client responses similar to those noted by Rogers (1961) have been observed: less anxiety or personal preoccupation, greater interest in the external environment, a better ability to engage in symmetrical dialogue, and a greater sense of well-being. In other words, the approach described herein elicits predictable client behavior in the form of self-disclosure, not in specifics, as in some controlling behavior modification techniques, but in terms of a general openness to engage in self-exploratory activity conducive to accessing deeply stored information. In turn, client correlative brain functions and logical reasoning processes appear to be automatically activated to revise meanings structuring the self and providing functional behavioral impulsion. As a result, clients, not therapists, ultimately choose the content and direction of their disclosure and are thus in control of their own self-revisions. Or, as Wexler (1974) puts it, by remaining within what the client has said, "we accord the person all the space." There is enormous power, he says, "in letting a person say what is inside" (p. 220).

This is not to suggest, however, that therapist attitudes play no part in therapy. Rather than being the immediate stimuli eliciting client change, therapist attitudes may more specifically guide the therapeutic process (Damasio, 1994, p. xv) by controlling inhibitive therapist behavior and promoting the kind of facilitative, nonconscious, nonverbal behavior—and asymmetry—described above. In other words, therapeutic attitudes appear to safeguard the therapeutic process by fostering asymmetrical dialogue and therapist interactive behaviors that are facilitative of client self-disclosure. This discursive interaction, facilitated especially by dominant eye contact, in turn appears to automatically engage the correlative function of the brain and/or the client's own reasoning processes to promote the automatic revision of meanings structuring the self and motivating behavior. In addition, the therapeutic attitudes may help ensure that such disclosure occurs at a pace the client can accommodate (depending upon his or her idiosyncratic history of experiences and meanings stored temporally in the brain) by promoting asymmetry within the relationship and thus respecting the client's direction in the self-revision process.

THE IDEOLOGICAL LEGACY

As for the longevity or endurance of Rogers' (1957) "necessary and sufficient conditions" and of Freud's "unconscious" in psychotherapeutic theory, Dennett (1991) explains why such "unquestioned" hypothetical constructs continually need to be tested for possible revision. Such a construct, he states:

> . . . Seems obvious until you look quite hard at what we might learn about the brain's activities and begin trying to imagine, in detail, an alternative model. Then what happens is rather like the effect of learning how a stage magician performs a conjuring trick. Once we take a serious look backstage, we discover that we didn't actually see what we thought we saw onstage. The huge gap between phenomenology and physiology shrinks a bit; we see that some of the "obvious" features of phenomenology are not real at all. (p. 434)

In short, assuming that these "obvious" features of our favorite therapies are factual rather than hypothetical and disregarding knowledge, from whatever source (Lazarus, 1992, p. 235), may have hindered theory revision and delayed paradigmatic realization thus resulting in the current nebulous *state of the art* described by R.D. Laing (1990):

Psychotherapy is what the practitioners of the dozens of accredited schools of psychotherapy say it is. All definitions imply an intention of the psychotherapist to help the client to resolve difficulties in living. I attempt to give undivided attention to *what goes on* in and between us: how we affect one another through vision, how we look, and move (kinesics), and how we sound (paralinguistics: the pitch, timbre, volume, rhythm, and tempo of our voices), as well as the content of what we say. (p. 206)

Laing's personal integrative eclectic definition notwithstanding, Norcross and Newman (1992) nevertheless maintain that definitions of psychotherapy integration generally "do not tell us what individual psychotherapists actually do or what it means to be an eclectic or integrative therapist" (p. 17). This final chapter therefore offers a possible "modus operandi" (Lazarus, 1992) based upon my clinical practice and supported by empirical research from disparate fields. Partial rationale for presenting what may (through further applied research and replication) prove to be a higher-order theory is offered by Prochaska and Diclemente (1992):

Although therapists have not struggled with all the particular problems faced by different clients, all therapists have had some experience with the processes of change. This is the common experiential ground that forms the basis of the relationship between therapist and client. In general, the therapist is seen as an expert on change—not in having all the answers, but in being aware of the critical dimensions of change and being able to offer some assistance in this regard. Clients have potential resources as self-changers, which must be used in order to effect a change. In fact, clients need to shoulder much of the burden of change. . . . (pp. 314-315)

HELPING CLIENTS
"SHOULDER THE BURDEN OF CHANGE"

Facilitating client self-disclosure as opposed to inhibiting it, being "non-interfering" (Maslow, 1976, p. 91), or simply getting "out of the way of the emergent patterns of healing" (Rossi, 1993,

p. 99), has been the focus of this book. As stated by Laing (1990): "My attempts to address myself with skillful means to the specifics of the other's difficulties calls on all the resources of my repertoire of learned and acquired techniques of effectiveness-through-harmlessness" (p. 207). However, in the past, it appears that empathy may have served as the therapist's main, if not only, tool for achieving this objective. With empathy, Jackendoff (1994) observes, human beings imagine "how they would feel and act in a comparable situation," an ability, he states, which "acts as a brake on inflicting harm." We are less apt to cause pain, he notes, "if we can imagine how it feels" (p. 217).

However, this book recommends moving beyond empathy and beyond the therapeutic relationship since, as Rogers (1967) intimates, these noble but global tools may be inadequate to address the overwhelming number and complexity of personal and interpersonal concerns currently facing humanity (not to mention the toll which the current nebulous state of affairs appears to be extracting from therapists and clients alike). The following statement by Carl Rogers, as quoted by Friedman (1992), emphasizes these limitations: "I have learned, especially in working with more disturbed persons, that empathy can be perceived as lack of involvement; that an unconditional regard on my part can be perceived as indifference; that warmth can be perceived as a threatening closeness, that real feelings of mine can be perceived as false" (p. 55).

Thus the need for *operationalization* through the behaviorally, biologically, and cognitively grounded procedure described herein which, in my clinical experience, has resulted in greater efficacy of the therapeutic process. Within the scientific essence of building upon previous knowledge, the thesis of this book therefore suggests that quality control within psychotherapeutic practice may be achieved through the integrative eclecticism of "observable" (Lazarus, 1992, p. 235) phenomena. That is, by employing the above specified nonverbal behaviors and interpersonal communication techniques, within an information processing perspective, access to deeper levels of stored information ostensibly occurs. In turn, autonomous growth processes within the client, in the form of constructivistic language and/or logical reasoning abilities, appear to be simultaneously activated to revise meanings, effect self-change, and motivate functional behavior and ideation.

In view of its empirical grounding (as well as the effectiveness evidenced in the author's own clinical practice), isolating ourselves within schools and disregarding knowledge from neurology and information processing (to echo Edelman's [1992] view presented in the introduction to this book) may have been scientifically "hazardous." As Wexler (1974) observes:

> Congruence has come to be seen as the equivalent of therapist self-expression, and therapists have come to think of their task as reacting to the client rather than understanding him. As a result, under the banner of being honest, egalitarian, and genuine in engaging in a "real" human encounter, a number of therapists from a client-centered orientation have used the concept of congruence as some sort of license for relying on the expression of their reactions to their clients as a therapeutic tool.
>
> In introducing and relying on the expression of their reactions, these therapists have not only abdicated the very potent processing functions they can play through the active use of empathic responding, but they have also significantly departed from the basic client-centered orientation in introducing material that is external to the frame of reference of the client. (p. 112)

Similarly, there is reason to believe that ignoring knowledge from the fields of interpersonal communication and nonverbal behavior may likewise have hindered efficacy in psychotherapy, further delaying paradigmatic realization. In particular, the effects of eye contact, which Argyle and Cook (1976) regard as "part of a broader pattern of behavior, which establishes closer relationships with other people" (p. 149), would appear to require closer scrutiny in psychotherapy process research. As Argyle and Cook maintain, it is possible that "gaze and mutual gaze are important in the development of trust and deeper relationships" (p. 165). Moreover, as Bloomer (1976) states, "Research data reveals complex, intimate, and mysterious relationships between eye and brain, showing that these two organs are linked in profound ways" (p. 32).

Adding to this accumulating biological knowledge in the visual sphere and its possible relevance to psychotherapy, is the relationship between vision and language. For example, Davis (1994) reports that the visual cortex's processing areas "play a role in written, signed, and verbal language." We receive the vast majority of our information about the world, Davis maintains, "through our sense of sight." He therefore concludes that the "visual processing area must, and does, contribute mightily to the vast influx of data that contributes to language." Without the visual cortex, he says, "we would not have much to talk, write, or sign about" (p. 135).

This possible vision language connection is also supported by the psychotherapeutic research finding that women reportedly "engage in and receive more self-disclosure than men" (Jourard, 1971, p. 37)—a characteristic which may, in turn, be related to the interpersonal communication finding by Ellsworth and Ludwig (1972), that women "engage in more overall eye contact" (p. 379) than men. In any event, such studies appear to argue in favor of the need for greater scrutiny of these universal variables in psychotherapy research.

A FINAL VARIABLE: LENGTH OF SESSION

Session length is the final variable discussed herein. As Rosenhan (1979) notes, "It has long been known that the amount of time a person spends with you can be an index of your significance to him." Furthermore, if he "initiates and maintains eye contact," Rosenhan maintains, "there is reason to believe that he is considering your requests and needs" (p. 230). In this respect, when clients were seen almost daily, Efran, Lukens, and Lukens (1990) state, "relatively short sessions (the 'therapeutic hour') made good general sense." However, they explain:

> . . . Clients are now seen at less frequent intervals, and it isn't always clear that the 50-minute hour (which, in some cases, has been further decreased to 45 minutes) is the most sensible arrangement. . . . Under strict time-limit rules, sessions have been ended abruptly while the client is in the middle of tear-

fully reliving a crucial experience of loss or enacting a full-blown tantrum. Such structures fail to provide clients with the opportunity to complete an important cycle of experience and to restore an appropriate public "face" before departing. Thus, this may result in *less* safety, rather than more. . . . (pp. 124-125)

In other words, such shorter sessions may make it difficult to access deeper levels of stored information or may interrupt the client in the midst of such accessing. As Shapiro (1995) states of her EMDR information processing technique, "Maintaining the traditional 50-minute hour also generally more than doubles the number of sessions needed for full remediation of clients complaints" (p. 99). In order to complete a "cycle of experience," therefore, Efran, Lukens, and Lukens (1990) suggest employing a more flexible time structure. As they explain:

We want our clients to understand that once certain processes have been allowed to begin, we will assume an obligation to see them through to completion, even if it takes more time than expected....

Our model of therapy is therefore more akin to that of a surgeon (or the internist) than to that of the psychiatrist. A surgical procedure isn't over until it's over, and internists rarely tell their patients to put their clothes back on and return the following week because an examination or procedure took longer than expected. Similarly, we like to end sessions at junctures that feel like natural stopping points, not when the clock hands reach a particular point. We confess that, under this plan, some of our sessions have gone on for two, three, or even four hours. (p. 125)

However, because a four-hour session, or even a three-hour one, is difficult for therapists to endure, this is probably one reason why the "therapeutic hour" has remained popular. (This drain on the therapist may also account, in part, for the rise in popularity of group and family therapy since, as Carl Whitaker [1989] observes, "the greater the number of people, the less need there is for a professional therapist" [p. 142]. And this is so, since, as previously noted, the group or the family, rather than the therapist or individual client, eventually assumes direction in the process.) In any event, in my experience, a two-hour session at the beginning of dyadic therapy appears to produce a better treatment effect (a phenomenon possibly analogous to the training effect produced by twenty minutes of continuous aerobic exercise). In this sense, the initial double session when clients are in crisis appears to reduce anxiety more effectively than two single interrupted therapeutic hours (the treatment effect also being more readily observable). At the same time, similar to Shapiro's (1995) EMDR findings, a resulting shortening of the overall length of treatment appears to occur.

That there exists support for such double session length is evidenced by existentialists who, as Prochaska (1979) points out, "may spend extended hours with the patient" (p. 95) when he or she is in crisis. And Dinkmeyer, Pew, and Dinkmeyer (1979) who report: "With a two-hour block of time, we are able to get into the relationship more deeply and still have enough time to bring about resolution" (p. 257). Also lending support to the treatment effect phenomenon of the double session are Stern and Marks (1973), who found that two hours of continuous exposure *in vivo* to an anxiety-evoking stimulus produced significantly more change than four interrupted half hours. In this regard, they conclude, "Duration of exposure is presumably important because it gives certain unidentified processes more time to work while exposure is going on" (p. 505).

These "unidentified processes" in psychotherapy may further parallel those categorized by Toukmanian (1992) as *automated* and *controlled*, which she describes as follows:

What this means is that relatively well-functioning individuals are prepared and able to engage in a variety of operations. Some of the operations provide the rapid detection of familiar or redundant information (i.e., automated processes). Others are performed within a time frame that is broad enough to allow a fuller exploration of the elements of a given situation (i.e., controlled processes). Thus, by bringing in a predominantly controlled mode of processing to bear on most of the available information, individuals further their schematic development, leading them to generate a richer perspective when construing similar situations on subsequent occasions. (pp. 82-83)

In this respect, therefore, the "controlled mode" would appear to be of particular relevance to the double session length in psychotherapy. As Toukmanian (1992) explains:

> The controlled mode is carried out more slowly. Once it is initiated, the perceiver engages in a variety of mental operations and performs a more reflective and deliberate exploration of a given situation; that is, he or she analyzes the information in more depth and develops a fuller and more differentiated representation of an experience. The contention here is that, although both modes are essential to human functioning, it is the controlled mode of processing that is instrumental in enhancing perceptual development and change. (pp. 81-82)

Furthermore, accessing this "controlled mode" may be a function of empathy or what Rice (1974) refers to as "the evocative response," whose purpose "is to stimulate the client to get deeper and more accurately into his own experience." In the process, she maintains, the therapist attempts to "register the fragments and synthesize them" (or helps the client resynthesize them). In other words, Rice says, the therapist does not "label the experience," but tries "to open it up" (p. 309).

THERAPEUTIC OUTCOME: A SUMMARY

Within an integrative eclectic perspective, Beutler and Consoli (1992) contend that psychotherapy "should not be considered as a process with a given beginning and a final end" (p. 280). Clients are best prepared to face the world, they say, "when they understand their difficulties within the context of an ongoing life struggle" (p. 280). In this sense, therefore, the client generally determines when therapy is no longer necessary. Near the end of therapy, for example, Rogers (1942) observed early on that the client usually becomes less preoccupied with his or her own personal concerns and shows interest in the external world, including the life of the therapist. In other words, the client appears better able to engage in two-way dialogue—the relationship having become more *symmetrical*—a factor which may account for subsequent improved interpersonal functioning seemingly resulting from improved intrapersonal communication.

Recapping thus far, Garfield's (1992) overview of the therapeutic transactions leading up to this final point in therapy tend to acquire greater meaning when viewed from an integrative information processing perspective. In his words:

> . . . As patients discuss their problems in the understanding and accepting climate of therapy, over time these problems appear less threatening. It is as if the process of bringing out concerns into the open and examining them or sharing them with the therapist lessen their impact. Problems may be perceived differently as the client discusses them. By having to communicate items that are disturbing, the individuals have to organize their experience and to be somewhat more objective and realistic in appraising their life situation. In terms of a learning orientation, client's anxieties about their difficulties are generally extinguished as they discuss them in the security of the therapeutic setting, with no negative consequences following. (p. 189)

Concluding this theory-building and/or construct-revision endeavor, suggesting how the "impact" of the client's disclosures may be "lessened," how clients may be helped to "organize their experience" more objectively and realistically, and how "anxieties" are likely "extinguished" has been the objective of this book. While verification of what may prove to be a higher-order theory awaits process and outcome research of the universal variables cited herein, it is presented at this time for heuristic research purposes and as a guide for integrative eclectic practice.

Supporting the thesis that "Knowledge grows from that which precedes it" (including self-knowledge), this book's objectives might in this sense be consistent with the personal construct theory of Neimeyer (1990), who states:

> . . . By providing a well-developed theory of personality that details the process of construing, the structural features of our construct systems, and the social embeddedness of our anticipatory efforts, construct theory coordinates the use of a wide variety of techniques. . . . As a result, while it continues to generate novel interventions, its technical eclecticism helps promote the integration of different psychotherapeutic traditions. . . . In the face of the sometimes bewildering variety of approaches to psychother-

apy, this effort to identify constructivist themes that help bridge different traditions may prove to be one of the most enduring contributions of personal construct theory. (p. 163)

Moreover, it may be precisely because psychotherapeutic theory has lacked adequate behavioral, biological, and cognitive grounding that the "bewildering" growth of therapies continues to occur—increasing the confusion which threatens to overwhelm the field and delaying convergence of scientific opinion. Beutler (1990) summarizes this state of affairs:

> There are dozens of different eclectic models and hundreds of purist theories of psychotherapy. . . . The empirical test has yet to be passed by any of these approaches.
> To pass the test of empirical veracity, it is not enough to build a model of treatment on past research. We must also construct prospective studies that will specifically test our assumptions. This work is just beginning, with many theorists beginning to test their own methods and others hoping to win by default and force of persuasion. As new findings evolve, all will be forced to incorporate them into their own viewpoints. In this process, it is inevitable that we will eventually move closer to one another. Indeed, this process of convergence is already beginning. (p. 231)

Paradigmatic realization having been elusive, however, it is ironic, and in some cases probably tragic, that after a century of employment in its molar state, psychotherapy still remains broadly defined as a "psychological procedure that results in an improvement in the functioning of the patient" (Furedy, 1990, p. 120). Concerning this indefinite state of affairs, Emmelkamp (1990) observes: "It is curious that society requires that the effects of drugs be thoroughly evaluated before they are prescribed but does not apply the same standards with respect to the prescription of psychotherapy" (p. 127). Furthermore, this lack of efficacy and quality control apparently continues to exist despite the fact that, as Furedy (1990) notes, we know what is scientifically required. To the extent that the procedure is to be considered to have a scientific basis, he says, "it must be specifiable as a set of repeatable operations that can be transmitted cognitively" (p. 120).

For this reason, focusing upon universal *observable* therapist variables may help explicate the "repeatable operations" as the interactive behaviors (therapist nonverbal behaviors) achieve *forefront materialization* and the cognitive components (client constructivistic language and logical reasoning abilities) become more discernible. Additionally, within this integrative eclectic framework, Hebb's (1949, 1959) studies of environmental enrichment, supported by such neurological work as that of Damasio (1994) (the use of neurons resulting in the growth of synaptic connections between neurons), may become salient. In fact, even in the absence of empirical verification through replication within dyadic clinical outcome trials, the approach described herein, and its underlying theory, already derive significant qualitative (Horowitz, 1994) empirical support from the diverse sources cited, as well as from my own clinical practice, suggesting it to be based less on faith than upon a scientific field theory. In this sense, it is therefore being offered as a possible "metaperspective" for the field whose formulation Lopez (1995) hypothesized to face a number of "challenges"—challenges which this book has attempted to meet:

> Beyond the task of integrating theories and models that variously emphasize cognitive, affective, and interpersonal dynamics, a metaperspective should also address important linkages between past learning experiences and present-day functioning, as well as between both these domains and behaviors that shape subsequent events and outcomes. . . . A relevant metaperspective should speak to important process and outcome issues in counseling and thus deepen our understanding of how client and counselor characteristics may interact to facilitate therapeutic change. (p. 396)

FUTURE RESEARCH PROSPECTS

Existing qualitative empirical evidence supporting this proposed "metaperspective" notwithstanding, Beutler and Consoli (1992) nevertheless observe that ultimately, for an integrative eclectic approach to prove more effective than the theories it attempts to integrate, "it must stand the empirical as well as clinical test." In their estimation, the constructs thereby revised, or devised, must be "useful to the clinician, verifiable to the scientist, and acceptable to a diversity of practitioners and theoreticians" (p. 293). No small test—but one toward which this proposed higher-order theory should be more amenable due to its adherence to scientific precepts, i.e., its emphasis on observables and upon empirical grounding.

Bergin and Strupp (1972) and, more recently, Davison and Lazarus (1994), further propose a means of achieving this scientific objective. As Bergin and Strupp state:

> . . . Ideas about change mechanisms are likely to derive either from clinical phenomena or from behavioral science research. They may then be subjected to testing, experimentation and refinement by means of analogue studies and single case experiments. . . . Once the morphology of [a] therapeutic agent and its effects on given symptoms are defined by means of quantitative case studies, then field trials on larger samples of homogeneous cases could be conducted to demonstrate its clinical usefulness. After clinical validity was established, the procedure could be incorporated into the repertoire of clinical practices. . . . The process is especially one of technique building and not simply technique testing. (pp. 432-434)

Similarly, Davison and Lazarus (1994) suggest:

> Only fine-grained study of individual cases permits us to relate therapeutic effect to specific patient characteristics.
>
> When an individual therapeutic effect follows a sequence of treatment methods within an appropriately controlled framework, numerous patient-therapist characteristics in whose context the effect took place can be specified. One can thus narrow down the particular patient and technique variables involved. Strictly speaking, specific inferences are valid only with respect to the individual case itself, but if one relates the particular individual's most relevant characteristics to similar attributes in other people, general theories can be formulated in terms of these common characteristics. . . . The basic emphasis is upon the documentation of clinical research, with special reference to objective ratings and the statistical study of the course of a given patient's treatment, in relatively concrete and operational terms. (p.166)

In this respect, therefore, because of its emphasis on observable phenomena, evidence for or against this psychotherapeutic approach and its underlying theory should, in any event, be more readily and reliably *quantified* to ensure that the research efforts are "mutually intelligible" and the results, "comparative and cumulative" (Orlinsky and Howard, 1978, p. 319). In the end, further empirical verification could contribute toward the more precise definition of psychotherapy which has eluded the field—a definition whose prerequisites are outlined by Norcross (1990):

> From an integrative perspective, an acceptable definition of psychotherapy will possess several necessary features (Norcross, 1987) beyond the obvious need for accuracy. First, the definition should be descriptive, operationalizing the clinical phenomena at hand. Second, it will be accessible, readily available to clinicians and researchers alike. Third, it will eventually be consensual, subject to agreement and verification by psychotherapists of diverse persuasions. And fourth, for want of a better phrase, our generic definition should be respectfully evenhanded. . . . The requirement that the methods be "derived from established psychological principles" is sufficiently broad to permit clinical and/or research validation. (pp. 218-219)

In the final analysis, what may emerge from such empirical research is the realization that while clients may be experts on their own self-revisions, therapeutic change is nevertheless facilitated by the asymmetric interactive expertise of the therapist which maximizes client self-disclosure, resulting in accessing deeply stored information. This asymmetric discursive interaction may in turn automatically activate constructivistic language capacities, neurological correlative functions, and logical reasoning abilities, within the client, to revise *meanings* and effect self-change—under the guidance of the therapist facilitative attitudes. As Rice (1974) observes of these "necessary and sufficient conditions":

> Although the specification of these three therapist conditions has had a sweeping influence on the whole psychotherapy field, the tendency has been to accept them as perhaps necessary but certainly not sufficient. They are seen by those not trained in client-

centered therapy as useful in establishing a climate of trust and nondefensiveness, but as a background for other interventions, rather than as active agents of change. (pp. 289-290)

Exploring these "other interventions," or operations, existing beyond empathy and the therapeutic relationship, has been the objective of this book—a therapeutic approach observed to result in what Weeks (1990) describes as the client's perception of *being* different rather than simply *"doing* something different." As Weeks explains, clients who are forced to change "will experience *doing* things differently without *being* different." However, in order to change the *meaning* of the behavior or symptom, he says, "the client must attribute the change to himself or herself—not to the therapist." Facilitating this "self-attributional process," Weeks further contends, "is psychotherapy at its best" (pp. 262-263).

In other words, implied in this "self-attributional process" is the contention that the client is the expert on changing or revising self-meanings. The therapist, on the other hand, more specifically possesses expertise in activating the "scanning process" (the interactive and discursive procedure for mobilizing the client's own correlative and logical reasoning resources to revise meanings and expand the self). It should be noted, however, that practiced in this way, change in psychotherapy is often more directly attributed by the client to him- or herself, with only indirect recognition being accorded the therapist (a process further empowering the client). Nevertheless, the change is especially observable to outside observers who know the client personally. Moreover, the efficacy which accrues from the therapist attending to what may prove to be the legitimate variables promoting change should result in greater client progress (psychotherapy's raison d'être) and, in the process, increased personal and professional satisfaction for the therapist.

CONCLUSION

In closing, the challenging field of psychotherapy is sustained by the work of many therapists and researchers, not only those cited in this volume, who serve as generators, employers, and custodians of knowledge through the language. However, to become comparative and cumulative, this knowledge must continue to transfer across ideological lines within a theoretically valid scientific framework. Given the previous long-standing insularity of the school-based approach to psychotherapy and the resulting delay in paradigmatic realization, however, we may have to remind ourselves that ideological obsession and therapist personas do not advance science. Only knowledge can claim that distinction—knowledge which is "boundaryless and infinite," which derives from rational authority, and which, in this indefinite field, needs to build upon previous knowledge through an *integrative eclecticism* within transtheoretical and common factors integration.

Bibliography

Adler, R. B. and Towne, N. (1990). *Looking Out, Looking In: Interpersonal Communication*, Sixth Edition. Fort Worth: Holt, Rinehart and Winston Inc.

Allport, G. W. (1955). *Becoming: Basic Considerations for a Psychology of Personality.* New Haven, CT: Yale University Press.

Allport, G. W. (1967). Attitudes. In M. Fishbein (Ed.), *Attitude, Theory and Measurement.* New York: Wiley.

Allport, G. W. and Vernon, P. E. (1933). *Studies in Expressive Movement.* New York: Macmillan Publishing Co., Inc.

Anderson, W. (1974). Personal growth and client-centered therapy: An information processing view. In D. Wexler and L. Rice (Eds.), *Innovations in Client-Centered Therapy.* New York: John Wiley and Sons.

Argyle, M. and Cook, M. (1976). *Gaze and Mutual Gaze.* Cambridge: Cambridge University Press.

Argyle, M., Salter, V., Nicholson, H., Williams, M., and Burgess, P. (1970). The communication of inferior and superior attitudes by verbal and nonverbal signals. *British Journal of Social and Clinical Psychology, 9,* pp. 222-231.

Arkowitz, H. (1992). A common factors therapy for depression. In J. C. Norcross and M. R. Goldfried (Eds.), *Handbook of Psychotherapy Integration.* New York: Basic Books.

Avila, D. L., Combs, A. W., and Purkey, W. W. (1977). *The Helping Relationship Sourcebook*, Second Edition. Boston: Allyn and Bacon.

Bakan, P. (1971). The eyes have it. *Psychology Today, 4,* April, pp. 64-67.

Bandler, R. and Grinder, J. (1979). *Frogs into Princes: Neuro-Linguistic Programming.* Moab, Utah: Real People Press.

Barretta, N., Barretta, P., and Bongiovanni, J. (1990). Understanding negotiable options. In J. Zeig and M. Munion (Eds.), *What Is Psychotherapy? Contemporary Perspectives.* San Francisco: Jossey-Bass Publishers.

Barton, A. (1974). *Three Worlds of Therapy: An Existential-Phenomenological Study of the Therapies of Freud, Jung, and Rogers.* Palo Alto, CA: Mayfield Publishers.

Bebout, J. (1974). It takes one to know one: Existential-Rogerian concepts in encounter groups. In D. Wexler and L. Rice (Eds.), *Innovations in Client-Centered Therapy.* New York: John Wiley and Sons.

Beck, A. P. (1974). Phases in the development of structure in therapy and encounter groups. In D. Wexler and L. Rice (Eds.), *Innovations in Client-Centered Therapy.* New York: John Wiley and Sons.

Beck, A. T. (1984). Cognitive therapy, behavior therapy, psychoanalysis, and pharmacotherapy: The cognitive continuum. In J. B. W. Williams and R. L. Spitzer

(Eds.), *Psychotherapy Research: Where Are We and Where Should We Go?* New York: Guilford.

Beitman, B. D. (1992). Integration through fundamental similarities and useful differences among the schools. In J. C. Norcross and M. R. Goldfried (Eds.), *Handbook of Psychotherapy Integration*. New York: Basic Books.

Bergin, A. E. and Lambert, M. J. (1978). The evaluation of therapeutic outcomes. In S. Garfield and A. Bergin (Eds.), *Handbook of Psychotherapy and Behavior Change: An Empirical Analysis*, Second Edition. New York: John Wiley and Sons.

Bergin, A. E. and Lambert, M. J. (1979). Counseling the researcher. *The Counseling Psychologist, 8 (3)*, pp. 53-56.

Bergin, A. E. and Strupp, H. H. (1972). *Changing Frontiers in the Science of Psychotherapy*. Chicago: Aldine.

Beutler, L. E. (1990). Systematic eclectic psychotherapy. In J. K. Zeig and W. M. Munion (Eds.), *What Is Psychotherapy? Contemporary Perspectives*. San Francisco: Jossey-Bass Publishers.

Beutler, L. E. and Consoli, A. J. (1992). Systematic eclectic psychotherapy. In J. C. Norcross and M. R. Goldfried (Eds.), *Handbook of Psychotherapy Integration*. New York: Basic Books.

Beutler, L. E. and Sandowicz, M. (1994). The counseling relationship: What is it? *The Counseling Psychologist, 22 (1)*, January, pp. 98-103.

Birdwhistell, R. L. (1970). *Kinesics and Context*. Philadelphia: University of Pennsylvania Press.

Bloom, F., Lazerson, A., and Hofstadter, L. (1985). *Brain, Mind, and Behavior*. New York: W. H. Freeman.

Bloomer, C. M. (1976). *Principles of Visual Perception*. New York: Van Nostrand Reinhold Co.

Bordin, E. S. (1974). *Research Strategies in Psychotherapy*. New York: Wiley.

Bowlby, J. (1979). *The Making and Breaking of Affectional Bonds*. London: Tavistock.

Bronowski, J. (1966). The logic of the mind. *American Scientist, 54*, pp. 1-14.

Brooks, W. D. and Emmert, P. (1976). *Interpersonal Communication*. Dubuque, IA: William C. Brown Co.

Butcher, J. N. and Koss, M. P. (1978). Research on brief and crisis-oriented therapies. In S. L. Garfield and A. E. Bergin (Eds.), *Handbook of Psychotherapy and Behavior Change: An Empirical Analysis*. New York: John Wiley and Sons.

Butler, J. M. (1974). The iconic mode in psychotherapy. In D. Wexler and L. Rice (Eds.), *Innovations in Client-Centered Therapy*. New York: John Wiley and Sons.

Carkhuff, R. R. (1977). *The Art of Helping III*. Amherst, MA: Human Resources Development Press.

Carkhuff, R. R. and Berenson, B. G. (1977). *Beyond Counseling and Therapy*. New York: Holt, Rinehart and Winston.

Cegala, D. J., Sokuvitz, S., and Alexander, A. F. (1979). An investigation of eye gaze and its relation to selected verbal behavior. *Human Communication Research*, *5 (2)*, pp. 99-108.

Clevenger, T. and Mathews, J. (1971). *The Speech Communication Process*. Glenview, IL: Scott, Foresman and Co.

Cochrane, C. T. and Halloway, A. J. (1974). Client-centered therapy and gestalt therapy: In search of a merger. In D. Wexler and L. Rice (Eds.), *Innovations in Client-Centered Therapy*. New York: Wiley.

Combs, A. W., Richards, A. E., and Richards, F. (1976). *Perceptual Psychology: A Humanistic Approach to the Study of Persons*. New York: Harper and Row.

Coren, S. (1992). *The Left-Hander Syndrome: The Causes and Consequences of Left-Handedness*. New York: The Free Press.

Coren, S. and Porac, C. (1978). The validity and reliability of self-report items for the measurement of lateral preference. *British Journal of Psychology, 69 (2)*, pp. 207-211.

Covey, S. R. (1990). *The Seven Habits of Highly Effective People: Restoring the Character Ethic*. New York: Simon and Shuster.

Damasio, A. R. (1994). *Descartes' Error: Emotion, Reason, and the Human Brain*. New York: Grosset/Putnam.

Danziger, K. (1976). *Interpersonal Communication*. New York: Pergamon Press.

Davis, J. (1994). *Mother Tongue: How Humans Create Language*. New York: Carol Publishing Group.

Davison, G. C. and Lazarus, A. A. (1994). Clinical innovation and evaluation: Integrating practice with inquiry. *Clinical Psychology: Science and Practice, 1 (2)*, Winter, pp. 157-168.

Davison, G. C. and Lazarus, A. A. (1995). The Dialectics of Science and Practice. In S. C. Hayes, V. M. Follette, R. M. Dawes and K. E. Grady (Eds.), *Scientific Standards of Psychological Practice: Issues and Recommendations*. Reno, NV: Context Press.

Dawkins, R. D. (1978). *The Selfish Gene*. New York: Granada Publishing Limited.

DeBerry, S. T. (1990). Humanistic existentialism. In J. K. Zeig and W. M. Munion (Eds.), *What is Psychotherapy? Contemporary Perspectives*. San Francisco: Jossey-Bass Publishers.

Dennett, D. C. (1991). *Consciousness Explained*. Boston: Little, Brown and Co.

Derlega, V. J. and Grzelak, J. (1979). Appropriateness of self-disclosure. In G. J. Chelune (Ed.), *Self-disclosure*. San Francisco: Jossey-Bass Publishers.

Derlerga, V. J., Hendrick, S. S., Winstead, B. A., and Berg, J. H. (1991). *Psychotherapy as a Personal Relationship*. New York: The Guilford Press.

de Shazer, S. (1990). Brief therapy. In J. K. Zeig and W. M. Munion (Eds.), *What Is Psychotherapy? Contemporary Perspectives*. San Francisco: Jossey-Bass Publishers.

Di Francesco, G. V. (1977). Interactive distance and eye contact in the counseling relationship. Unpublished Doctoral Dissertation. Lehigh University. Bethlehem, PA.

Dinkmeyer, D. C., Pew, W. L., and Dinkmeyer, D. C. Jr. (1979). *Adlerian Counseling and Psychotherapy.* Monterey, CA: Brooks/Cole.

Dittman, A. T. (1972). *Interpersonal Messages of Emotion.* New York: Springer.

Dittman, A. T. and Llewellyn, L. G. (1968). Relationship between vocalizations and head nods as listener responses. *Journal of Personal and Social Psychology, 9,* pp. 79-84.

Dreikurs R. (1967). *Psychodynamics, Psychotherapy, and Counseling.* Chicago: Alfred Adler Institute.

Dubois, R. (1990). Self-healing: A personal history. In R. Ornstein and C. Swencionis (Eds.), *The Healing Brain: A Scientific Reader.* New York: The Guilford Press.

Edelman, G. M. (1992). *Bright Air, Brilliant Fire: On the Matter of the Mind.* New York: Basic Books.

Edelson, M. (1994). Can psychotherapy research answer this psychotherapist's questions? In P. F. Talley, H. H. Strupp, and S. F. Butler (Eds.), *Psychotherapy Research and Practice: Bridging the Gap.* New York: Basic Books.

Efran, J. S. (1968). Looking for approval: Effects on visual behavior of approbation from persons differing in importance. *Journal of Personality and Social Psychology, 10,* pp. 21-25.

Efran, J. S., Lukens, M. D., and Lukens, R. J. (1990). *Language, Structure, and Change: Frameworks of Meaning in Psychotherapy.* New York: W. W. Norton and Co.

Eisenberg, A. M. (1975). *Living Communication.* Englewood Cliffs, NJ: Prentice-Hall.

Ekman, P. and Friesen, W. W. (1968). Nonverbal behavior in psychotherapy research. In J. M. Shlien (Ed.), *Research in Psychotherapy,* Volume 3, Washington, DC: American Psychological Association.

Ekman, P. and Friesen, W. W. (1975). *Unmasking the Face: A Guide to Recognizing Emotions from Facial Clues.* Englewood Cliffs, NJ: Prentice-Hall.

Elliott, R. and Anderson, C. (1994). Simplicity and complexity in psychotherapy research. In R. L. Russell (Ed.), *Reassessing Psychotherapy Research.* New York: The Guilford Press.

Elliott, T. R. and Marmarosh, C. (1995). Social-cognitive processes in behavioral health: implications for counseling. *The Counseling Psychologist, 23 (4),* October, pp. 666-681.

Ellis, A. (1973). *Humanistic Psychotherapy: The Rational-Emotive Approach.* New York: McGraw-Hill.

Ellsworth, P. C. and Ludwig, L. M. (1972). Visual behavior and social interaction. *Journal of Communication, 22,* pp. 375-403.

Ellsworth, P. C. and Ross, L. (1975). Intimacy in response to direct gaze. *Journal of Experimental Social Psychology, 11,* pp. 592-613.

Emelkamp, P. M. (1990). An experimental clinical approach. In J. K. Zeig and W. M. Munion (Eds.), *What Is Psychotherapy? Contemporary Perspectives.* San Francisco: Jossey-Bass Publishers.

Epstein, M. (1995). Opening up to happiness. *Psychology Today, 28 (4),* pp. 42-46.

Exline, R. V. and Eldridge, C. (1967). Effects of two patterns of a speakers visual behavior upon the authenticity of his verbal message. Paper presented to the Eastern Psychological Association. Boston: Unpublished paper, Department of Psychology, University of Delaware.

Exline, R. V., Ellyson, S. L., and Long, B. (1975). Visual behavior as an aspect of power role relationships. In P. Pilner, L. Krames, and T. Alloway (Eds.), *Advances in the Study of Communication and Affect,* Volume 2. New York: Plenum Press.

Exline, R. V. and Fehr, B. J. (1978). Applications of semiosis to the study of visual interaction. In A. W. Siegman and S. Feldstein (Eds.), *Nonverbal Behavior and Communication.* Hillsdale, NJ: Lawrence Erlbaum Associates, Publishers.

Exline, R. V. and Winters, L. C. (1965). Affective relations and mutual glances in dyads. In S. Tompkins and C. Izard (Eds.), *Affect, Cognition, and Personality: Empirical Studies.* New York: Springer.

Eysenck, H. J. (1952). The effects of psychotherapy: An evaluation. *Journal of Consulting Psychology, 16,* July, pp. 319-324.

Eysenck, H. J. (1966). *The Effects of Psychotherapy.* New York: International Science Press.

Feldman, L. B. and Powell, S. L. (1992). Integrating therapeutic modalities. In J. C. Norcross and M. R. Goldfried (Eds.), *Handbook of Psychotherapy Integration.* New York: Basic Books.

Ferrara, K. W. (1994). *Therapeutic Ways with Words.* New York: Oxford University Press.

Fishbein, M. and Laird, J. (1979). Concealment and disclosure: Some effects of information control on the person who controls. *Journal of Experimental Social Psychology, 15,* pp. 114-121.

Fisher, A. B. (1978). *Perspectives on Human Communication.* New York: Macmillan.

Fisher, M. (1990). The shared experience and self-disclosure. In G. Stricker and M.Fisher (Eds.), *Self-disclosure in the Therapeutic Relationship.* New York: Plenum Press.

Frank, J. D. (1965). Discussion papers by H. J. Eysenck: The effects of psychotherapy. *International Journal of Psychotherapy, 1,* pp. 150-152.

Frankl, V. E. (1963). *Man's Search for Meaning. An Introduction to Logotherapy.* New York: Washington Square Press.

Fretz, B. R. (1966). Postural movements in a counseling dyad. *Journal of Counseling Psychology, 13,* pp. 335-343.

Freud, S. (1957). *A Metaphysical Supplement to the Theory of Dreams.* Standard Edition 14. London: Hogarth Press. (Original work published in 1917.)

Freud, S. (1957). "Wild" psychoanalysis. In J. Strachey (Ed. and Trans.), *The Standard Edition of the Complete Psychological Works of Sigmund Freud,* Volume 11. London: Hogarth Press. (Original work published in 1910.)

Friedman, M. (1992). *Dialogue and the Human Image: Beyond Humanistic Psychology.* Newbury Park, CA: Sage.

Furedy, J. J. (1990). Biofeedback and the case for pure empirical validation. In J. K. Zeig and W. M. Munion (Eds.), *What Is Psychotherapy? Contemporary Perspectives*. San Francisco: Jossey-Bass Publishers.

Gale, A., Lucas, B., Nissim, R., and Harpham, B. (1972). Some EEG correlates of face-to-face contact. *British Journal of Social and Clinical Psychology, 11*, pp. 326-332.

Galin, D. (1979). The two modes of consciousness and the two halves of the brain. In D. Goleman and R. Davidson (Eds.), *Consciousness: The Brain, States of Awareness, and Alternate Realities*. New York: Irvington Publishers.

Gandelman, R. (1992). *Psychobiology of Behavioral Development*. New York: Oxford University Press.

Gardner, H. (1993). *Creating Minds: An Anatomy of Creativity Seen Through the Lives of Freud, Einstein, Picasso, Stravinsky, Eliot, Graham, and Ghandi*. New York: Basic Books.

Garfield, S. L. (1990). Multivariant eclectic psychotherapy. In J. K. Zeig and W. M. Munion (Eds.), *What Is Psychotherapy? Contemporary Perspectives*. San Francisco: Jossey-Bass Publishers.

Garfield, S. L. (1992). Eclectic psychotherapy: A common factors approach. In J. C. Norcross and M. R. Goldfried (Eds.), *Handbook of Psychotherapy Integration*. New York: Basic Books.

Garfield, S. L. and Bergin, A. E. (1971). Personal therapy, outcome, and some therapist variables. *Psychotherapy: Theory, Research and Practice, 18*, pp. 251-253.

Garfield, S. L. and Bergin, A. E. (1978). *Handbook of Psychotherapy and Behavior Change: An Empirical Analysis*, Second Edition. New York: John Wiley and Sons.

Garfield, S. L. and Bergin, A. E. (1986). *Handbook of Psychotherapy and Behavior Change: An Empirical Analysis*, Third Edition. New York: John Wiley and Sons.

Gelso, C. J. (1979). Research in counseling: Methodological and professional issues. *The Counseling Psychologist, 8 (3)*, pp. 7-35.

Gelso, C. J. and Carter, J. A. (1985). The relationship in counseling and psychotherapy: Components, consequences, and theoretical antecedents. *The Counseling Psychologist, 13*, pp. 155-243.

Gendlin, E. T. (1962). *Experiencing and the Creation of Meaning*. New York: Free Press.

Gendlin, E. T. (1970). A short summary and some long predictions. In J. T. Hart and T. M. Tomlinson (Eds.), *New Directions in Client-Centered Therapy*. Boston: Houghton Mifflin.

Gendlin, E. T. (1974). Client-centered and experiential psychotherapy. In D. A. Wexler and L. N. Rice (Eds.), *Innovations in Client-Centered Therapy*. New York: John Wiley and Sons.

Gergen, K. J. and Kaye, J. (1992). Beyond narrative in the negotiation of therapeutic meaning. In S. McNamee and K. J. Gergen (Eds.), *Therapy as Social Construction*. Newbury Park, CA: Sage.

Ginsburg, S. W. and Arrington, W. (1948). Aspects of psychiatric clinic practice. *American Journal of Orthopsychiatry, 18*, pp. 322-333.

Gladstein, G. A. (1974). Nonverbal communication and counseling/psychotherapy: A review. *The Counseling Psychologist, 4*, pp. 35-37.

Goble, F. (1970). *The Third Force: The Psychology of Abraham Maslow*. New York: Grossman Publishers.

Goffman, E. (1964). *Behavior in Public Places*. Glencoe, IL: The Free Press.

Goldberg, C. (1992). *The Seasoned Psychotherapist: Triumph over Adversity*. New York: W. W. Norton and Company.

Goldfried, M. R., Castonguay, L. G., and Safran, J. D. (1992). Core issues and future directions in psychotherapy integration. In J. C. Norcross and M. R. Goldfried (Eds.), *Handbook of Psychotherapy Integration*. New York: Basic Books.

Goldfried, M. R. and Newman, C. F. (1992). A history of psychotherapy integration. In J. C. Norcross and M. R. Goldfried (Eds.), *Handbook of Psychotherapy Integration*. New York: Basic Books.

Goldstein, A. P. and Shipman, W. G. (1961). Patient expectancies, symptom reduction, and aspects of the initial psychotherapeutic interview. *Journal of Clinical Psychology, 17*, pp. 129-133.

Gottman, J. and Markman, H. (1978). Experimental designs in psychotherapy research. In S. Garfield and A. Bergin (Eds.), *Handbook of Psychotherapy and Behavior change: An Empirical Analysis*, Second Edition. New York: John Wiley and Sons.

Graves, J. R. and Robinson, J. D. (1976). Proxemic behavior as a function of inconsistent verbal and nonverbal messages. *Journal of Counseling Psychology, 23*, pp. 333-338.

Greenberg, J. (1994). Psychotherapy research: A clinician's view. In P. Talley, H. Strupp, and S. Butler (Eds.), *Psychotherapy Research and Practice: Bridging the Gap*. New York: Basic Books.

Greenberg, L. S. (1994). The investigation of change: Its measurement and explanation. In R. L. Russell (Ed.), *Reassessing Psychotherapy Research*. New York: The Guilford Press.

Gregory, R. L. (1977). *Eye and Brain: The Psychology of Seeing*. London: Weidenfeld and Nicholson.

Griffin, J. M. (1978). The effect on self-disclosure of seating position, related differences in eye contact, and promise of feedback. Unpublished Doctoral Dissertation. Philadelphia: Temple University.

Grosch, W. N. and Olsen, D. C. (1994). *When Helping Starts to Hurt: A New Look at Burnout Among Psychotherapists*. New York: W. W. Norton and Company.

Gross, H. S. (1972). Toward including listening in a model of the interview. In A. W. Siegman and B. Pope (Eds.), *Studies in Dyadic Communication*. New York: Pergamon Press.

Guidano, V. F. (1987). *Complexity of the Self: A Developmental Approach to Psychotherapy and Theory*. New York: Guilford.

Gutsch, K. U. (1990). Cognitive psychotherapy. In J. K. Zeig and W. M. Munion (Eds.), *What Is Psychotherapy? Contemporary Perspectives.* San Francisco: Jossey-Bass Publishers.

Haase, R. and Tepper, D. (1972). Nonverbal components of empathic communication. *Journal of Counseling Psychology, 19,* pp. 417-424.

Haley, J. (1963). *Strategies of Psychotherapy.* New York: Grune and Stratton.

Harper, R. G., Wiens, A. N., and Mattarazzo, J. D. (1978). *Nonverbal Communication: The State of the Art.* New York: John Wiley and Sons.

Harre, R. and Gillett, G. (1994). *The Discursive Mind.* Thousand Oaks, CA: Sage.

Harris, T. A. (1969). *I'm OK—You're OK: A Practical Guide to Transactional Analysis.* New York: Harper and Row.

Havens, L. (1994). Some suggestions for making research more applicable to clinical practice. In P. F. Talley, H. H. Strupp, and S. F. Butler (Eds.), *Psychotherapy Research and Practice: Bridging the Gap.* New York: Basic Books.

Hayes, S. T. (1990). Contextual behavior therapy. In J. K. Zeig and W. M. Munion (Eds.), *What Is Psychotherapy? Contemporary Perspectives.* San Francisco: Jossey-Bass Publishers.

Hebb, D. O. (1949). *The Organization of Behavior: A Neuropsychological Theory.* New York: Wiley.

Hebb, D. O. (1959). Intelligence, brain functions, and the theory of mind. *Brain, 82,* June, pp. 260-275.

Hess, E. H. (1975a). The role of pupil size in communication. *Scientific American, 233,* pp. 110-119.

Hess, E. H. (1975b). *The Tell-Tale Eye: How Your Eyes Reveal Hidden Thoughts and Emotions.* New York: Van Nostrand Reinhold Co.

Hill, C. (1994). What is the therapeutic relationship? A reaction to Sexton and Whiston. *The Counseling Psychologist, 22 (1),* January, pp. 90-97.

Horowitz, M. J. (1994). Psychotherapy research and the views of clinicians. In P. Talley, H. Strupp, and S. Butler (Eds.), *Psychotherapy Research and Practice: Bridging the Gap.* New York: Basic Books.

Jackendoff, R. (1994). *Patterns in the Mind: Language and Human Nature.* New York: Basic Books.

Jaffe, J. (1978). Parliamentary procedure and the brain. In A. W. Siegman and S. Feldstein (Eds.), *Nonverbal Behavior and Communication.* Hillsdale, NJ: Lawrence Erlbaum Associates.

James, W. T. (1932). A study of the expression of body posture. *Journal of General Psychology, 7,* pp. 405-437.

Jensen, J. P., Bergin, A. E., and Greaves, D. W. (1990). The meaning of eclecticism: New survey and analysis of components. *Professional Psychology: Research and Practice, 21,* pp. 124-130.

Jones, E. E., Cumming, J. D., and Horowitz, M. J. (1988). Another look at the nonspecific hypothesis of therapeutic effectiveness. *Journal of Consulting and Clinical Psychology, 56,* pp. 48-55.

Josephs, L. (1990). Self-disclosure in psychotherapy and the psychology of the self. In G. Stricker and M. Fisher (Eds.), *Self-disclosure in the Therapeutic Relationship*. New York: Plenum Press.

Jourard, S. (1968). *Disclosing Man to Himself*. New York: D. Van Nostrand.

Jourard, S. (1971). *Self-disclosure: An Experimental Analysis of the Transparent Self*. New York: John Wiley and Sons.

Jourard, S. (1974). *Healthy Personality*. New York: Macmillan Publishers.

Kaul, T. J. and Schmidt, L. D. (1971). Dimensions of interviewer trustworthiness. *Journal of Counseling Psychology, 18*, pp. 542-548.

Kelly, G. (1955). *The Psychology of Personal Constructs*. New York: Norton.

Kelly, G. (1963). *A Theory of Personality*. New York: Norton.

Kendon, A. (1967). Some functions of gaze-direction in social interaction. *Acta Psychologica, 26*, pp. 22-63.

Kendon, A. (1972). Some relationships between body motion and speech. An analysis of an example. In A. W. Seigman and B. Pope (Eds.), *Studies in Dyadic Communication*. New York: Pergamon Press.

Kendon, A. and Cook, M. (1969). The consistency of gaze patterns in social interaction. *British Journal of Psychology, 60 (4)*, pp. 481-494.

Kernberg, O. F. and Clarkin, J. F. (1994). Training and the integration of research and clinical practice. In P. Talley, H. Strupp, and S. Butler (Eds.), *Psychotherapy Research and Practice: Bridging the Gap*. New York: Basic Books.

Key, M. R. (1975). *Paralanguage and Kinesics: Nonverbal Communication*. Metuchen, NJ: The Scarecrow Press.

Kiesler, D. (1979). Commentary on Gelso's Research in counseling: Methodological and professional issues. *The Counseling Psychologist, 8 (3)*, pp. 44-47.

Kiesler, D. (1994). Standardization of intervention: The tie that binds psychotherapy research and practice. In P. Talley, H. Strupp, and S. Butler (Eds.), *Psychotherapy Research and Practice: Bridging the Gap*. New York: Basic Books.

Kimura, D. (1993). *Neuromotor Mechanisms in Human Communication*. New York: Oxford University Press.

Knapp, M. L. (1978). *Nonverbal Communication in Human Interaction*. New York: Holt, Rinehart and Winston.

Kolden, G. G., Howard, K. I., and Maling, M. S. (1994). The counseling relationship and treatment process and outcome. *The Counseling Psychologist, 22 (1)*, January, pp. 82-89.

Kornhuber, H. H. (1988). The human brain: From dream and cognition to fantasy, will, conscience, and freedom. In H. J. Markowitsch (Ed.), *Information Processing by the Brain: Views and Hypotheses from a Physiological-Cognitive Perspective*. Toronto: Hans Hüber Publishers.

Kosslyn, S. M. and Koenig, O. (1992). *Wet Mind: The New Cognitive Neuroscience*. New York: The Free Press.

Kovac, D. and Horkovic, G. (1970). How to measure lateral preference. *Studia Psychologica, 12*, pp. 5-11.

Kuhn, T. (1970). *The Structure of Scientific Revolutions*, Second Edition. Chicago: University of Chicago Press.

Laing, R. D. (1990). The love of wisdom. In J. K. Zeig and W. M. Munion (Eds.), *What Is Psychotherapy? Contemporary Perspectives.* San Francisco: Jossey-Bass Publishers.

Lambert, M. J. (1992). Psychotherapy outcome research: Implications for integrative and eclectic therapists. In J. C. Norcross and M. R. Goldfried (Eds.), *Handbook of Psychotherapy Integration.* New York: Basic Books.

Lambert, W. W. and Lambert, W. E. (1964). *Social Psychology.* Englewood Cliffs, NJ: Prentice-Hall.

Lambert, M. J., Shapiro, D., and Bergin, A. (1986). The effectiveness of psychotherapy. In S. Garfield and A. Bergin (Eds.), *Handbook of Psychotherapy and Behavior Change,* Third Edition. New York: Wiley.

Lang, W. A. and West, L. W. (1980). Human nature, sociobiology, and counselling. *The Canadian Counsellor, 14 (3),* pp. 167-173.

Langs, R. J. (1990). Communicative approach to psychoanalysis and psychotherapy. In J. K. Zeig and W. M. Munion (Eds.), *What Is Psychotherapy? Contemporary Perspectives.* San Francisco: Jossey-Bass Publishers.

Lankton, S. R. (1990). Ericksonian strategic therapy. In J. K. Zeig and W. M. Munion (Eds.), *What Is Psychotherapy? Contemporary Perspectives.* San Francisco: Jossey-Bass Publishers.

Lansford, E. (1986). Weakenings and repairs of the working alliance in short-term psychotherapy. *Professional Psychology: Research and Practice, 17,* pp. 364-366.

Larson V. A. (1987). An exploration of psychotherapeutic resonance. *Psychotherapy, 24,* pp. 321-324.

Lazarus, A. A. (1967). In support of technical eclecticism. *Psychological Reports, 21,* pp. 415-416.

Lazarus, A. A. (1976). *Multimodal Behavior Therapy.* New York: Springer.

Lazarus, A. A. (1989). *The Practice of Multimodal Therapy.* Baltimore: Johns Hopkins University Press.

Lazarus, A. A. (1992). Multimodal therapy: Technical eclecticism with minimal integration. In J. C. Norcross and M. R. Goldfried (Eds.), *Handbook of Psychotherapy Integration.* New York: Basic Books.

Lazarus, A. A. (1993a). Theory, subjectivity, and bias: Can there be a future? *Psychotherapy, 30 (4),* Winter, pp. 674-677.

Lazarus, A. A. (1993b). Tailoring the therapeutic relationship, or being an authentic chameleon. *Psychotherapy, 30 (3),* Fall, pp. 404-409.

Leger, F. J. (1989). *A Behavioral and Biological Approach to Counseling and Psychotherapy: The Dominant Eye Phenomenon.* New York: Carlton Press.

Lewin, K. K. (1965). Nonverbal cues and transference. *Archives of General Psychiatry, 12,* pp. 391-394.

Lieberman, M., Yalom, Y. D., and Miles, M. (1973). *Encounter Groups: First Facts.* New York: Basic Books.

Lietaer, G. (1992). Helping and hindering processes in client-centered/experiential psychotherapy: A content analysis of client and therapist postsession perceptions. In S. G. Toukmanian and D. L. Rennie (Eds.), *Psychotherapy Process Research: Paradigmatic and Narrative Approaches.* Newbury Park, CA: Sage.

Lister, J. (1970). School counselling: For better or for worse? *Counseiller Canadien, 4,* January, pp. 33-39.

Livermore, B. (1992). Build a better brain. *Psychology Today, 25(5),* September/October, pp. 40-48.

Long, M. E. (1992). The sense of sight. *National Geographic, 182 (5)*, pp. 3-42.

Lopez, F. G. (1995). Contemporary attachment theory: An introduction with implications for counseling psychology. *The Counseling Psychologist, 23,* July, pp. 395-415 .

Lord, C. (1974). The perception of eye contact in children and adults. *Child Development, 45*, pp. 1113-1117.

Lord, C. and Haith, M. (1974). The perception of eye contact. *Perception and Psychophysics, 16 (3),* pp. 413-416.

Luborsky, L. (1987). Research can affect clinical practise—a happy turnaround. *The Clinical Psychologist, 40, (3),* pp. 56-60.

Lynch J. J. (1985). *The Language of the Heart: The Body's Response to Human Dialogue.* New York: Basic Books.

Lynch, J. J. (1990). The broken heart: The psychobiology of human contact. In R. Ornstein and C. Swencionis (Eds.), *The Healing Brain: A Scientific Reader.* New York: The Guilford Press.

Mahoney, M. J. (1990). Developmental cognitive therapy. In J. K. Zeig and W. M. Munion (Eds.), *What Is Psychotherapy? Contemporary Perspectives.* San Francisco: Jossey-Bass Publishers.

Mahoney, M. J. (1991). *Human Change Processes: The Scientific Foundations of Psychotherapy.* New York: Basic Books.

Malan, D. H. (1976). *Toward the Validation of Dynamic Psychotherapy: A Replication.* New York: Plenum.

Malcolm, J. (1981). *Psychoanalysis: The Impossible Profession.* New York: Knopf.

Maling, M. S. and Howard, K. I. (1994). From research to practice to research to . . . . In P. F. Talley, H. H. Strupp and S. F. Butler (Eds.), *Psychotherapy Process Research: Bridging the Gap.* New York: Basic Books.

Maloney, C. (1976). *The Evil Eye.* New York: Columbia University Press.

Marmor, J. (1971). Dynamic psychotherapy and behavior therapy: Are they irreconcilable? *Archives of General Psychiatry, 24,* pp. 22-28.

Martin, J. (1992). Cognitive-mediation research on counseling and psychotherapy. In S. G. Toukmanian and D. L. Rennie (Eds.), *Psychotherapy Process Research: Paradigmatic and Narrative Approaches.* Newbury Park, CA: Sage.

Maslow, A. H. (1965). *Eupsychian Management.* Homewood, IL: Dorsey.

Maslow, A. H. (1970). *Motivation and Personality,* Second Edition. New York: Harper and Row.

Maslow, A. H. (1976). *Religions, Values, and Peak-Experiences.* New York: Penguin Books.

Mead, G. H. (1962). *Mind, Self, and Society from the Standpoint of a Social Behaviorist.* Chicago: University of Chicago Press.

Mehrabian, A. (1968). Inference of attitudes from the posture, orientation, and distance of a communicator. *Journal of Consulting and Clinical Psychology, 32,* pp. 296-308.

Mehrabian, A. (1970). *Tactics of Social Influence.* Englewood Cliffs, NJ: Prentice-Hall.

Mehrabian, A. (1972). *Nonverbal Communication.* Chicago: Aldine-Atherton.

Mehrabian, A. and Ferris, S. (1967). Inference of attitudes from nonverbal communication in two channels. *Journal of Consulting Psychology, 31,* pp. 248-252.

Meltzoff, J. and Kornreich (1970). *Research in Psychotherapy.* New York: Atherton Press.

Messer, S. B. (1992). A critical examination of belief structures in integrative and eclective psychotherapy. In J. C. Norcross and M. R. Goldfried (Eds.), *Handbook of Psychotherapy Integration.* New York: Basic Books.

Miller, R., Brickman, P., and Bolen, D. (1975). Attribution versus persuasion as a means of modifying behavior. *Journal of Personality and Social Psychology, 31,* pp. 430-441.

Neimeyer, R. A. (1990). Personal construct therapy. In J. K. Zeig and W. M. Munion (Eds.), *What Is Psychotherapy? Contemporary Perspectives.* San Francisco: Jossey-Bass Publishers.

Nichols, M. P. (1995). *The Lost Art of Listening.* New York: The Guilford Press.

Norcross, J. C. (1990). Eclectic-integrative psychotherapy. In J. K. Zeig and W. M. Munion (Eds.), *What Is Psychotherapy? Contemporary Perspectives.* San Francisco: Jossey-Bass Publishers.

Norcross, J. C. and Goldfried, M. R. (Eds.) (1992). *Handbook of Psychotherapy Integration.* New York: Basic Books.

Norcross, J. C. and Newman, C. F. (1992). Psychotherapy integration: Setting the context. In J. C. Norcross and M. R. Goldfried (Eds.), *Handbook of Psychotherapy Integration.* New York: Basic Books.

Norton, R. and Pettegrew, L. (1979). Attentiveness as a style of communication: A structural analysis. *Communication Monographs, 46,* March, pp. 13-26.

Nye, R. D. (1975). *Three Views of Man: Perspectives from Sigmund Freud, B. F. Skinner, and Carl Rogers.* Monterey, CA: Brooks/Cole.

Omer, H. (1994). *Critical Interventions in Psychotherapy.* New York: W. W. Norton and Co., Inc.

Orlinsky, D. E. (1994). Research-based knowledge as the emergent foundation for clinical practice in psychotherapy. In P. F. Talley, H. H. Strupp, and S. F. Butler (Eds.), *Psychotherapy Research and Practice: Bridging the Gap.* New York: Basic Books.

Orlinsky, D. E. and Howard, K. I. (1978). The relation of process to outcome in psychotherapy. In S. L. Garfield and A. E. Bergin (Eds.), *Handbook of Psychotherapy and Behavior Change: An Empirical Analysis.* New York: John Wiley and Sons.

Orlinsky, D. E. and Russell, R. L. (1994). Tradition and change in psychotherapy research: Notes on the fourth generation. In R. L. Russell (Ed.), *Reassessing Psychotherapy Research.* New York: The Guilford Press.

Ornstein, R. (1993). *The Roots of the Self: Unraveling the Mystery of Who We Are.* New York: HarperCollins.

Ornstein, R. and Swencionis, C. (1990). What is the healing brain? In R. Ornstein and C. Swencionis (Eds.), *The Healing Brain: A Scientific Reader.* New York: The Guilford Press.

Palmer, L. (1976). Inability to wink an eye and eye dominance. *Perceptual and Motor Skills, 42 (3, part 1),* June, pp. 825-826.

Papouchis, N. (1990). Self-disclosure and psychotherapy with children and adolescents. In G. Stricker and M. Fisher (Eds.), *Self-disclosure in the Therapeutic Relationship.* New York: Plenum Press.

Parloff, M., Waskow, I., and Wolfe, B. (1978). Research on therapist variables in relation to process and outcome. In S. Garfield and A. Bergin (Eds.), *Handbook of Psychotherapy and Behavior Change: An Empirical Analysis.* New York: John Wiley and Sons.

Patterson, C. H. (1959). *Counseling and Psychotherapy: Theory and Practice.* New York: Harper and Row.

Paul, G. (1969). Behavior modification research: Design and tactics. In C. M. Franks (Ed.), *Behavior Therapy: Appraisal and Status.* New York: McGraw-Hill.

Penfield, W. and Roberts, L. (1959). *Speech and Brain Mechanisms.* Princeton, NJ: Princeton University Press.

Peres, H. (1947). An investigation of non-directive group therapy. *Journal of Consulting Psychology, 11,* 159-172.

Perez, J. F. (1965). *Counseling: Theory and Practice.* Reading, MA: Addison-Wesley.

Perez, J. F. (1968). *The Initial Counseling Contact.* Guidance monograph series. Boston: Houghton-Mifflin.

Perls, F., Hefferline, R., and Goodman, P. (1977). *Gestalt Therapy: Excitement and Growth in the Human Personality.* New York: Crown Publishers.

Perrett, D., Smith, P., Potter, D., Mistlin, A., Head, A., Milner, A., and Jeeves, M. (1985). Visual cells in the temporal cortex sensitive to face view and gaze direction. *Proceedings of the Royal Society of London, Series B, 223,* pp. 293-317.

Peterfreund, E. (1971). Information systems and psychoanalysis: An evolutionary biological approach to psychoanalysis. *Psychological Issues, 7,* monograph 25 and 26.

Phillips, E. L. (1990). The delivery system as prime therapeutic determinant. In J. K. Zeig and W. M. Munion (Eds.), *What Is Psychotherapy? Contemporary Perspectives.* San Francisco: Jossey-Bass Publishers.

Phillips, G. M. and Metzger, N. J. (1976). *Intimate Communication.* Boston: Allyn and Bacon.

Porac, C. and Coren, S. (1976). The dominant eye. *Psychological Bulletin, 83 (5),* pp. 880-897.

Porac, C. and Coren, S. (1979). Monocular asymmetries in recognition after an eye movement: Sighting dominance and dextrality. *Perception and Psychophysics, 25 (1),* pp. 55-59.

Price, R. H. (1978). *Abnormal Behavior: Perspectives in Conflict*. New York: Holt, Rienhart, and Winston.

Prochaska, J. O. (1979). *Systems of Psychotherapy: A Transtheoretical Analysis*. Georgetown: The Dorsey Press.

Prochaska, J. O. and DiClemente, C. C. (1992). The transtheoretical approach. In J. C. Norcross and M. R. Goldfried (Eds.), *Handbook of Psychotherapy Integration*. New York: Basic Books.

Rachlin, H. (1994). *Behavior and Mind: The Roots of Modern Psychology*. New York: Oxford University Press.

Reamy-Stephenson, M. (1990). Strategic-systemic family therapy. In J. K. Zeig and W. M. Munion (Eds.), *What Is Psychotherapy? Contemporary Perspectives*. San Francisco: Jossey-Bass Publishers.

Reece, M. M. and Whitman, R. N. (1962). Expressive movements, warmth, and verbal reinforcement. *Journal of Abnormal and Social Psychology, 64*, pp. 234-236.

Rennie, D. and Toukmanian, S. (1992). Explanation in psychotherapy process research. In S. Toukmanian and D. Rennie (Eds.), *Psychotherapy Process Research: Paradigmatic and Narrative Approaches*. Newbury Park, CA: Sage.

Rhodes, R. H. and Greenberg, L. (1994). Investigating the process of change: Clinical applications of process research. In P. F. Talley, H. H. Strupp, and S. F. Butler (Eds.), *Psychotherapy Research and Practice: Bridging the Gap*. New York: Basic Books.

Rice, L. N. (1965). Therapist's style of participation and case outcome. *Journal of Consulting Psychology, 29*, pp. 155-160.

Rice, L. N. (1974). The evocative function of the therapist. In D. Wexler and L. Rice (Eds.), *Innovations in Client-Centered Therapy*. New York: John Wiley and Sons.

Rice, L. N. (1992). From naturalistic observation of psychotherapy process to micro theories of change. In S. G. Toukmanian and D. L. Rennie (Eds.), *Psychotherapy Process Research: Paradigmatic and Narrative Approaches*. Newbury Park, CA: Sage.

Rice, L. N. and Wagstaff, A. K. (1967). Client voice quality and expressive style as indexes of productive psychotherapy. *Journal of Consulting Psychology, 31*, pp. 557-563.

Richards, L., Burlingame, G. M., Barlow, S., and Lambert, M. J. (1990). Comparison of group interactions of improvers and deteriorators on the SASB. Paper presented at the Society for Psychotherapy Research, Wintergreen, VA.

Riesen, A. H. (1966). Sensory deprivation. In E. Stellar and J. M. Sprague (Eds.), *Progress in Physiological Psychology*, Volume 1. New York: Academic Press.

Riesen, A. H. (1975). *The Developmental Neuropsychology of Sensory Deprivation*. New York: Academic Press.

Robertiello, R. C. (1990). Dynamically based integrative approach. In J. K. Zeig and W. M. Munion (Eds.), *What Is Psychotherapy? Contemporary Perspectives*. San Francisco: Jossey-Bass Publishers.

Robson, K. S. (1967). The role of eye-to-eye contact in maternal-infant attachment. *Journal of Child Psychology and Psychiatry, 8*, pp. 13-21.

Rogers, C. R. (1942). *Counseling and Psychotherapy.* Boston: Houghton-Mifflin.

Rogers, C. R. (1951). *Client-centered Therapy.* Boston: Houghton-Mifflin.

Rogers, C. R. (1957). The necessary and sufficient conditions of therapeutic personality change. *Journal of Consulting Psychology. 21,* pp. 95-103.

Rogers, C. R. (1959). A theory of therapy, personality, and interpersonal relationships as developed in the client-centered framework. In S. Koch (Ed.), *Psychology: A Study of a Science,* Volume 3, *Formulations of the Person and the Social Context.* New York: McGraw-Hill.

Rogers, C. R. (1961). *On Becoming a Person.* Boston: Houghton-Mifflin.

Rogers, C. R. (1965). A theory of therapy, personality, and interpersonal relations as developed in the client-centered framework. In G. Lindzey and C. S. Hall (Eds.), *Theories of Personality: Primary Sources and Research.* New York: John Wiley and Sons Inc.

Rogers, C. R. (1967). The interpersonal relationship: The core of guidance and learning to be free. In C. R. Rogers and B. Stevens (Eds.), *Person to Person: The Problem of Being Human. A New Trend in Psychology.* Lafayette, CA: Real People Press.

Rogers, C. R. (1972). Communication: Its blocking and its facilitation. In H. Altmann (Ed.), *Readings in Human Relationships.* Berkeley, CA: McCutchan Publishing Co.

Rogers, C. R. (1975). Issues in contemporary psychology. In R. I. Evans (Ed.), *Carl Rogers: The Man and His Ideas.* New York: E. P. Dutton and Co.

Rogers, C. R. (1977). *On Personal Power.* New York: Dell Publishers.

Rogers, C. R. and Skinner, B. F. (1956). Some issues concerning the control of human behavior: A symposium. *Science, 124,* pp. 1057-1066.

Roll, W. V., Schmidt, L. D., and Kaul, T. J. (1972). Perceived interviewer trustworthiness among black and white convicts. *Journal of Counseling Psychology, 19,* pp. 537-541.

Rosenhan, D. L. (1979). On being sane in insane places. In C. Torniero (Ed.), *Readings In Psychology 79/80.* Guilford, CT: Dushkin Publishing Co.

Rossi, E. L. (1990). Psychobiological psychotherapy. In J. K. Zeig and W. M. Munion (Eds.), *What Is Psychotherapy? Contemporary Perspectives.* San Francisco: Jossey-Bass Publishers.

Rossi, E. L. (1993). *The Psychobiology of Mind-Body Healing: New Concepts of Therapeutic Hypnosis.* New York: W. W. Norton and Co.

Russell, R. L. (1994). Critically reading psychotherapy process research: A brief renactment. In R. L. Russell (Ed.), *Reassessing Psychotherapy Research.* New York: The Guilford Press.

Sacks, O. (1995). The man who mistook his life for a what? *Psychology Today.* May/June, pp. 28-33.

Safran, J. D. and Muran, J. C. (1994). Toward a working alliance between research and practice. In P. F. Talley, H. H. Strupp, and S. F. Butler (Eds.), *Psychotherapy Research and Practice: Bridging the Gap.* New York: Basic Books.

Sage, W. (1979). The split brain lab. In C. Torniero (Ed.), *Readings in Psychology 79/80.* Guilford, CT: Dushkin Publishers.

Sanford, R. (1990). Client-centered psychotherapy. In J. K. Zeig and W. M. Munion (Eds.), *What Is Psychotherapy? Contemporary Perspectives*. San Francisco: Jossey-Bass Publishers.

Sapir, E. (1927). The unconscious patterning of behavior in society. In E. S. Drummer (Ed.), *The Unconscious: A Symposium*. New York: Knopf.

Sarles, H. B. (1975). A human ethological approach to communication: Ideas in transit around the Cartesian impasse. In A. Kendon, R. Harris, and M. Key (Eds.), *Organization of Behavior in Face-to-Face Interaction*. Chicago: Aldine.

Scheflen, A. E. (1973). *Communicational Structure: Analysis of a Psychotherapy Transaction*. Bloomington, IN: Indiana University Press.

Schwartz, G. E. (1978). Psychobiological foundations of psychotherapy and behavior change. In S. Garfield and A. Bergin (Eds.), *Handbook of Psychotherapy and Behavior Change: An Empirical Analysis*. New York: John Wiley and Sons.

Selltiz, C., Wrightsman, L., and Cook, S. (1976). *Research Methods in Social Relations*. New York: Holt, Rinehart and Winston.

Sexton, T. L. and Whiston, S. C. (1994). The status of the counseling relationship: An empirical review, theoretical implications, and research directions. *The Counseling Psychologist, 22 (1)*, January, pp. 6-78.

Shaffer, J. B. (1978). *Humanistic Psychology*. Englewood Cliffs, NJ: Prentice-Hall Inc.

Shapiro, A. and Morris, L. (1978). The placebo effect in medical and psychological therapies. In S. Garfield and A. Bergin (Eds.), *Handbook of Psychotherapy and Behavior Change: An Empirical Analysis*. New York: John Wiley and Sons.

Shapiro, F. (1995). *Eye Movement Desensitization and Reprocessing: Basic Principles, Protocols, and Procedures*. New York: Guilford Publications, Inc.

Shapiro, J. (1968). Relationships between visual and auditory cues of therapeutic effectiveness. *Journal of Clinical Psychology, 24*, pp. 236-239.

Siegel, J. C. and Sell, J. M. (1978). Effects of objective evidence of expertness and nonverbal behavior on client-perceived expertness. *Journal of Counseling Psychology, 25*, 188-192.

Siegel, R. and Grinvald, A. (1992). A window on the brain. *Discover*, July, p. 16.

Siegman, A. W. and Feldstein, S. (Eds.) (1978). *Nonverbal Behavior and Communication*. Hillsdale, NJ: Lawrence Erlbaum Associates.

Siegman, A. W. and Pope, B. (Eds.) (1972). *Studies in Dyadic Communication*. New York: Pergamon Press.

Simon, J. C. (1990). Criteria for therapist self-disclosure. In G. Stricker and M. Fisher (Eds.), *Self-disclosure in the Therapeutic Relationship*. New York: Plenum Press.

Skinner, B. F. (1953). *Science and Human Behavior*. New York: Macmillan.

Skinner, B. F. (1979). Why aren't we using science to change behavior? In C. Torniero (Ed.), *Readings In Psychology 79/80*. Guilford, CT: Dushkin Publishing Co.

Smedslund, J. (1995). Psychologic: Common sense and the pseudoempirical. In J. A. Smith, R. Harre, and L. Van Langenhove (Eds.), *Rethinking Psychology*. Thousand Oaks, CA.: Sage Publications.

Smith, H. C. (1966). *Sensitivity to People*. New York: McGraw-Hill Co.

Smith-Hanen, S. S. (1977). Effects of nonverbal behaviors on judged levels of counselor warmth and empathy. *Journal of Counseling Psychology, 24*, pp. 87-91.

Solomon, G. F. (1990). Emotions, stress, and immunity. In R. Ornstein and C. Swencionis (Eds.), *The Healing Brain: A Scientific Reader.* New York: The Guilford Press.

Spence, D. P. (1994). The failure to ask hard questions. In P. Talley, H. Strupp, and S. Butler (Eds.), *Psychotherapy Research and Practice: Bridging the Gap.* New York: Basic Books.

Spengler, P., Strohmer, D., Dixon, D., and Shivy, V. (1995). A scientist-practitioner model of psychological assessment: Implications for training, practice, and research. *The Counseling Psychologist, 23 (3),* July, pp. 506-534.

Spitz, R. (1965). *The First Years of Life.* New York: International Universities Press.

Staats, A. W. (1981). Paradigmatic behaviorism, unified theory construction methods, and the zeitgeist of separatism. *American Psychologist, 36*, pp. 239-256.

Staples, F. R. and Sloane, R. B. (1970). The relation of speech patterns in psychotherapy to empathic ability, responsiveness to approval, and disapproval. *Diseases of the Nervous System, 31*, pp. 100-104.

Stefflre, B. and Matheny, K. B. (1968). *The Function of Counseling Theory.* Boston: Houghton-Mifflin.

Steinfield, G. J. (1980). *Target Systems: An Integrative Approach to Individual and Family Therapy.* Jonesboro, TN: Pilgrimage.

Stern, R. S. and Marks, I. M. (1973). A comparison of brief and prolonged flooding in agoraphobics. *Archives of General Psychiatry, 28*, p. 210.

Stiles, W., Shapiro, D., and Elliott, R. (1986). Are all psychotherapies equivalent? *American Psychologist, 41*, pp. 165-180.

Stiles, W., Shapiro, D., and Harper, H. (1994). Finding the way from process to outcome: Blind alleys and unmarked trails. In R. Russell (Ed.), *Reassessing Psychotherapy Research.* New York: Guilford.

Stricker, G. (1990). Self-disclosure and psychotherapy. In G. Stricker and M. Fisher (Eds.), *Self-disclosure in the Therapeutic Relationship.* New York: Plenum Press.

Strong, S. R. (1978). Social psychological approach to psychotherapy research. In S. L. Garfield and A. E. Bergin (Eds.), *Handbook of Psychotherapy and Behavior Change: An Empirical Analysis.* New York: John Wiley and Sons.

Strong, S. R. (1995). From Social Psychology: What? *The Counseling Psychologist. 23 (4),* October, pp. 686-690.

Strong, S. R. and Matross, R. P. (1973). Change processes in counseling and psychotherapy. *Journal of Counseling Psychology, 20*, pp. 25-37.

Strong, S. R., Yoder, B., and Corcoran, J. (1995). Counseling: A social process for constructing personal powers. *The Counseling Psychologist, 23 (2),* April, pp. 374-384.

Strupp, H. H. (1973). *Psychotherapy: Clinical, Research, and Theoretical Issues.* New York: Jason Aronson.

Strupp, H. H. (1978). Psychotherapy research and practice: An overview. In S. L. Garfield and A. E. Bergin (Eds.), *Handbook of Psychotherapy and Behavior Change: An Empirical Analysis.* New York: John Wiley and Sons.

Strupp, H. H. and Bergin, A. E. (1973). New directions in psychotherapy research. In H. H. Strupp, *Psychotherapy: Clinical, Research, and Theoretical Issues*. New York: Jason Aronson.

Sullivan, H. S. (1970). *The Psychiatric Interview*. New York: W. W. Norton and Co.

Tepper, D. T. and Haase, R. F. (1978). Verbal and nonverbal communication of facilitative conditions. *Journal of Counseling Psychology, 25 (1)*, pp. 35-40.

Thoresen, C. E. (1974). Behavioral means and humanistic ends. In M. J. Mahoney and C. E. Thoresen (Eds.), *Self-control: Power to the Person*. Monterey, CA: Brooks Cole.

Tipton, R. M. and Rymer, R. A. (1978). A laboratory study of the effects of counselor eye-contact on client-focused and problem-focused counseling styles. *Journal of Counseling Psychology, 23 (3)*, pp. 200-204.

Tomkins, S. S. (1963). *Affect, Imagery, Consciousness*, Volume III, *The Negative Effects*. New York: Springer.

Toukmanian S. G. (1992). Studying the client's perceptual processes and their outcomes in psychotherapy. In S. G. Toukmanian and D. L. Rennie (Eds.), *Psychotherapy Process Research: Paradigmatic and Narrative Approaches*. Newbury Park, CA: Sage.

Trout, D. L. and Rosenfeld, H. M. (1980). The effect of postural lean and body congruence on the judgement of psychotherapeutic rapport. *Journal of Nonverbal Behavior, 4 (3)*, pp. 176-190.

Truax, C. B. and Carkhuff, R. R. (1965). Client and therapist transparency in the psychotherapeutic encounter. *Journal of Counseling Psychology, 12*, pp. 3-8.

Truax, C. B. and Carkhuff, R. R. (1967) *Toward Effective Counseling and Psychotherapy: Training and Practice*. Chicago: Aldine.

Truax, C. B. and Carkhuff, R. R. (1968). Experimental manipulation of therapeutic conditions. In L. Litwack, R. Getson, and G. Saltzman (Eds.), *Research in Counseling*. Itasca, IL: Peacock Publishers.

Truax, C. B. and Mitchell, K. M. (1971). Research on certain therapist interpersonal skills in relation to process and outcome. In A. E. Bergin and S. L. Garfield (Eds.), *Handbook of Psychotherapy and Behavior Change: An Empirical Analysis*. New York: John Wiley and Sons.

Vandenbos, G. R. and Karon, B. P. (1971). Pathogenesis: A new therapist personality dimension related to therapeutic effectiveness. *Journal of Personality Assessment, 35*, pp. 252-260.

Vaughn, D. R. and Burgoon, M. (1976). Interpersonal communication in the therapeutic setting: Mariah or messiah? In G. R. Miller (Ed.), *Explorations in Interpersonal Communication*. London: Sage.

Vinogradov, S. and Yalom, I. D. (1990) Self-disclosure in group psychotherapy. In G. Stricker and M. Fisher (Eds.), *Self-disclosure in the Therapeutic Relationship*. New York, Plenum Press.

Wachtel, P. L. (1990). Psychotherapy from an integrative psychodynamic perspective. In J. K. Zeig and W. M. Munion (Eds.), *What Is Psychotherapy? Contemporary Perspectives*. San Francisco: Jossey-Bass Publishers.

Wachtel, P. L. and McKinney, M. K. (1992). Cyclical psychodynamics and integrative psychodynamic therapy. In J. C. Norcross and M. R. Goldfried (Eds.), *Handbook of Psychotherapy Integration.* New York: Basic Books.

Watzlawick, P. (1978). *The Language of Change: Elements of Therapeutic Communication.* New York: Basic Books.

Watzlawick, P. and Beavin, J. (1977). Some formal aspects of communication. In P. Watzlawick and J. Weakland (Eds.), *The Interactional View.* New York: W. W. Norton.

Weeks, G. R. (1990). Paradox. In J. K. Zeig and W. M. Munion (Eds.), *What Is Psychotherapy? Contemporary Perspectives.* San Francisco: Jossey-Bass Pub-lishers.

Wexler, D. (1974). A cognitive theory of experiencing, self-actualization, and therapeutic process. In D. Wexler and L. Rice (Eds.), *Innovations in Client-Centered Therapy.* New York: John Wiley and Sons.

Wexler, D. and Rice, L. (Eds.) (1974). *Innovations in Client-Centered Therapy.* New York: John Wiley and Sons.

Whitaker, C. (1989). *Midnight Musings of a Family Therapist.* New York: W. W. Norton and Co.

Whitely, J. and Fretz, B. (1980). *The Present and Future of Counseling Psychology.* Monterey, CA: Brooks Cole.

Williamson, E. G. (1959). The meaning of communication in counseling. *Personnel and Guidance Journal, 36,* p. 6.

Yalom, I. D. (1975). *The Theory and Practice of Group Psychotherapy.* New York: Basic Books.

Zeig, J. K. and Munion, W. M. (1990). What is psychotherapy? In J. K. Zeig and W. M. Munion (Eds.), *What Is Psychotherapy? Contemporary Perspectives.* San Francisco: Jossey-Bass Publishers.

Zimring, F. M. (1974). Theory and practice of client-centered therapy: A cognitive view. In D. Wexler and L. Rice (Eds.), *Innovations in Client-Centered Therapy.* New York: John Wiley and Sons.

Index

Order Your Own Copy of
This Important Book for Your Personal Library!

BEYOND THE THERAPEUTIC RELATIONSHIP
Behavioral, Biological, and Cognitive Foundations of Psychotherapy

_____ in hardbound at $49.95 (ISBN: 0-7890-0291-4)

_____ in softbound at $24.95 (ISBN: 0-7890-0292-2)

COST OF BOOKS_____

OUTSIDE USA/CANADA/
MEXICO: ADD 20%_____

POSTAGE & HANDLING_____
(US: $3.00 for first book & $1.25
for each additional book)
Outside US: $4.75 for first book
& $1.75 for each additional book)

SUBTOTAL_____

IN CANADA: ADD 7% GST_____

STATE TAX_____
(NY, OH & MN residents, please
add appropriate local sales tax)

FINAL TOTAL_____
(If paying in Canadian funds,
convert using the current
exchange rate. UNESCO
coupons welcome.)

☐ **BILL ME LATER:** ($5 service charge will be added)
(Bill-me option is good on US/Canada/Mexico orders only;
not good to jobbers, wholesalers, or subscription agencies.)

☐ Check here if billing address is different from
shipping address and attach purchase order and
billing address information.

Signature_____

☐ **PAYMENT ENCLOSED: $**_____

☐ **PLEASE CHARGE TO MY CREDIT CARD.**

☐ Visa   ☐ MasterCard   ☐ AmEx   ☐ Discover
☐ Diner's Club

Account # _____

Exp. Date _____

Signature _____

Prices in US dollars and subject to change without notice.

NAME _____

INSTITUTION _____

ADDRESS _____

CITY _____

STATE/ZIP _____

COUNTRY _____ COUNTY (NY residents only) _____

TEL _____ FAX _____

E-MAIL_____
May we use your e-mail address for confirmations and other types of information? ☐ Yes   ☐ No

Order From Your Local Bookstore or Directly From
The Haworth Press, Inc.
10 Alice Street, Binghamton, New York 13904-1580 • USA
TELEPHONE: 1-800-HAWORTH (1-800-429-6784) / Outside US/Canada: (607) 722-5857
FAX: 1-800-895-0582 / Outside US/Canada: (607) 772-6362
E-mail: getinfo@haworth.com
PLEASE PHOTOCOPY THIS FORM FOR YOUR PERSONAL USE.